TRANSLATION EFFECTS

INTERVENTIONS: NEW STUDIES
IN MEDIEVAL CULTURE

Ethan Knapp, Series Editor

TRANSLATION EFFECTS

*Language, Time, and Community
in Medieval England*

~

Mary Kate Hurley

THE OHIO STATE UNIVERSITY PRESS
COLUMBUS

Copyright © 2021 by The Ohio State University.
All rights reserved.

Library of Congress Cataloging-in-Publication Data
Names: Hurley, Mary Kate, author.
Title: Translation effects : language, time, and community in medieval England / Mary Kate Hurley.
Other titles: Interventions: new studies in medieval culture.
Description: Columbus : The Ohio State University Press, [2021] | Series: Interventions: new studies in medieval culture | Includes bibliographical references and index. | Summary: "Reinterprets the translation of medieval texts such as *Orosius*, Ælfric's *Lives of Saints*, Ælfric's *Homilies*, Chaucer, Trevet, Gower, and *Beowulf*, through translation effects, observable traces which show how writers reimagined the political, cultural, and linguistic communities in which their texts were consumed"—Provided by publisher.
Identifiers: LCCN 2021003037 | ISBN 9780814214718 (cloth) | ISBN 0814214711 (cloth) | ISBN 9780814281284 (ebook) | ISBN 0814281281 (ebook)
Subjects: LCSH: English literature—Old English, ca. 450–1100—History and criticism. | Literature, Medieval—Translations—History and criticism.
Classification: LCC PR173 .H87 2021 | DDC 813/.0872909—dc23
LC record available at https://lccn.loc.gov/2021003037

Other identifiers: 9780814257951 (paper) | 081425795X (paper)

Cover design by Laurence J. Nozik
Text design by Juliet Williams
Type set in Adobe Minion Pro

For my mother, who taught me to speak with my own voice.
For Gillian, who taught me to hear Old English in its own voice.
For Tricia, who taught me to find my scholarly voice.
And for Lily, who taught me to enjoy every single syllable.

CONTENTS

Acknowledgments ix

INTRODUCTION 1
CHAPTER 1 What Orosius Said: Temporal Heterogeneity in the Old English *Orosius* 25
CHAPTER 2 Sanctity and Soil: Ælfric's *Life of Oswald, King and Martyr* 53
CHAPTER 3 Communities of the Page in the Ælfrician Homiletic Corpus 90
CHAPTER 4 Becoming England: The Northumbrian Conversion in Trevet, Gower, and Chaucer 125
CHAPTER 5 *Beowulf*'s Collectivities 151

Coda 183
Bibliography 189
Index 209

ACKNOWLEDGMENTS

ACKNOWLEDGMENTS TELL A story of how writing an academic book, as lonely as it can sometimes be, is the work of multitudes. The people I thank here have been friends, teachers, readers, and fellow writers over many years—I cannot possibly express how grateful I am to them all.

I owe more than I can ever say to Gillian Overing: teacher, mentor, and friend, she models the kind of scholarly generosity and capaciousness I hope to emulate. Early encouragement also came from Gale Sigal and Scott Klein, who both supported my overly ambitious ideas. In the New York City and the Columbia University medieval communities, my work found its first audiences and most tenacious mentors. First and foremost, Patricia Dailey's dedication and commitment to my work helped move it forward. Her optimism and hard work made me a far better scholar and writer than I would have been otherwise. Thanks are also due to Chris Baswell, Susan Boynton, Susan Crane, Consuelo Dutschke, Joan Ferrante, Eleanor Johnson, Richard Sacks, and Paul Strohm: to study with such medievalists was a privilege. Robert Hanning's humane and generous spirit taught me how to shape a good academic life and how to trust my scholarly instincts. Members of the Columbia Medieval Guild, past and present, have been constant interlocutors and companions. Special thanks to Carolyn Dinshaw, who accepted an Old English paper in a Middle English context. Martin K. Foys has consistently helped me refine my ideas, and his tireless advocacy for the field, and for me within it, gave me the courage I needed to make bigger claims. Kathleen Davis's work gave mine its heart: this book would not exist without her brilliant scholarship and mentorship. Indeed, the Colloquium on Early Medieval Studies came into being as I arrived in New York, and I could not have asked for a better group of scholars to guide me into my field. Patricia Dailey, Hal Momma, Kathleen Davis, and Stacy Klein are, simply put, the Old English dream team.

Rutgers University, Barnard College, Cooper Union, and Yale University all provided employment prior to my time at Ohio University. Yale also provided material and spiritual nourishment to a young itinerant medievalist, and I owe a deep debt of gratitude to Alastair Minnis, Ian Cornelius, Ardis Butterfield, and Jessica Brantley for accepting me into the Yale fold from 2011 to 2013. Roberta Frank's kindness and generosity will always exceed my ability to thank her: I aspire endlessly to her inimitable combination of social grace and scholarly style.

The team at The Ohio State University Press has been essential to this work: special thanks to Ana Maria Jimenez-Moreno and everyone there. Series editor Ethan Knapp's enthusiasm for this project was evident from our first meetings—I am so grateful for his support. Anonymous readers helped me to improve this work tremendously, and I am grateful for their labor. Financial support to pursue and present this work has come from fellowships at Columbia, grants from the International Society for the Study of Early Medieval England and the New Chaucer Society, the E. K. Rand Grant from the Medieval Academy of America, and the International Travel Fund at Ohio University. Chapter One appeared in *The Journal of English and Germanic Philology* and is reprinted here (with revisions) by permission. Parts of Chapter Two appeared in the volume *The Politics of Ecology* (OSU Press, 2016), and is similarly reprinted here (with revisions) by permission. An excerpt from James Arthur's poem "A Local History" from *The Suicide's Son* is used by permission of Signal Editions/Véhicule Press and the author. Small excerpts from Chapters One and Five appeared, in heavily revised form, on *In the Middle* and *Old English in New York,* as well as on Asa Mittman and Shyama Rajendran's blog. I thank the medieval blogging community of the late aughts for their support of that incipient work. Librarians, archivists, and curators at OU, Wake Forest, Yale, Columbia, the Bodleian Library, the British Library, Lambeth Palace Library, Cambridge University Library, Trinity College Library, Cambridge, and Corpus Christi College Library, Cambridge have made this research possible, from locating rare materials, to facilitating ILL requests, to trusting me with 1000-year-old books. My work would be literally impossible without them; so would all our work.

OU colleagues deserving special thanks include Edmond Y. Chang, Marsha Dutton, Heather Edwards, Sherrie Gradin, Eric LeMay, Brian MacAllister, Dinty W. Moore, Patrick O'Keeffe, Beth Quitslund, and Ryan Shepherd. Graduate students in my "Community, Collectivity, Ecology," "Narrative Time and Worldbuilding," and Old English language and literature courses deserve thanks for their intrepid engagement with texts that often went well beyond their own areas of study. I learned more from them than they ever could from me. Anne Bramley helped me find my way back into this work—her support was constant and invaluable. Gregory Tolliver and Kira Hall were the most able research assistants I could have asked for: working with them made my book far better than it would have been otherwise (although any lingering infelicities are my own).

Audiences at Wake Forest, Bates College, the Marco Institute for Medieval and Renaissance Studies at University of Tennessee-Knoxville, Trinity University, and Purdue University have all provided useful feedback for this project. Fellow medievalists and other scholars have been encouraging and exacting— and always in precisely the ways I most needed. Heartfelt thanks, therefore, to Anya Adair, Suzanne Conklin Akbari, Gania Barlow, Emma Bérat, Liza Blake, Brantley Bryant, John Burden, Mary Clayton, Jill Clements, Donna Beth Ellard, Heide Estes, Bruce Gilchrist, Shannon Godlove, Steve Harris, Derrick Higganbotham, Bruce Holsinger, Matthew Hussey, Miriam Jacobson, Drew Jones, Eileen Fradenburg Joy, A. B. Kraebel, Clare Lees, Roy Liuzza, Leslie Lockett, Ruen-Chuan Ma, Brian O'Camb, Dana Oswald, Mo Pareles, Daniel C. Remein, Benjamin A. Saltzman, Elizabeth Scala, Randy Schiff, Samantha K. Seal, Kathleen Smith, Larry Swain, Erin Sweany, Joseph Taylor, Carla María Thomas, Elaine Treharne, Erica Weaver, and Eric Weiskott. My co-bloggers at *In the Middle*—Jeffrey J. Cohen, Jonathan Hsy, Leila K. Norako, Karl Steel, and Cord J. Whitaker—have been inspiring interlocutors for over a decade now. Frederick Bengtsson, Jennifer Garrison, Ruth Lexton, Elizabeth Frame (and family), and Emily Shortslef all pulled double duty over the years as friends and colleagues, reading drafts and cheering me on when I needed it most.

Every scholar of Old English should have a *weorod*. Irina Dumitrescu, Denis Ferhatović, and Jordan Zweck have been my constant collaborators, editors, and friends these past years. This book would not exist without their encouragement, scholarly prowess, taste for good food, and friendship. I did the work, guys.

Academic work often takes one away from family life through travel, time in the library, and hours spent poring over the words of the dead rather than listening to those of the living. Thanks to my family-in-law, Bob, Linda, and

Catherine Osborne, for tolerating more than one holiday in which I spent more time working than celebrating. My grandmothers—Joan Hurley and Lorraine Ahearn, both readers to the last—are a constant source of inspiration, and are deeply missed. My aunt and godmother Lorraine Ahearn (Jr.) was the first person to push me harder in my writing at the tender age of twelve, and I'm proud to call her my Dr. Aunt. My sister Beth Cox always lent an ear while I worked out problems far beyond her interests. She is a *very* patient sister. Gina Marie Hurley—my medievalist sister—has been critic, interlocutor, and friend since she was old enough to correct my grammar (a very long time). It's a privilege to share a field with her. My parents Daniel and Christine Hurley have always encouraged me to pursue even the most unlikely of dreams. This book is a testament to the spirit of curiosity and learning with which they raised my sisters and me.

Finally, and most importantly: Nicholas Osborne's generosity and love have made my career possible. He's my first and last editor, sharpener of every argument, and corral-er of rogue commas. As a pandemic unfolded and my work life moved into our house, he did the lion's share of the childcare, the cooking, and pretty much everything else while I completed this book. He has my deepest thanks and love. Rory—our dog—(mostly) patiently endured this book's writing and revision process, insisting on walks when I needed them and naps (for her) the rest of time. And Lillian Claire—you arrived three days after your mama finished this book, and your first years unfolded in tandem with its final revision. I hope the stories you inherit from us help you build a better world. And since you've heard all of this book during naps and long, otherwise quiet, afternoons together, it is dedicated to you, alongside the inspiring women who helped me write my academic story.

INTRODUCTION

THIS STUDY REINTERPRETS a central feature of medieval textual production: translation. It demonstrates that medieval texts—from the ninth century to the fifteenth—often leave observable traces of the translation process that reveal their imagined political, cultural, and linguistic communities. I term these traces "translation effects" and argue that their presence creates imagined textual communities that are temporally heterogeneous and geographically expansive.[1] Such effects have a range of ramifications for the communities they help create. Sometimes translation effects lend authority to a translation, such as when the Old English *Orosius* invokes the voice of the historian Paulus Orosius to both describe and judge past cultures. In other moments, they imply an audience linked not by time or location but rather by access to shared cultural knowledge, such as Ælfric of Eynsham's *Lives of the Saints*'s repeated references to stories already known from Bede's *Historia Ecclesiastica*. These indications of the work of translation give insight into the way medieval readers and writers pursued their craft. By examining translation effects, modern scholars can better understand how medieval translations imagine community.

---

1. See Venuti, "Translation, Community, Utopia," in Venuti, *Translation Studies Reader*; Bassnett, *Translation Studies*; Ríkharðsdóttir, *Medieval Translations*, 53–54.

Considering translation effects calls attention to a fundamental difference between modern and medieval translation. Scholars of modern translation have long acknowledged what Lawrence Venuti calls the illusion of the translator's "invisibility."[2] This invisibility is achieved via "transparency," the characteristic of translations that masks their translators' role in creating them.[3] Yet according to Venuti, invisibility also enacts a form of violence: domesticating translations transforms the foreign into the familiar and in so doing elides fundamental differences between cultures and silences minority voices.[4] Moreover, "no translation can provide direct or unmediated access to the source text," no matter how transparent the translator attempts to make their work.[5]

But transparency was not necessarily a virtue for many medieval translators.[6] In fact, many of them actually celebrated the *visibility* of translation, transmission, and the reception of stories from other times, places, and languages. For example, take Chaucer's avowal of fidelity to his *auctor* Lollius in *Troilus and Criseyde*.[7] Much critical ink has been spilled over the identification of Lollius, the probability that Lollius did not exist, and the possibility that his invocation may be meant to obscure Chaucer's reliance on Boccaccio for his narrative. Yet as Bella Millett observes, despite Chaucer's deferral to Lollius, he still creates an author-figure with whom modern readers might feel familiar.[8] Moreover, the author that Chaucer creates in his fiction is also self-consciously positioned as a translator.

In fact, Chaucer explicitly refers to his method of drawing on Lollius's work as that of transferring a narrative between "tonges."[9] Regardless of

---

2. See Venuti, *Translator's Invisibility*.

3. Venuti defines transparency as a quality that elides the presence of translation at all: an "effect of a fluent translation strategy, of the translator's effort to insure easy readability by adhering to current usage, maintaining continuous syntax, fixing a precise meaning" (*Translator's Invisibility*, 1). See also Kratz, "Interview with Norman Shapiro."

4. See Venuti, *Translator's Invisibility*, 13–20; Bassnett, *Translation*, 81–103.

5. See Venuti, *Translator's Invisibility*, xiii.

6. For example, see Campbell and Mills, *Rethinking Medieval Translation*, 1–20. Campbell and Mills note that while ideas of transparency, foreignization, and the tension between strangeness and familiarity are deeply influential in modern translation studies, "They arguably apply to a relatively restricted range of cultural and political circumstances" (4). See also Campbell, "Scandals of Medieval Translation," in Fenster and Collette, *The French of England*.

7. I owe a debt of gratitude to Jennifer Garrison, who first drew my attention to Lollius.

8. Bella Millett argues that this author figure is "a writer confident of his own powers of invention and adaptation, untroubled by scruples about the intrinsic value of fiction, and prepared to entertain his readers even at the expense of strict morality" ("Chaucer, Lollius," 103). Alastair Minnis advances a contrary view: see Minnis, *Medieval Theory of Authorship*, 209.

9. Chaucer positions himself similarly in Book I, 393–95. See Machan, "Chaucer as Translator," in Ellis, *Medieval Translator*, 57.

whether Lollius is actually fictive, Chaucer deploys a modesty topos that foregrounds not his invention but rather the words of his *auctor*. He asks his audience to "Disblameth me, if any word be lame, / For as myn auctor seyde, so sey I" (Book II, 17–18).[10] While drawing attention to his *auctor*, Chaucer also highlights translation: "No sentiment I this endite / But out of Latyn in my tonge it write" (Book II, 13–14). The act of translation becomes a figure for the kind of decentering of authority that Chaucer asks the reader to accept. Alongside a theory of authorship, we see a theory of the translator emerge in these lines: a figure who attempts to claim his own invisibility even as he alerts readers to his presence.[11]

A central goal of this monograph is to demonstrate that although such choices—which draw attention to the presence of translation—might seem jarring to a modern audience, they perform important cultural work in medieval texts. Translation effects foreground translation as an act even when they do not technically perform it. They are not aberrations affecting a translation's quality, however, but moments of literary invention that imagine new textual communities.

Analyzing translation effects, therefore, contributes to a broader scholarly reinterpretation of medieval translation as a dynamic, "multilingual process" rather than a static, "monolingual product."[12] Translators are never moving simply from one language to another.[13] Rather, they operate in a broader cultural context that includes issues of linguistic transfer but is not reducible to them.[14] Translations can therefore give insight into cultural considerations that exceed the purely linguistic. Moreover, translation in medieval England was always already understood as something that was more than the sum of its linguistically transferred parts. Martin Irvine demonstrates that the most explicit exposition of a theory of translation in the pre-Conquest period—that of King Alfred's *Preface* to the *Pastoral Care*—"was driven by two historical

---

10. All Middle English text from Chaucer's *Troilus and Criseyde* is drawn from Benson, *Riverside Chaucer*.

11. Minnis argues that Chaucer was "an author who hid behind the 'shield and defence' of the compiler" (*Medieval Theory of Authorship*, 209–10).

12. See Warren, "Translation," in Strohm, *Middle English*, 52. Warren argues persuasively that medieval translation studies would benefit from a move to "set aside the very notion that 'originals' are worth more [than] their translations, 'originality' more than repetition, 'uniqueness' more than similarity [by] placing texts in relation to each other via strategic alliances that depend less on genre and language than on culture" (51).

13. Ríkharðsdóttir, *Medieval Translations*, 55.

14. For examples, see Copeland, *Rhetoric, Hermeneutics, and Translation*; Stanton, *Culture of Translation*; Irvine, *Making of Textual Culture*; Ríkharðsdóttir, *Medieval Translations*; Major, "Ælfric and Self-Translation," in Dinkova-Brunn and Major, *Teaching and Learning*; Taylor, "Rewriting," in Tether and McFayden, *Handbook of Arthurian Romance*.

forces: practical need in the face of a decline in Latin literacy and [a newly] emerging national and linguistic identity."[15] Even in the period, the cultural ramifications of—and motivations for—translation are inseparable from the work of linguistic transfer. The present study will therefore not seek to interrogate the linguistic transfer of medieval texts (a topic already much studied).[16] Rather it will examine how the products of linguistic transfer retain traces of that process and how those traces, taken together, create a cultural statement of imagined community that is premised on that community's extension in both time and space.[17]

Alfred's *Preface* illustrates how that extension works both in early medieval English history and the history of Christianity writ large:[18]

> Ða gemund ic hu sio æ wæs ærest on Ebrisc geðiode funden, & eft, þa þa hie Crecas geleornodon, þa wendon hi hie on hiora ægen geðiode ealle, & eac ealle oðre bec. And eft Lædenware swa same, siððan hi hie geleornodon, hi hie wendon ealla ðurh wise wealhstodas on hiora agen geðeode. & eac ealla oðra Cristena ðioda sumne dæl hiora on hiora agen geðiode wendon. (4–6)[19]

> Then I remembered how the law was first found in the language of the Hebrews, and after, when the Greeks had learned it, then they translated it all into their own language, and also all other books. And afterward the Romans in the same way, after they had learned them, they translated them all through wise translators into their own language. And also all other Christians peoples translated some part [of the law] into their own language.

---

15. See Irvine, *Making of Textual Culture*, 418.

16. For recent work that does engage with linguistic aspects of translation in Old English, see *inter alia* Kozuka, "Element Order in Old English Translation," in Hasaka et al., *Phases of the History of English*; Waite, "Translation Style"; Sato, "Ælfric's Linguistic and Stylistic Alterations"; Sato, "Ælfric's Lexical Alterations"; Timofeeva, "Late Old English Idiom vs. ablativus absolutus"; Taylor, "Contact Effects of Translation."

17. See Bassnett, *Translation*; Campbell, "Scandals of Medieval Translation," in Fenster and Collette, *The French of England*; Campbell, "Time of Translation"; Griffin, "Time of the Translator."

18. Davis argues that "as this passage traverses political geography and Christian history, each people emerges as participating in Scriptural truth when its 'own' (*agen*) language becomes the embodiment of Scripture" ("Performance of Translation Theory," in Boenig and Davis, *Manuscript, Narrative, Lexicon*, 154).

19. Old English text of the *Preface* to the *Pastoral Care* is drawn from Sweet, *King Alfred's West-Saxon Version of the Pastoral Care*. Throughout this book, all translations from Old English are my own unless otherwise noted.

This marked moment of *translatio studii, translatio imperii* seems to legitimize the task that Alfred undertakes in the larger translation project that the *Preface* inaugurates.[20] Because the English can no longer adequately understand the Latin language, Alfred suggests, "Forðy me ðyncð betre, gif iow swa ðyncð, ðæt we eac suma bec, ða þe nidbeðyrfesta sien eallum monnum to witanne, þæt we þa on ðæt geðeode wenden þe we ealle gecnawan mægen" (6) [Therefore it seems to me better, if you also think so, that we translate some books—those which are most needful for all men to know—into a language that we may all understand]. In making these claims, Alfred inscribes knowledge written in English into a longer Christian tradition, one that will allow the past learning that he claims has "fallen off" (*opfeallan*) among the English people to be reclaimed in the present.[21]

The *Preface* repairs to a past that authorizes the king's present decision to make a rebirth of learning a key feature of his reign. As Kathleen Davis has persuasively shown, the *Preface* engages in protonationalist discourse. It imagines and creates a unified kingdom where previously there was none by appealing to a fictionalized and idealized past.[22] Translation—signified by the verb *wendan*, which Alfred uses repeatedly to indicate the kind of work he both emulates and undertakes—is more than simply a linguistic tool to combat an increasingly ill-educated populace. Rather, when Alfred "turns" these Latin books into English ones, he also imagines a new community.[23]

---

20. For further work on the imperial project and authority of the Old English translation of the *Pastoral Care*, see Davis, "National Writing"; Discenza, "Alfred's Verse Preface to the *Pastoral Care*." On the preface itself, see Stanley, "King Alfred's Prefaces"; Irvine, *Making of Textual Culture*, 415–20. For a recent reading of the *Preface* that takes it to refer to books of scripture, see Anlezark, "King Alfred's Educational Reform."

21. See Davis, "Performance of Translation Theory," in Boenig and Davis, *Manuscript, Narrative, Lexicon*, 160. As Davis demonstrates, "this carefully detailed sequence corresponds closely to Alfred's sequential description of his own translation process" (154). This parallelism, Davis shows, is part of what legitimates his choice to translate at all. See also Irvine, who argues that "what Alfred lamented had 'fallen off' was the grammatical culture England was famous for in the later seventh and eighth centuries, a culture of *grammatica*, ecclesiastical learning, Christian literature, and law" (*Making of Textual Culture*, 419). Yet, of course, the *Preface* may exaggerate the problem: Davis notes that "Alfred's bleak description of a national decline in literacy has seemed exaggerated and curiously inaccurate [. . .] especially since he drew several scholars from Mercia and so must have known that literacy was in a relatively better state there, and also because his own works indicate access to a rich literary tradition" ("National Writing," 624).

22. Davis, "National Writing," 623.

23. For a full account of the vocabulary that Alfred uses to denote translation—and most importantly, its relationship to the Latin vocabulary denoting the same—see Davis, "Performance of Translation Theory," in Boenig and Davis, *Manuscript, Narrative, Lexicon*, 158–59.

Alfred's work retrospectively identifies and brings into being an *Angelcynn* in the past that never existed.[24] Yet his *Preface* also creates a *present* community, one that can only exist within the *Preface* itself. Drawn together through both a lack of learning and a king's proposed remedy for that lack, the community of *Angelcynn* in the *Preface* reaches across time when it traverses languages. As Davis suggests, it looks backward to Christian hegemony as a foundational principle, as well as to the ubiquity of learning that a shared commitment to the Latin language facilitated (at least as Alfred imagines).[25] And yet multilingualism defines this group, not monolingualism.[26] Latin texts must be turned—translated—to English. These actions will bridge past and present, and bring back the supposedly better times that Alfred appeals to with his program. Importantly, however, they also endow the *Angelcynn* with a transtemporal and transgeographical identity, one made legible in the Christian genealogy of translation that Alfred outlines. In translating the law into the vernacular, the *Angelcynn* join a community that extends across both time and space, beginning with the Hebrews, and continuing through Greece, Rome, and even all of Christendom.[27] That community is one based in access to shared texts. Through the translation, the past will be brought back into consonance with the present through the conversions that translation makes possible, an outcome that is in part brought to fruition by calling attention to the act of translation and its consequences.

The *Preface* to the *Pastoral Care* thus dramatizes some of the concerns that this monograph will explore. Most importantly, it demonstrates how translation can imagine temporally expansive communities, communities that can cohere around texts but that can also only be strictly present in the text itself. In this case, the work of translation inscribes Alfred's incipient England into a Christian community defined by its relationship to multiple languages. That community stretches from the pre-Christian era, which only saw the law in the Hebrew language, through to the Christian present. On the one hand, this

---

24. Davis, "National Writing."

25. Irvine also argues that Alfred's great innovation here is that he "invokes the assumptions and values of *grammatica* and transfers them to a written English culture, or, rather, he reinvents *grammatica* as a discipline of both languages, incorporating English in an educational program previously limited to Latin texts" (*Making of Textual Culture*, 417–18).

26. Indeed, as Davis points out, "the legitimation of each translation, and hence of the Christian identity of the people it represents, resides in the careful process of learning and interpretation exercised by the *wise wealhstodas*" ("Performance of Translation Theory," in Boenig and Davis, *Manuscript, Narrative, Lexicon*, 154).

27. For an account of how the concept of "cristendom" might fulfill a community-forming function in terms of race and ethnicity, see Harris, *Race and Ethnicity in Anglo-Saxon Literature*.

genealogy creates a sense of continuity that is facilitated by translation. On the other hand, as with all instances of *translatio* in the Middle Ages, it also highlights the breaks with the past—beginning but not ending with language itself—that necessitate a reenvisioning of the contours of community.[28]

TRANSLATION EFFECTS

Translation's ubiquity in medieval literature can belie the complexity of the work it performs. Translation is, fundamentally, interpretation.[29] It requires a thinking mind to transfer a text in one language not only into a different language but also into a different culture. If we approach translations as a negotiated series of interactions between humans and texts, we can better understand their temporal, textual, and community-oriented interests. Therefore, rather than describing translation as a simple relationship between a source text and a translated one, I suggest that focusing on the textual communities that translations imagine within themselves allows scholars better access to the multifaceted reality that produced these textual objects.[30] Traces of the interpretive process remain, in both the most transparent translations of the Middle Ages and in those it might be tempting to describe as "mere" paraphrase. By attending to these traces that medieval translators left—intentionally or not—in their work, we regain a sense of the complexity of medieval translation and how it negotiates fundamental questions of identity and history.[31]

---

28. See Stahuljak, "Medieval Fixers," in Campbell and Mills, *Rethinking Medieval Translation*. Stahuljak notes that "medieval *translatio* [. . .] does not highlight or theorize issues of linguistic difference and identity and it rarely gives us the privilege of seeing the human being behind translation" (148).

29. Most translation theorists of the twentieth century and beyond subscribe to this view of translation as interpretation. Among others, see Steiner, "Hermeneutic Motion," in Venuti, *Translation Studies Reader*; Jakobson, "On Linguistic Aspects of Translation," in Venuti, *Translation Studies Reader*; Benjamin, "Task of the Translator," in Bullock and Jennings, *Selected Writings Volume 1*. See also Copeland, *Rhetoric, Hermeneutics, and Translation*; Stanton, *Culture of Translation*; Irvine, *Making of Textual Culture*.

30. For further considerations, see Warren, "Translation," 52.

31. For a full account of translation in the period and its relationship to both identity and culture, see: Steiner, *After Babel*; Stanton, *Culture of Translation*; Beer, *Medieval Translators and Their Craft*; Beer, *Translation Theory and Practice*; Djordjević, "Mapping Medieval Translation," in Weiss et al., *Medieval Insular Romance*; Davis, "National Writing"; Discenza, *King's English*; Thijs, "Early Old English Translation"; Bately, "Literary Prose," in Szarmach, *Old English Prose*; Copeland, *Rhetoric, Hermeneutics, and Translation*; Ríkharðsdóttir, *Medieval Translations*; Fisher, *Scribal Authorship*; Irvine, *Making of Textual Culture*.

The reason I call these traces "translation effects" is because they do not necessarily point to instances of interlinguistic translation, although they can.[32] Rather, they deploy the trappings of translation to suggest the act of narrative transmission between times and cultures. Take, for example, the most famous Old English poem, *Beowulf*. It begins not by introducing its eponymous hero and his exploits, but rather with an invocation of a textual community shared by narrator and listener: "Hwæt, we Gar-Dena in geardagum / þeodcyninga þrym gefrunon"[33] (1–2) [Hwæt! We have heard of the glory of the Spear-Danes in days of yore, the kings of the people]. The inclusivity of this "we" transcends time and space. Every person who hears or reads that line can be included in the textual community it imagines. By the same measure, however, the "we" that the poem invokes can only ever be fictive, as fleeting as the story that the imagined group hears recited. This community exists only in its members' knowledge of stories from the past carried across time. *Beowulf* is not a translation in the strictest sense: it is not a narrative that has been retold in a language other than its original. But the allusion to stories of "Spear-Danes" in an Old English poem is nevertheless a translation *effect* because it calls attention to the existence of a source tradition while also positing the group of readers and listeners—the "we"—who have heard these stories before.

This kind of community can only exist because the text itself imagines its extent.[34] It exists in a multilingual and multitemporal milieu. Thus, the historical specificity that helps define traditionally conceived textual communities is not as salient a feature for the ones I study in this book.[35] Scholars usually understand textual communities as groups that form in relation to a given text—or in the medieval period, groups that form in relation to a learned interpreter of that text for those who cannot read or understand it without assistance.[36] Yet texts can, in themselves, imply communities that the narrative imagines: they may be contemporary communities who will use the translated text, but they can also be communities that no longer exist or do not exist

---

32. My inspiration for the term translation effects comes from the work of Joel Fineman on subjectivity effects in early modern drama. See Fineman, *Shakespeare's Perjured Eye* and *Subjectivity Effect*. For a different use of the same phrase, see Taylor, "Contact Effects of Translation."

33. Old English text from *Beowulf* is drawn from Fulk et al., *Klaeber's Beowulf*.

34. Here I draw on Benedict Anderson's influential definition of the nation as an "imagined political community," in which "members of even the smallest nation will never know their fellow-members, meet them, or even hear of them, yet in the minds of each lives the image of their communion" (*Imagined Communities*, 6).

35. Brian Stock's definition of these "textual communities" remains the most influential. See Stock, *Implications of Literacy* and *Listening for the Text*.

36. See particularly Stock, *Implications of Literacy*, 522–30.

yet.³⁷ In translations, these imagined communities often include the audiences or even authors of the source text, recreated in a new linguistic and cultural context. For medieval texts such as those that I study here, these imagined communities frequently exceed the historical community of readers or users that formed around the text in the time of its dissemination. Regardless of whether "we" share anything else with *Beowulf*'s long-dead original listeners, "we" as much as "they" have putatively heard the stories of the Spear-Danes because the poem says we have. Translation effects call such communities into being.

How are these communities constituted and what are their attributes? Raymond Williams's description of "the warmly persuasive word to describe an existing set of relationships, or the warmly persuasive word to describe an alternative set of relationships,"³⁸ highlights the difficulty of finding a definition of community that is both capacious enough to fit the uses to which the word is put and specific enough to have clear meaning. For the purposes of my argument, therefore, I propose a relatively specific usage that operates when translation effects do. First, these textual communities are imagined communities.³⁹ A translation requires its translator to imagine a future group who will need the text being transferred—a group that might exist, but might only be a wished-for community for whom this text will be necessary. Second, these imagined textual communities specifically share an interest in an identity based on a shared history, fictional or otherwise. That shared identity is formed in relationship to texts—for example, Alfred's imagined future that would need his translations—but it is also forged by them. Translation effects, that is, both indicate the community that their texts form and create it by their imaginative engagement with the past.

Finally, the communities imagined by translation share the trait of temporal heterogeneity—"a fuller, denser, more crowded *now*."⁴⁰ A source text will always precede its translation. At a minimum, therefore, the source and its translation will imagine communities of two different times—and often different places, languages, religions, and other cultural markers. Therefore, translators must necessarily make choices about how to alter, expand, or remain

---

37. See Anderson, *Imagined Communities*. Although Anderson's concept is based on the modern nation state, the capacity to imagine a group identity is not alien to the Middle Ages.

38. Williams, *Keywords*, 76. For an alternative definition of community based in medieval confessional practice, see Hurley, "Confession and the Creation of Community in Medieval Romance."

39. See Anderson, *Imagined Communities*; Stock, *Implications of Literacy*; Stock, *Listening for the Text*.

40. Dinshaw, *How Soon Is Now?*, 4. For the use of Dinshaw's "asynchrony" to examine translation, see Campbell, "Time of Translation," 7.

faithful to the earlier narrative they transmit. By choosing to produce a translation rather than a putatively original work, translators must also imagine that this work will be as important to a contemporary audience as it was to its original one: they "[create] a domestic community of interest around the translated text."[41] Yet this shared appeal necessarily implies that the audience of the original text and the audience of the translation will overlap in meaningful ways.

In order to reach these audiences, translators must make specific choices, which are often indicated by translation effects. These can encompass the initial invocation of the "we" in *Beowulf* discussed above as well as the assertion that a passage of the Old English *Orosius* is what "Orosius said" (*cwæð Orosius*) in its Latin source. They can range from the suggestion that a story being retold in Trevet's Anglo-Norman *Chronicle* can also be found in old Saxon books to the emendations and alterations that accrue in manuscripts over time. In each case, these moments of translation simultaneously demonstrate their assumption of a community that will inherit these retold stories and their insistence on that community's extension in time and space.

My focus on these temporally heterogeneous communities and the translation effects that reveal them affords scholars of medieval literature the opportunity to recontextualize our understanding of translation overall. By treating source and translation as relatively independent works, I demonstrate the robust character of the tradition of translation both within and beyond early medieval England. Therefore, while I do employ a measure of source study, I do so not to pin down the "real" context of a work or its purported meaning (although such studies are valuable). Rather, I use the methodologies of source study to demonstrate the vitality of translations themselves, the way that their alterations, emendations, additions, and subtractions create different visions of community and of time. As a whole, this monograph reveals how translation imagines the temporally heterogeneous communities it seeks to create.

This approach responds to present directions in studies of medieval translation. Michelle Warren has provocatively suggested that scholars might reimagine the medieval literary tradition productively by viewing translations as "an aesthetic grouping independent from authorial and generic categories."[42] Here, Warren opens the possibility of evaluating and understanding translations as cultural objects in their own right and as valuable resources for understanding how medieval cultures imagined their worlds. If translations are accorded "the same critical value" as texts in other genres, their study can

---

41. See Venuti, "Translation, Community, Utopia," 477.
42. Warren, "Translation," 51.

reveal heretofore undervalued dimensions of how these texts interact with, are shaped by, and respond to the world in which they were written.[43] Translation becomes a fertile ground for understanding how medieval authors envisioned the communities their work imagines. My study reveals the depth of insight available in medieval translation by embracing the heterogeneous temporalities and expansive geographies that the genre produces.

There are several projects that lie beyond the scope of the present study. First, this book does not aim to be a comprehensive study of medieval translation: indeed, multiple such studies already exist, and each lays crucial groundwork for the present volume.[44] Second, this book does not attempt to understand translation as an endeavor predominantly rooted in linguistic imperatives. Finally, it does not attempt to resurrect a theory of translation out of pre-Conquest England.[45] Rather, through a series of case studies, I argue that translation effects offer an important new heuristic for understanding medieval translation.

To do so, I engage texts that were written both pre- and post-Conquest. I have not chosen these texts based on any historical or textual connection, although they all consider the history of the community that they call (in their various languages) England. Rather, my corpus is defined by a breadth of approach to translation itself, ranging from direct Latin-to-Old-English translation to more metaphorical instances of narrative transmission. By including a diverse selection of texts that all nonetheless include translation in some guise, I demonstrate the ubiquity of translation effects within the textual culture of early medieval England.

To that end, my work proceeds in three interlocking parts. The first segment examines literal translation in the Old English *Orosius* and Ælfric's *Lives of the Saints* and the methods by which these texts expand their imagined communities across time and geographical space. The second part of the book takes up translation as it appears in texts that transmit stories across the Norman Conquest, specifically examining the manuscript tradition of Ælfric's homilies and the transmission history of the "Life of Constance" in Trevet, Chaucer, and Gower. By shifting my focus to a manuscript tradition that extends to both sides of the Conquest and a narrative that reimagines the

---

43. Warren, "Translation."

44. See especially Copeland, *Rhetoric, Hermeneutics, and Translation*; Beer, *Translation Theory and Practice*; Weiss et al., *Medieval Insular Romance*; Blumenfeld-Kosinski et al., *Politics of Translation*; Beer, *Medieval Translators and Their Craft*.

45. For partial examples of this strain of criticism, see Stanton, *Culture of Translation*; Butler, *Language and Community*; Discenza, *King's English*; Irvine, *Making of Textual Culture*; Thijs, "Early Old English Translation."

pre-Conquest era as a vital component of post-Conquest identity, I emphasize the centrality of both Old English texts and subsequent envisionings of the period to emerging narratives of community in Middle English. The final section of the book redirects its inquiry back to Old English literature, focusing on *Beowulf*. Although *Beowulf* is not literally a translation, I argue that it figures narrative transmission as a primary feature of communal identity. It therefore demonstrates the metaphorical impact of translation rather than the more literal uses I study in the first four chapters. *Translation Effects* as a whole demonstrates how various kinds of medieval translations create community across time and geography.

TRANSLATION STUDIES AND THE MIDDLE AGES

My analysis of translation effects contributes to scholarship concerning the imbrication of translation and power in the Middle Ages. Before turning to the study of *translatio* in the period, however, it is important to note that such questions are not insulated from the present. Indeed, our work as medievalists requires careful attention to present-day reimaginings of the period and its work, which often illustrate the modern inheritance of the inextricable relationship between knowledge and (imperial) power. Thus, it is important to note a change in terminology that I have adopted in this book. As my work on medieval English translation reached its conclusion, an important and long overdue conversation regarding scholarly terminology and identity in the study of pre-Conquest England reached a tipping point.[46] This conversation regarded the field's traditional use of the term "Anglo-Saxon" to describe the people who lived and wrote in pre-Conquest England: a term which, as Mary Rambaran-Olm has pointed out, "gained popularity in the eighteenth and nineteenth century as a means of connecting white people to their supposed origins."[47] A number of scholars have pointed to the racist underpinnings of the term in the United States, the United Kingdom, and throughout the world: its usage often promotes a vision of ethnic continuity with the past and consequently excludes people of color from both our field and its scholarship.[48] In

---

46. Although this conversation reached its tipping point in 2019–20, queries about the use of the term "Anglo-Saxon" reach much further into the collective bibliography of our field: Susan Reynolds, among many earlier commentators, reminded us in 1985 that "if we want to call them that, we ought to think hard about what we mean, and what others may think we mean, by the name we have chosen to use" ("'Anglo-Saxon' and 'Anglo-Saxons,'" 414).

47. Rambaran-Olm, "Rejecting 'Anglo-Saxon' Studies," in *History Workshop*.

48. The racist underpinnings of the term "Anglo-Saxon" have received copious attention; therefore, I cite only a selection of the most recent works here: Rambaran-Olm, "[Early Eng-

a study of how translations—indeed, of how the deployment of mythologies and narratives—can build and sustain communities as well as undermine and destroy them, it would be unethical not to acknowledge this ongoing conversation. It would be even more so not to change my scholarly practice to reflect the kind of community I want my work to build. As a result, I have excised references to this term in my own argument. I have preserved it in the work of scholars that I cite in my footnotes to reflect the change in thinking the field is undergoing. It is, ultimately, a very small alteration to make in pursuit of a more vibrant and diverse scholarship for our field.

Turning back to the Middle Ages, the concept of *translatio* itself explicitly links *studium* and *imperium* as "a nexus of a will to knowledge and technologies of power."[49] Indeed, the very formulation *translatio studii et translatio imperii* formulates the deep imbrication of the act of translation with cultural inheritance and identity: the question of whose access to knowledge is licit. Yet modern translation theory poses some obstacles to the student of medieval translation: both the conditions of production and their philosophical underpinnings render such connections quite difficult, yet not impossible to pursue.[50] For example, Rita Copeland's foundational work demonstrates "the ways in which translation articulates the relationship between academic and vernacular cultures in the Middle Ages."[51] Building from this insight, scholars have gone beyond tracing theories of translation or relationships between texts to illuminate the role of translation as both a product and producer of medieval culture. As Emily Butler and Jonathan Hsy have shown, the reach of translation was limited neither to one time nor to one social milieu. Rather, translations could evoke linguistic difference to imagine communities across

---

lish Studies], Academia, and White Supremacy"; Miyashiro, "Race, Settler Colonialism, and Medieval Heritage Politics" and "Decolonizing Anglo-Saxon Studies"; Remein, "ISAS Should Probably Change Its Name"; Ellard, *Anglo-Saxon(ist) Pasts, postSaxon Futures*; Oosthuizen, *Emergence of the English*, 3–6.

49. Stahuljak, "Medieval Fixers," in Campbell and Mills, *Rethinking Medieval Translation*, 148. Yet while it "theorized the origin and effect" of the transmission of these objects, it elided "its medium, that is, human agency" (Stahuljak, 148). Perhaps most influentially, Jacques LeGoff notes that "the transfer of power, the *translatio imperii*, was above all a transfer of knowledge and culture, a *translatio studii*" (*Medieval Civilization*, 171). See also Curtius, *European Literature and the Latin Middle Ages*, 28–29.

50. Campbell and Mills explore the complexity introduced when medieval translation interfaces with modern theories of translation. See Campbell and Mills, *Rethinking Medieval Translation*, 4–5. See also Campbell, "Scandals of Medieval Translation," in Fenster and Collette, *The French of England*.

51. Copeland, *Rhetoric, Hermeneutics, and Translation*, 8.

time, or they could indicate a readership for whom multilinguality was an indelible part of their world.⁵²

These and similar studies inform my argument that translations—on their own terms—were an essential component of Old English literary culture and its reception in the later Middle Ages. Old English scholars have traditionally confined their work on translation to source study or have focused their energy on engaging Old English translation theory through discussions of prefaces to translated works and commentaries. I do not suggest that either approach is without merit; indeed, such studies deepen our understanding of the period and its relationship to the texts it recreated. However, such approaches must be supplemented by careful theoretical inquiry into the ramifications of translation itself—and scholars of Old English are increasingly undertaking such work. For example, Davis's germinal work on King Alfred deploys postcolonial theory to situate the *Preface* to the *Pastoral Care* as an aspirational exercise in community building. She shows that the work of translation in early medieval England always had far-reaching social and political implications that existed in excess of linguistic transfer.⁵³

I assert that one of the implications of translation lies in the extended temporalities that attend its imagined communities. These temporalities encompass more than a simple linear relationship between prior source text and later translated version. My work in this vein expands on research by Robert Stanton, who argues compellingly that the idea of translation was central to literary production in early medieval England and that translation was thus part of the cultural mindset of the period.⁵⁴ His attention to Old English translation in contexts beyond the Alfredian circle and in excess of source study provides an important template for subsequent writers to think through translation. Nicole Guenther Discenza's work on the Old English translation of the *Boethius,* for example, approaches translation through the concept of authority: the cultural capital of a Latin text enhances the authority of the Old English translation.⁵⁵ Rebecca Stephenson's work on Ælfric of Eynsham and Byrhtferth of Ramsey explores the political ramifications of multilingualism in the context of the Benedictine reform, arguing that this context reveals the interrelatedness of English and Latin literary production in the period.⁵⁶

---

52. Butler, *Language and Community*; Hsy, *Trading Tongues*. Butler demonstrates that the linguistic distance enacted between languages was part of how such texts imagined communities across time. Hsy argues that the intersections of mercantile language and multilingualism is part of an important nexus of poetic production in the period.

53. Davis, "National Writing."

54. Stanton, *Culture of Translation.*

55. Discenza, *King's English.*

56. Stephenson, *Politics of Language.* See also O'Brien, *Reversing Babel.*

Translation Effects expands on these crucial scholarly interventions in several important ways. First and foremost, I take a capacious approach to what scholars might typically define as translation. Rather than focus solely on texts that have clear sources (Latinate or otherwise) translated into a vernacular language, I include both these kinds of traditional translations as well as works that use the figure of narrative transmission as part of their self-positioning, even though they might not have an obvious source text. This range of texts demonstrates how translation and its vicissitudes become thematized in medieval literature. Because translation effects refer to the rhetoric of textual translation rather than its fact, my methodology is broadly comparative. I utilize comparisons between the vernacular and Latin versions of Paulus Orosius's world history as well as between Bede and Ælfric's lives of King Oswald. But the remainder of my argument presents how translation effects imagine textual communities outside of—or in addition to—the context of direct source text analysis. My chapter on the Ælfrician homiletic manuscripts, for example, analyzes individual manuscripts in the homiletic tradition to examine how certain interventions into manuscripts respond to ideas of both literal translation and narrative transmission. My consideration of Chaucer's *Man of Law's Tale* examines a post-Conquest narrative that rehearses pre-Conquest English history, transforming its subject matter to create a temporally heterogeneous vision of the past. *Beowulf* presents a test case for considering translation effects in texts that foreground a figure of translation even in the absence of an identifiable source or explicit acknowledgement of a text being the product of translation. My consideration of *Beowulf* shows us that even in these conditions, translation effects by themselves are essential means by which medieval narratives create their imagined textual communities.

MY FIRST CHAPTER, "What Orosius Said," defines how the translation effect works as a heuristic for studying translations. I use a straightforward example of a translation effect from the Old English *Orosius* as a case study of the textual communities such effects can create—in this case, an audience extended in time. This ninth-century translation of a fifth-century Latin world history is usually treated as a paraphrase of its source text, a secondary artifact with less literary interest than its predecessor. My reconsideration of it reveals, however, that it is a complex literary work in its own right. I demonstrate that the *Orosius* highlights its own status as a translation by using a phrase that repeatedly upsets the authority of the Old English text: *cwæð Orosius*, or "Orosius said." This phrase, along with other moments of first-person narration in the text, punctures the illusion of a purely faithful translation by calling attention to the distance between the voices of translator and narrator. I argue that the inclusion of what "Orosius said" enlarges the temporal boundaries of community by assuming an audience that identifies with the history, culture, and language of both fifth-century Rome and ninth-century England.

Using this reading of the *Orosius* to establish the terms of my argument, in my second chapter I turn to Ælfric of Eynsham's *Lives of the Saints* in order to understand the deployment of translation effects in a broader set of works. Where Chapter One examines the manipulation of a Latin text translated into an Old English context, Chapter Two, "Saints and Soil," turns to the more recent English past in order to consider how translation effects might serve a specific political purpose—in this case, by imagining England as the site of a persistent religious community that transcends momentary lapses in belief. It addresses Ælfric's use of translation, particularly his handling of both Late Antique exemplars and English saints drawn from the work of Bede. I argue that Ælfric's inclusion of the *Life of Oswald, King and Martyr*—the hagiography of a Northumbrian king whose holiness is inextricably bound to the land he died on and for—stakes a claim for England's membership in a larger group of Christian nations. Ælfric's translation of Bede's narrative retells the story of both the king's martyrdom and the holy soil his relics produce. By doing so, Ælfric connects temporally disparate groups: the English contemporaries of the saints and the later audiences that studied the saints and their works. The translation effects in this chapter—such as the explicit identification of the story's most important location as being named in "englisc" (rather than in Latin)—combine discourse markers with the transferability of both saintly relics and narratives to create communities that cohere across time and geographical space.

Where the first two chapters of this book look at translation as it appears in narrative, Chapter Three, "Communities of the Page," turns to the manuscript tradition of Ælfric of Eynsham's homilies, which extends from the tenth to the twelfth century. It addresses how later audiences translated Ælfric for their own purposes by amending, annotating, and glossing manuscripts of his work. By considering the multiple emendations, erasures, insertions, and marginalia in these manuscripts as translation effects—in the sense that they each represent a mind responding to the presence of translation—this chapter demonstrates how readers interacted with the textual communities created by manuscripts. While these annotated manuscripts would not traditionally be considered translations, I argue that they give insight into the way that medieval audiences engaged with received narratives. These manuscript additions reflect and constitute a transtemporal community of creators and users of the codex itself. This chapter elucidates how the copyists and users of these homiletic texts across the Middle Ages understood their own work as part of an asynchronous conversation centered on the transmission of stories.

In contrast to the opening chapters, which establish the frequent appearance of translation effects across a range of time periods and a variety of genres rooted in early medieval England, Chapter Four, "Becoming England," examines the extension of textual communities across the Norman Conquest. It demonstrates that a post-Conquest setting might alter conversations about the pre-Conquest past through the emergence of a new vernacular. This exchange begins in Nicholas Trevet's Anglo-Norman *Chronicle* and its narrative of the life of Constance—a Roman princess who journeys to Northumbria (among other places), where she converts the Northumbrians before becoming their queen. The story of Constance and her journeys is later taken up by John Gower in his *Confessio Amantis* and Geoffrey Chaucer in his *Man of Law's Tale*. Each of the three narratives grapples with questions of linguistic identity and community, positioning translation within the story not only as an act of interpretation that transmits foundational texts but also as a method for creating and sustaining communities across time. By shifting focus to a post-Conquest narrative that is fundamentally concerned with understanding the legacy of pre-Conquest England, this chapter argues that the retellings of the "Life of Constance" demonstrate the long cultural memory of both conversion and linguistic difference that marks the period. I demonstrate how Chaucer, and to a lesser extent Gower, reshape Trevet's narrative to create a clear future for a Christian England out of its non-Christian past.

The foregoing analyses of medieval authors reconceptualizing their source narratives and the pasts from which they emerge serve as a model for modern scholars seeking to reconsider the canonical texts of the medieval past. In a move that deliberately unsettles traditional literary history, my final chapter, "*Beowulf*'s Collectivities," returns to pre-Conquest literature and its most celebrated work: *Beowulf*. I include *Beowulf* as the end point of my work both as an homage to and critique of its centrality in Old English literature. Included in most surveys and anthologies of English literature as one of the first English poems, *Beowulf* cannot be dated with any precision and addresses Scandinavian rather than English subject matter. And while the poem is not explicitly a translation, it frequently deploys translation effects, and by doing so, thematizes its investment in the inheritance of stories. These translation effects emphasize communities that for one reason or another are threatened and do not endure. These narratives are often contained in segments of the text—traditionally referred to as "digressions"—that do not actively involve the exploits of the character Beowulf in his narrative present. The dominant scholarly reading of the digressions in *Beowulf* casts them as attempts to bolster human communities within the poem by reiterating shared narratives and relaying knowledge that these communities need. However, they more frequently outline a series of connections that articulate the inevitable dispersal these communities face, foregrounding the thematic fragility of human social bonds based on inherited narratives. I argue that the translation effects in *Beowulf* create a community of listeners or readers that understand more than the poem's characters can, and so perceive the potential for the endurance of community but also its possible loss.

My coda considers one final translation effect from *Beowulf*, the Roman mosaic floors that appear in the hall of Heorot. A literal inheritance from another time, these floors suggest how translations accrete cultural meaning: they are the ground on which future cultures build. Translations may well alter, expand, or change that past; they may or may not be aware of the structures on which their own societies rest. But as manifestations of translation effects, *Beowulf*'s mosaic floors show us how a text reimagines its own past and, in so doing, creates communities that rely both on that past and on the alterations it accrues. By ending my monograph with *Beowulf*, I show that translation effects endure even when textual transmission fails.

CÆDMON'S *HYMN*: BEGINNING (WITH) TRANSLATION[57]

To illustrate the kinds of concerns that translation effects foreground, consider one of the most iconic moments in Old English literature: Cædmon's *Hymn*. An illiterate cowherd, ashamed that he cannot create verses in the manner of his counterparts, leaves a gathering where his compatriots all sing songs in turn. He falls asleep, and in his dream, an unknown person commands him to sing. He sings a song of Creation: the poem we call "Cædmon's *Hymn*." Upon waking, he tells his reeve about the dream, who brings him to an abbess. He is then "bidden to describe his dream in the presence of a number of the more learned men and also to recite his song so that they might all examine him and decide upon the nature and origin of the gift of which he spoke" (417).[58] When he does so, the heavenly provenance of his miraculous gift is clear to all

---

57. This segment of my introduction owes much to conversations with Shannon Godlove, who pointed out to me how central translation is to the narrative of Cædmon at the ICMS Kalamazoo in 2017.

58. "iussus est, multis doctioribus uiris praesentibus, indicare somnium et dicere carmen, ut uniuersorum iudicio quid uel unde esset quod referebat probaretur" (*HE* IV.24.416). Latin text and English translations from Bede's *Ecclesiastical History* are drawn from Colgrave and Mynors, *Bede's Ecclesiastical History*.

concerned. Cædmon goes on to live a long and productive life, creating verses based on biblical stories, his miraculous talent indicative of his holiness.

The transmission history of Cædmon's *Hymn* is less simple than its narrative, however. In the present day, Cædmon's *Hymn* is a representative Old English work in the *Norton Anthology of English Literature (Volume A: Medieval)*: in fact, it is the first Old English work to appear. But the first extant version of the *Hymn* is a prose Latin paraphrase in Bede's *Historia Ecclesiastica*. It only later became an Old English poem as a marginal addition in various manuscripts.[59] At the outset of a chronologically organized anthology of English literature, we find a poem whose earliest extant copy is neither in English nor in verse; fittingly, it is part of a narrative about a poet who performs a complex act of translation, mediating between God and man. He even undertakes a career as a translator, devoting the rest of his life to creating vernacular verse out of Latinate lore.

Unsurprisingly, the *Norton Anthology* lingers on questions of translation in its presentation of the Old English hymn. Most notably, it comments explicitly on the problem of translation in conveying the poem: because of its "formulaic style" that uses eight separate phrases to describe God, the *Hymn* "provides a richness of texture and meaning difficult to convey in translation."[60] The introduction highlights that Bede, too, shared some concerns about translating Old English poetry: it states that because "no literal translation of poetry from one language to another is possible without sacrifice of some poetic quality,"[61] Bede chose instead to provide a Latin paraphrase. That is, Bede's narrative provides the sense of the words, but not their order.

This introductory point becomes rather ironic because of the anthology's attention to the manuscript history of the hymn. It notes that "several manuscripts of Bede's *History* contain the Old English text in addition to Bede's Latin version."[62] However, in the anthology, only the West Saxon version of the poem appears, to the exclusion of Bede's "Latin version" (and other Old English versions as well). Yet it retains Bede's careful disclaimer, "This is the general sense but not the exact order of the words that he sang in his sleep;

---

59. For an analysis of the relationship between the poem and prose, as well as its status as translation and liturgical hymn, see the following: Altman, "Hymnody, Graphotactics"; O'Donnell, "Bede's Strategy in Paraphrasing"; Holsinger, "Liturgical Invention and Literary Tradition."

60. Greenblatt, *Norton Anthology: Volume A*, 29. I am far from the first literary critic to note the strangeness of how Cædmon's *Hymn* is presented in the Norton's version of the *Historia Ecclesiastica*. See Kiernan, "Reading Cædmon's 'Hymn.'"

61. Greenblatt, *Norton Anthology: Volume A*, 29. For more on the relationship between English and Latin, see Dumitrescu, "Bede's Liberation Philology."

62. Greenblatt, *Norton Anthology: Volume A*, 30.

for it is impossible to make a literal translation, no matter how well-written, of poetry into another language without losing some of the beauty and dignity."[63] Bede's hesitation to translate directly is undercut by the presence of the Old English poem in the *Norton Anthology*.

Given that Bede's original concerns are retained—indeed, they appear directly after the insertion of the West Saxon version of the poem and its interlinear English translation—the editorial decisions concerning the presentation of Cædmon's *Hymn* in the *Norton Anthology* have several interdependent effects. First and foremost, they erase Bede's own response to the problem of translation, which was of course not to focus on a word-for-word translation but rather to translate and legitimize a sense-for-sense translation of an important work.[64] More intriguingly, however, two specific moments in this edited version of the *Hymn* mark the interplay of temporalities that translation produces. In the interlinear translation, bold italics emphasize the alliteration of the lines, but they also highlight the interventions of a modern editor into the poem. No Old English manuscript would feel the need to stress the alliteration in this way; moreover, Old English poetry is not written in lineated form in its manuscript attestations. This method of writing poetry responds explicitly to modern concerns about poetic convention and genre, rather than medieval ones. Second, the contrast between an interlinear translation (which suggests a kind of linguistic equivalence) and the fact that both the introduction and Bede's subsequent Latin text note the impossibility of such an endeavor draws attention to the fact of translation itself. Despite its appearance, *all* of Bede's writing that appears in the *Norton Anthology* is a translation, one that through editorial choice eschews fidelity to Bede in favor of the very poetry he elided. These two disjunctions in turn emphasize the interaction of times—Cædmon's, Bede's, the time of the poetic version of the hymn, and the time of the modern English anthology. In so doing, they remind us that we experience Cædmon's work at a remove from its origin, one that makes it both temporally and linguistically complex. These are translation effects: they only exist because of the linguistic distance that is simultaneously referred to and erased in the *Norton Anthology*. They come into focus because the translating work of the edition leaves traces in its final form.

The temporal complexity of translation as it pertains to Cædmon's *Hymn*, however, is not limited to its modern anthologization. Even at the time of its inscription—both in Bede's narrative of the miracle and its manuscript

---

63. Bede, "Story of Cædmon," in Greenblatt, *Norton Anthology: Volume A*, 31.
64. Similar choices are made, famously, by King Alfred in the *Preface* to the *Pastoral Care* and Jerome's "Letter to Pammachius," which lays out similar concerns. See Jerome, "Letter to Pammachius," in Venuti, *Translation Studies Reader*.

context—the *Hymn*'s multiple temporalities were part and parcel of its relationship to translation. As Katherine O'Brien O'Keeffe observes, because of the poem's manuscript distribution, the *Hymn* allows scholars to explore "the transformation of a work as it passes from an oral to literate medium, [. . .] the consequent development of a text in Old English, and [. . .] the presuppositions underlying the way a text was to be read."[65] To these I would add another area of scholarly inquiry. Taken in concert with its later status as the "first" English poem (as established, for our purposes, in the *Norton Anthology*), Cædmon's *Hymn* and its textual development offer a compelling example of the temporalities that attend translation and the translation effects that bring such temporalities to light.

Although scholars have often remarked on the transmission of Cædmon's *Hymn* from the Latin of Bede's *Historia* into the Old English poem that modern students encounter in the *Norton Anthology*, they less commonly observe how deeply Bede's consideration engages with questions of translation beyond his concern about the vicissitudes of trying to translate poetry.[66] In his dream, Cædmon creates heavenly verses that praise the creator. However, when he is asked to perform for the learned men, he is not asked to compose, but rather to translate: "Exponebantque illi quendam sacrae historiae siue doctrinae sermonem, praecipientes eum, si posset, hunc in modulationem carminis **transferre**" (*HE* IV.24.418) [They then read to him a passage of sacred history or doctrine, bidding him to make a song out of it, if he could, in metrical form (417–19)] (*emphasis mine*). Although in their translation Colgrave and Mynors use the sense of *transferre* that has to do with making or transferring one thing into another, the word also carries another semantic range pertinent to our discussion here: "to put, transfer, or render into another language, translate, [. . .] to transfer into another form of expression."[67] Indeed, *transferre* is where our modern form of "translate" comes from. Here it carries a dual connotation. First, it means to transfer from one cultural milieu into another, as Cædmon creates Old English poetry from sacred stories. Second, it suggests

---

65. O'Brien O'Keeffe, *Visible Song*, 24.

66. Irvine is an important exception: he argues that Cædmon's activities are part of the literate—and textual—*grammatica* tradition. Further, he suggests that Cædmon himself functions as a kind of glossator. See Irvine, *Making of Textual Culture*, 431–35. Osborn also argues that the *Hymn* itself performs a kind of "translocation" of biblical material into Germanic praise poetry: see Osborn, "Translation, Translocation." See also Kaušikaitė and Solomonik-Pankrašova, "Vernacular Translation as *Enarratio Poetarum*"; O'Donnell, "Bede's Strategy in Paraphrasing"; Orchard, "Poetic Inspiration and Prosaic Translation" in Toswell and Tyler, *Doubt Wisely*.

67. Ashdown et al., *Dictionary of Medieval Latin from British Sources*, s.v. *transferre*[6]. Hereafter, I cite this dictionary as DMLBS.

translation from one form to another, changing the putatively prose narratives the wise men give to Cædmon to the metrical song they ask him to create.

That the central thrust of the meaning of *transferre* has to do with linguistic translation is not surprising. The learned men tell Cædmon stories, most probably after they themselves translate holy scripture from Latin into a vernacular. They then ask Cædmon to translate those stories into a new form, moving from prose to divinely inspired poetry. The Old English version of the narrative uses a verb that carries the same connotations: "Þa rehton heo him 7 sægdon sum halig spell 7 godcundre lare word: bebudon him þa, gif he meahte, þæt he in swinsunge leoþsonges þæt **gehwyrfde**" (IV.25, p. 344) [Then they told him and recited some holy stories and words of holy wisdom: they bid him then, if he could, that he turn them into melodious songs] (*emphasis mine*).[68] As in the Latin version of the text, the description of Cædmon's task has a wide semantic range, in this case concerning turning one thing into another. But again, this range encompasses linguistic considerations alongside cultural ones: *gehwyrfan* can also mean "to turn, render, translate (stories, doctrine [. . .])."[69] At the paradigmatic moment of poetic production, we also encounter a paradigmatic account of translation.

As I suggested at the outset of my analysis of the *Hymn*, translation is a central concern not only of Bede's version but also of the Old English translation thereof. Yet how does this moment of translation constitute a translation effect? After Bede introduces the story of Cædmon's *Hymn* and his paraphrase in the *Historia Ecclesiastica*, he foregrounds not the content of the hymn, but the method by which he transmits it:

> Hic est sensus, non autem ordo ipse uerborum, quae dormiens ille canebat; neque enim possunt carmina, quamuis optime conposita, ex alia in aliam linguam ad verbum sine detrimento sui decoris ac dignitatis transferri. (*HE* IV.24.416)

> This is the sense, but not the order of the words which he sang as he slept.; For it is not possible to translate verse, however well composed, literally from one language to another without some loss of beauty and dignity. (417)

Again using the word *transferre*, Bede avers that translation is only ever a partial enterprise. Any translator is bound to lose something when translating verse. Yet Bede goes further by suggesting that translating *the sense* of

---

68. Old English text from Miller, *Old English Version of Bede's Ecclesiastical History*.
69. Cameron et al., *Dictionary of Old English*, s.v. *gehwyrfan*[A.11]. This dictionary is hereafter cited as the DOE.

the words *will* preserve the materials in question: the exact song Cædmon sang while he slept is ultimately unnecessary to the narrative. Bede's careful delineation of the difference between Latin and English, prose and poetry, constitutes a translation effect: he emphasizes that he has performed translation, even if the absence of a prior record of the *Hymn* suggests Bede may have created it wholesale.[70] For Bede, the preservation of the "original" version of the poem no longer matters.

Yet the transmission history of the *Hymn* suggests that later copyists did not agree with Bede's assessment: the copyists of even very early manuscripts like the "Leningrad Bede" (Saint Petersburg, Russian National Library, Q.v.I.18)[71] and Cambridge University Library Kk.5.16[72] use marginal additions to recreate the lost hymn, either copying from other versions of the same text or creating the Old English words whole cloth from Bede's initial Latin paraphrase.[73] Instead of translating sense-for-sense *rather* than word-for-word, these later copyists of the *Historia Ecclesiastica* translate using both possibilities: the Latin paraphrases, translating sense-for-sense, while the marginal Old English creates from the Latin paraphrase an illusion of a word-for-word translation. Indeed, Kevin Kiernan has influentially argued that the copyists of the Leningrad and Cambridge University Library manuscripts utilize Bede's Latin paraphrase of Cædmon's song to *recreate its words*.[74] They translate Bede's Latin paraphrase back into the Old English Bede himself would deem irrecoverable. In a sense, they rewrite—across both time and geographical distance in the case of the West Saxon versions of the hymn—the very

---

70. Several scholars have made this assertion. Most famously, Kiernan observes that "the possibility that the Old English versions we have inherited in this way began as glosses, or reverse translations of Bede's Latin paraphrase, warrants more attention than it has yet received" ("Reading Cædmon's 'Hymn,'" 162). Similarly, Irvine surveys the manuscript context of the piece and concludes that "we must also allow for the possibility that the 'Hymn,' in both dialects, is a gloss or reverse translation of Bede's Latin paraphrase" (*Making of Textual Culture*, 434). See also Mitchell, "Cædmon's Hymn, Line 1"; O'Donnell, "Bede's Strategy in Paraphrasing"; Altman, "Hymnody, Graphotactics."

71. Ker no. 122, Gneuss-Lapidge no. 846. For manuscript numbers, description, and bibliography, see Ker, *Catalogue of Manuscripts*; Gneuss and Lapidge, *Anglo-Saxon Manuscripts*.

72. Ker no. 25, Gneuss-Lapidge no. 25.

73. O'Brien O'Keeffe's review of the hymn's manuscript setting remains the most comprehensive study of its reception in the period. According to O'Brien O'Keeffe, Saint Petersburg, Russian National Library Q.v.I.18 and Cambridge University Library Kk.5.16 are "the earliest witnesses to the text of Caedmon's *Hymn*" ("Orality and the Developing Text," 9). In the "Leningrad" Bede, the text of the hymn is written "in three long lines across the bottom margin of fol. 107r" (10). In the Cambridge University Library manuscript, it appears on the "first three lines of fol. 128v, a sort of addendum to the text of the history" (11). Schott also gives a sensitive reading of the relationship between Latin prose and English, marginal verse as part of the "intimacy of texts" ("Intimate Reading," 32–36). See also Irvine, *Making of Textual Culture*, 434.

74. Kiernan, "Reading Caedmon's 'Hymn.'"

Old English that Bede's Latin version elides. In so doing, they create a new model of textual community: one that can recover the past, in certain ways, by reinventing it.[75]

MY READING OF the many translations and transmissions of Cædmon's *Hymn* models the core interests of this monograph. On the one hand, translation is a method of movement across languages with an interest in transmitting certain key narratives to a readership removed in time and space from the originators of those narratives. On the other hand, translation is also fundamentally oriented toward building a community—including contemporaries of both the originators and the translators—and extending it across centuries, languages, and geographies through the transmission of important narratives. They create these communities, in part, through the traces of translation they reveal to the careful reader, which function as sites of multiple times and geographies.

I have used Cædmon's *Hymn* to summarize my introductory ideas in part because its position at the so-called "beginning" of Old English poetry demonstrates how central translation is to the corpus—and not just in texts that are "traditional" translinguistic translations. Cædmon's *Hymn* shows how the material conditions of a text (translated or not) create a temporally heterogeneous imagined textual community. In his careful avowal that poetic translation will always alter the text it seeks to transmit, Bede draws attention to his interpretive activities. Then in the margins of the manuscripts of the *Historia Ecclesiastica*, anonymous scribes take up the mantle of transmission and go about pursuing their *own* interpretations. A community of the page emerges in the careful work of these scribes, who when faced with the inadequacy of translation to convey poetic force, chose to invent the poem the manuscript elided. This choice creates an asynchronous conversation through translation, unfolding across time and language, on a single manuscript page.

The chapters that follow explore how such interventions create communities that stretch beyond their own immediate locale. These communities vary in language from Latin and Old English to Middle English and Anglo-Norman. They range in time from the ninth century to the fifteenth. They occur in works deemed canonical to the history of English literature and in the margins of texts that modern students rarely (if ever) read. But in each case, across time, space, and linguistic difference, these communities exist only because of the impulse to share an old story with a new audience. These communities emerge in translation.

---

75. See Bassnett, *Translation*; See also Griffin, "Time of the Translator," 34.

CHAPTER 1

What Orosius Said
Temporal Heterogeneity in the Old English *Orosius*

IN A PARTICULARLY startling moment of the Old English *Orosius*, the translator inserts an interjection into what otherwise might be confused for a faithful translation: "Gesecgað me nu, Romane, cwæð Orosius" (IV.x, p. 103) [Tell me now, Romans, said Orosius].[1] This command is surprising for several reasons. First, the translation uses a discourse marker—*cwæð Orosius*—that calls the entire status of the translation into question. It uses this construction throughout the text, and not only in moments of direct address, which makes it a rather strange addition to the translation. Second, it energetically insists on its object of address: the Romans from whom Orosius demands an answer. And finally, it reveals this demand's strange temporality: Orosius asks for an answer from these Romans "now." That he does so in ninth- or tenth-century Old English seems to matter little.[2] If Orosius said *this*, what does that mean for the rest of the text? Put another way: whose words does this phrase introduce, for whom are they written, and to what time do they belong?

In this chapter, I lay out some of the central concerns of this book by exploring these and ancillary questions regarding the Old English *Orosius*,

---

1. All Old English text is from Bately, *Old English Orosius*.
2. According to Godden, the *Orosius* can be dated to "sometime in the late ninth or early tenth century." I agree with this dating, but for the purposes of clarity simply refer to the Old English text's audience as being located "in the ninth century." Godden, *Old English History of the World*, xi.

a translation of fifth-century Roman historian Paulus Orosius's *Historiarum adversum paganos libri septem*. Orosius wrote his Christian universal history in order to counter Roman claims that the empire's conversion to Christianity brought about the sack of the city in 410 CE. To make its case, the text "presents a systematic catalogue of human misery from the Creation to the early fifth century, and repeatedly emphasizes the relative superficiality of contemporary suffering in comparison with the catastrophes of the past."[3]

The Old English *Orosius* retains this agenda, despite its vastly different historical context. One of the seven so-called "Alfredian translations,"[4] it is not what modern translation scholars call a purely "transparent" translation. That is, the Old English *Orosius*—like its Alfredian companions—is not a perfect stand-in for its Latin source. This approach is not surprising: most medieval translations do not attempt or value transparency in their work, focusing instead on other concerns such as authority or creativity. In this case, transparency usefully distinguishes between modern and medieval translation practices. Janet Bately argues that the Old English *Orosius* is perhaps best understood as a paraphrase rather than as a translation *per se*: the translator renders his subject not word-for-word but rather sense-for-sense, and exhibits "no hesitation in making radical but unacknowledged alterations to his primary source."[5] Yet the *Orosius*'s paraphrastic qualities would likely not have rendered it less of a translation in the eyes of its Old English readers. Moreover, the translator himself attributes the content of the *Orosius* to the *Historiae* despite his lack of concern with fidelity to it. Most prominently, he achieves this via his repeated use of a translation effect: the phrase *cwæð Orosius* [Orosius said].

The translator of the Old English *Orosius* repeats the *cwæð Orosius* construction forty-six times over the course of its six books. Its use serves several rhetorical purposes. Although the *cwæð* construction purports to indicate a first-person quotation of Paulus Orosius, it is ironically most often not a direct translation from the *Historiae*. Because the words that follow this phrase are frequently not at all what Orosius said, they draw attention to the addition of an extra-narrative voice in the Old English text. I call this figure the *Orosius-*

---

3. Merrills, *History and Geography in Late Antiquity*, 39–40.

4. For scholarly considerations of the Old English *Orosius* with particular regard to its status as an "Alfredian translation," see Leneghan, "*Translatio Imperii*"; Tyler, "Writing Universal History," in Campopiano and Bainton, *University Chronicles in the High Middle Ages*; Bately, "Old English *Orosius*," in Discenza and Szarmach, *Companion to Alfred*; Godden, "*Orosius* and Its Sources"; Harris, "Alfredian World History"; Kretzschmar, "Adaptation and *anweald*"; Bately, "World History and the Anglo-Saxon *Chronicle*"; Bately, "King Alfred and the *Orosius*."

5. Bately, *Old English Orosius*, xciii.

narrator.⁶ Because it draws attention to the hand of the translator, the presence of the *cwæð Orosius* is somewhat puzzling: as a translation, the entirety of the Old English *Orosius* is meant to be what "Orosius said." Why, then, does this construction occur and what effect does it have on the narrative?

I argue that the presence of the *cwæð Orosius* demonstrates that the Old English text constructs an audience located in two distinct times: the fifth-century Roman world of Paulus Orosius and the ninth-century Old English-speaking world for whom his work was among the books deemed "most needful to know."⁷ The text rewrites the identity and message of the historical Orosius and his *Historiae* for the Old English future into which the *Orosius*-narrator speaks by collocating two temporally distinct textual communities into a single imagined one.⁸ While this audience resembles Brian Stock's idea of a textual community, the key difference between it and the communities that Stock examines is historical reality. Whereas Stock referred to specific localizable groups who used the texts he studied, and although there may well have been historical textual communities that formed around the *Orosius*, we have little-to-no access to their composition.⁹ Therefore, the textual communities I am interested in are best framed as imagined, or "virtual"—that is, they are formed by an anticipated readership within the text rather than an extant one outside of it.¹⁰ An analysis of the Old English *Orosius* thus serves to estab-

---

6. The author-figure is an effect produced by the text and should be distinguished from the historical figure Paulus Orosius, however much the text wishes to fuse them together. For clarity's sake, I refer to the author Paulus Orosius and his Latin *Historiae*. I refer to the Old English translation as the *Orosius*, and the author-figure therein as the *Orosius*-narrator.

7. Sweet, *King Alfred's West-Saxon Version of the Pastoral Care*, 6. My interest in the collocation of different temporalities in the Old English *Orosius* owes much to Strohm, *Theory and the Premodern Text*. Strohm argues that "no text fails to bear within itself a range of alien temporalities, imported into its bounds as unavoidable part and parcel of the words and images of which it is made." Therefore, each text "harbors different notions of time" (Strohm, 81). In this view of textual representation and production, the text becomes a collection not merely of words, stories, or characters, but of times as well: the narrative present is always "held hostage to the past and future" (Strohm, 81). Fafinski divides the temporalities of the Old English *Orosius* into the *nu* of early medieval England and the *nunc* of fifth-century Rome. See Fafinski, "Faraway, So Close."

8. See Anderson, *Imagined Communities*.

9. Stock, *Implications of Literacy*, 522–30. Stock describes such communities as "groups of people whose social activities are centered around texts, or, more precisely, around a literate interpreter of them" (Stock, 522).

10. My understanding of the "virtuality" of the textual communities formed by the Old English *Orosius* is particularly indebted to the work of Martin K. Foys. See Foys, *Virtually Anglo-Saxon*. In his consideration of the Cotton Map, Foys argues that in relation to the Orosian geography it attempts to represent, "the plotting of narrative lines on geographic lines (and vice versa) calls attention to how the narratives of written histories and geographies construct a reality at least one plane removed from the 'primary world'" (Foys, 127). The reality

lish one of the primary functions of translation effects: to alter how readers perceive community and time in translations.

ROME AND EARLY MEDIEVAL ENGLAND

The contextual background of the *Historiae* deeply informs the translation of the Old English *Orosius*. Paulus Orosius wrote his world history partly to address—and to rebuke—the discontent that some citizens of the Roman Empire felt. These citizens purportedly attributed the sack of Rome by Alaric the Goth in 410 CE to the empire's conversion to Christianity.[11] The *Historiae* was written as a companion piece to Saint Augustine's *City of God* and includes an introductory preface addressed to Augustine, Orosius's mentor. Orosius asserts that he wrote his book because "Nanctus sum enim praeteritos dies non solum aeque ut hos graues, uerum etiam tanto atrocius miseros quanto longius a remedio uerae religionis alienos" (I.Prol.2) [I found that the days gone by were as fraught as the present, and all the more horribly wretched as they were further from the salvation of True Religion (33.14)].[12] From the very beginning of the *Historiae,* Orosius avers that the only proper reading of history is a Christian one. Such a reading shows that the past was, in a sense, destitute. The further back one looks in history, the worse the situation was. Per Orosius, this deterioration is a result of the increasing distance from Christianity and its salutary effects on history.

In Orosius's view, understanding and insight into the meaning of historical events cannot exist without the acknowledgment of Christ as both an historical and hermeneutic figure. Orosius reveals the evils of the past to be all the more heinous when seen from a Christian viewpoint. He suggests that the pre-Christian world did not know how to read history—a trait they share with contemporary non-Christians: "Qui cum futura non quaerant, praeterita autem aut obliuiscantur aut nesciant" (I.Prol.2) [They do not look to the future and have either forgotten or are ignorant of the past (32.9)]. His implicit argument is that contemporary non-Christians cannot correctly interpret the past

---

thus constructed "dissolves temporal distinctions, [. . .] expands the reality of its Anglo-Saxon counterpart, and attempts to open up its future" (Foys, 146).

11. For a full account of the historical milieu of Paulus Orosius and his impetus for writing his *Historiae*, see Bately, *Old English Orosius*, xciii–xciv. See also Orosius, *Seven Books of History against the Pagans*, ed. and trans. Deferrari, xv–xx.

12. This preface was either omitted or lost from the Old English text. All Latin text from the *Historiae* is drawn from Orosius, *Historiarum Adversum Paganos Libri Septem*, ed. Zangemeister. English translations are from Paulus Orosius, *The Seven Books of History against the Pagans*, ed. and trans. Fear.

because they cannot appreciate the inevitability of a future that is destined by the divine.[13]

A defining structural feature of both the Latin *Historiae* and the Old English *Orosius* is that both texts historically locate all events with reference to the number of years they occurred before or after the building of Rome. In the Old English text, each chapter begins with either "Ær ðam þe Romeburg getimbred wæs" [Before the city of Rome was built] or "Æfter ðam þe Romeburg getimbred wæs" [After the city of Rome was built], followed by the relevant number of winters, or years.[14] These references to Rome function in part "[to evoke] that city's centrality in western Christendom,"[15] as Nicholas Howe suggests. Moreover, the dating of each event in the *Orosius* in terms of the founding of Rome suggests continuity between the Roman Empire and the early medieval English, who were partial inheritors of the Roman tradition of historiography.[16]

Because the Roman world fell into decay between the writing of the *Historiae* and the writing of the Old English *Orosius*, the translation preserves what M. R. Godden terms a "monument to the fallen Roman world, a snapshot of a moment when the empire tottered on the brink of dissolution and yet contemporaries could insist that all was well."[17] Godden is one of the few scholars to specifically consider the phrase *cwæð Orosius*, arguing that it demonstrates

---

13. Orosius clearly saw himself in the same tradition as Augustine in terms of his understanding of the relation of human history to divine providence; however, Orosius's conception of *historia* differs significantly from his mentor's and is generally considered less sophisticated. See Rohrbacker, *Historians of Late Antiquity*, 147–48. On the key differences between Augustine's and Orosius's conceptions of history, see Bittner, "Augustine's Philosophy of History," in Matthews, *Augustinian Tradition*.

14. For both Paulus Orosius and the Old English translator, the entirety of history is structured around the building of Rome rather than Christ's birth. Although the nativity is given significant attention in the Latin text, the Old English translation drastically reduces its presence to no more than a passing mention (VI.i, p. 132).

15. Howe, "Rome: Capital of Anglo-Saxon England," 158. For Howe, the translation of so many prominent Latin works into the vernacular under Alfred constitutes a "forced program of modernization that sought to reconnect the badly educated and peripheral Anglo-Saxons to the center of Christian belief and culture" (158).

16. As Leneghan argues, the text takes a special interest in empires and their rise and fall, which he connects to the expansion of Wessex in the tenth century as an explicit instance of *translatio imperii*. See Leneghan, "*Translatio Imperii*"; Tyler, "Writing Universal History," in Campopiano and Bainton, *Universal Chronicles*.

17. Godden, "Rewriting the Sack of Rome," 61. The translation can thus preserve the irony of the Latin context while simultaneously adding to it the knowledge, in non-verbal apposition, of what Orosius could not have known or predicted—that Rome would indeed fall, and that Alaric's conquest was not simply a gentle admonishment from God—because it does not follow the logic of the worldview he presents. See also Howe, *Migration and Mythmaking*, 176, for the idea of an "appositive geography."

that the Old English translator was very aware of the vast difference between his historical moment and that of Paulus Orosius.[18] With the exception of the Old English *Historia Ecclesiastica*, which uses "cwæð Beda" a handful of times, the *Orosius* is unique among the Alfredian translations for its use of this peculiar phrase.[19] Its use creates what Godden terms a "distancing" effect in the translation, indicating that the material that follows is not "taken from the Latin originals; it is often sheer invention by the translator."[20] What Godden terms a distancing effect might also be termed a translation effect—a moment in which a text draws attention to itself as a translation, regardless of whether or not it actually is one. In the Old English *Orosius*, the *cwæð Orosius* invokes an author-figure to claim words that Paulus Orosius could never have said in an Old English he could not have spoken. The *cwæð Orosius* thus allows the text to stage the intermingling of two times: Orosius's Rome, which had not yet fallen, and Alfred's England, with its uncertain future. The result is a composite conception of early English identity within the translated text.

As a translation effect, the *cwæð* construction performs a similar function to the prefaces in other Old English translations. Nicole Discenza argues that prefaces transfer authorial power from Latin authors to Old English translators, whether the preface is original to the Old English or is a translation from Latin.[21] In transferring this authority, the prefaces also draw attention to the following text *as a translation* in two distinct senses: not only one between languages but also one that is a movement or "carrying over" of power and authority.[22] The absence of any preface to the Old English *Orosius*, however, necessitates the location of the translator's authority in another form, which I argue can be found in the *Orosius*-narrator.[23] Because what follows the *cwæð* does not necessarily belong to the "original" Latin text, however, its use indicates the presence of both the narrator and also another authoritative voice, one that is not entirely coterminous with it: the Old English translator who

---

18. Godden, "Rewriting the Sack of Rome," 61–62. For a consideration of a similar phrase's translation work in the Old English *Historia Ecclesiastica*, see Rowley, "'Ic Beda' . . . 'Cwæð Beda.'"

19. Although the *Dialogues*, the *Soliloquies*, and the *Boethius* all use a similar phrase with their respective Latin authors, they are different in kind from the *Orosius* because they are all in the form of dialogues, and thus the author of the Latin texts speaks routinely throughout the works.

20. Godden, "Rewriting the Sack of Rome," 62; "Did King Alfred Write Anything?," 7.

21. Discenza, "Construction of Anglo-Saxon Authority."

22. For more on the influence of *translatio studii, translatio imperii*, see Copeland, *Rhetoric, Hermeneutics, and Translation*, 105–7. See also Introduction, n. 48, this volume.

23. The geographical preface has attracted much attention from scholars; however, it does not fulfill the same function as the more traditional preface in the Latin *Historiae*. See Leneghan, "*Translatio Imperii*."

refers to the narrator. This voice speaks across time: it invents what "Orosius said" while inevitably demonstrating the text's distance from the historian who purportedly said it.

Examining the *cwæð* construction as a translation effect reveals the *Orosius*-narrator as an author-figure with specific tasks to perform in relation to the history he writes. These tasks exist in addition to and in excess of the simple report of events. First, the *cwæð Orosius* portrays the *Orosius*-narrator as a purveyor of knowledge and therefore as a figure who carries narrative authority. Second, it depicts the *Orosius*-narrator as the *compilator* of his work: he decides how the history he writes will and, moreover, *ought* to be written.[24] As a composer, the *Orosius*-narrator performs several crucial tasks that are associated with narrative boundaries. He decides when and where to begin and end both individual narratives and the books in which he records them. Similarly, he delimits the boundaries of what should and should not be included in history.

These first two functions of the *cwæð* construction create a volitional role for the *Orosius*-narrator. In so doing, they evoke the final function of the *cwæð Orosius*: the creation of an authorial voice that not only relates information but also renders judgment upon it. This third use of the *cwæð Orosius* characterizes the historian as a judge. He stands as the arbiter of what is worthy of record and what ought to be left out, including distinctions between Christian and non-Christian worldviews. These three narrative effects—portraying the *Orosius*-narrator as a master of knowledge, a shaper of historical writings, and the arbiter of good and evil—are often all at work in the same occurrence of the *cwæð* construction.

Such uses of the phrase *cwæð Orosius* signal moments of cultural interpretation. Attention to them alters our critical perception of the *Orosius* to better account for the multitemporal valences of translation. When collated, they allow for a modern reading of the text that reaches beyond the historiographical narrative to enable an understanding of the Old English interpretation of the *Historiae*.[25] The Old English text uses translation effects to position the

---

24. Irvine, *Making of Textual Culture*, 242. See also Copeland, who argues that the role of the *compilator* was to gather "together the opinions of others rather than setting forth his own" (*Rhetoric, Hermeneutics, and Translation*, 196). In this sense, the *Orosius*-narrator's work as *compilator* draws indirectly on the same tradition as Isidore's *Etymologiae* and Jerome's *Liber quaestionum hebricarum in Genesim*. See Lindsay, *Isidori Hispanlensis episcopi Etymologiarum sive Originum libri XX*; for a translation, see Barney et al., *Etymologies of Isidore of Seville*. See Hieronymus, *Hebraicae quaestiones in libro Geneseos*. For a translation, see Hayward, "Saint Jerome's Hebrew Questions."

25. Here I draw on particularly useful work done in the introduction to Tyler and Balzaretti, *Narrative and History*. They suggest "that conventions were maintained, not by abstract

Orosius-narrator as a voice that both narrates and comments upon the history of the world. This characterization portrays the *Orosius*-narrator as part of a tradition of historical commentary but simultaneously changes how the text is received in its future. The translation modifies the text's portrayal of Roman history and serves to change the implied audience members' self-perception as inheritors of a "Roman" tradition.[26] Translation effects in the *Orosius* reshape both the text and its implied audience.

WHAT OROSIUS SAID

Collating what "Orosius said" in the Old English *Orosius* demonstrates some of the temporal implications of the text that are made apparent because of the presence of translation effects and the author-figure they construct. The text portrays this figure both as a writer who explicitly states his reasons for abridging certain stories or ending books at specific junctures (often with obsessive clarity) and as a moral authority who stands not only willing but eager to judge the past he records. Understanding these roles of the *Orosius*-narrator as they are created by the *cwæð* construction begins to reveal the entangled eras to which this figure speaks.

In each of the forty-six appearances of the *cwæð* construction, the Old English text invokes the *figure* of Paulus Orosius, without necessarily relying on his Latin words to do so. The most straightforward way that the text uses the *Orosius*-narrator is in terms of the knowledge he conveys as an historian. The *cwæð* construction asserts control over the process of recording history and forecloses the possibility of alternative narratives. The use of the *cwæð* construction to demonstrate the author's skillful manipulation of the writing of his text reveals another dimension of the historian's work, one that is broadly related to the assumption that history must be understood in the way that the *Orosius*-narrator portrays it. This control extends to the *Orosius*-narrator's ability—perhaps even responsibility—to judge the worth of the past he records.

The transmission of knowledge signaled by the *cwæð* construction first appears at the very beginning of the translation, where it indicates an authoritative geographical demarcation. The *Orosius*-narrator outlines the view of the world's geography accepted by *ure ieldran* (our ancestors): "Ure ieldran ealne

---

diplomatic, poetic, or hagiographic traditions, but by people who found the conventions useful in shaping lived experience" (8).

26. For a particularly fruitful discussion of the function of the narrator in Old English poetry, see Parks, "'I Heard' Formulas." See also VanderBilt, "Translation and Orality."

þisne ymbhwyrft þises middangeardes, cwæþ Orosius, swa swa Oceanus utan ymbligeþ, þone [mon] garsæcg hateð, on þreo todældon 7 hie þa þrie dælas on þreo tonemdon: Asiam 7 Europem 7 Affricam, þeah þe sume men sæden þæt þær nære buton twegen dælas: Asia 7 þæt oþer Europe" (I.i, p. 8) [Our ancestors divided into three parts all of Middle Earth, said Orosius, around which Oceanus—which men call *garsecg*—lies outside, and they distinguished the three parts with three names: Asia and Europe and Africa, although some said that there were but two parts, Asia and the other, Europe]. Here, the *Orosius*-narrator comments on past cartographic practices which, despite variation, might also be considered accepted truth.[27] Yet the *cwæð* construction also foregrounds the act of translation, in which the Latin *Oceanus* is explicitly glossed with the Old English *garsecg*. Meanwhile, the grammatical construction of the phrase raises the question of temporality in the text vis-à-vis the construction of authority. Both the *cwæð* construction and the verb *hatan* appear in the past tense. At the very moment in which the text highlights a question of authority by invoking the proper name of Paulus Orosius and the idea of what "Orosius said," it also dislodges the identification of this knowledge with the past by translating *Oceanus* with an Old English term Paulus Orosius and his contemporaries could not have used, placing the language in a Roman past in which it has no real context.[28]

The *cwæð Orosius* sometimes also positions the *Orosius*-narrator as an authority who is part of a larger system of knowledge-making, a use that is most evident when the text presents the *Orosius*-narrator as a second-hand witness to the information in question. The verb *hyran* identifies the *Orosius*-narrator as someone who has heard of the event he reports. When the *Orosius*-narrator describes a particularly war-torn era (approximately 298 BCE) in the pre-Christian Roman Empire, the Old English direct citation of his words is indicated by the *cwæð* construction:

Eac ic hierde to soþum secgan, cwæð Orosius, þæt hit na nære on ðæm dagum mid Romanum buton gewinne, oþþe wið oþra folc, oþþe on him selfum mid monigfealdum wolum & moncwealmum. (Book III.x, p. 75)

---

27. Other occurrences are similar: the *cwæð* construction appears in Book III.v (58) in the context of the doors of Janus and what they stood for; in Book IV.xiii (112) with regard to the size and description of the city of Cartaina; and in Book VI.xxxvii (155) to bring the history of the ancients into the present of Orosius's fifth-century Roman Empire.

28. Discenza argues that this moment in the text is particularly disruptive to readers, who would initially identify with the "ure" of "ure ieldran" only to experience a discomfiting mélange of both Latin and Old English terms and expectations (*Inhabited Spaces*, 110–11).

> Also I have heard it said as a truth, said Orosius, that it was not only in those days among the Romans that there were wars with other folk, but also that amid themselves there were manifold evils and manslaughters.

The significance of this assertion of second-hand knowledge has less to do with factual reporting than it does with the interpretation of what transpired. The use of *ic hierde* suggests the presence of a transmitted history by indicating a moment in the text at which the *Orosius*-narrator reports "a truth" that he has heard from another source. The result is the construction of the *Orosius*-narrator as an authority figure in the text and as a figure with knowledge of the historical events in question—a knowledge he possesses because he has learned of them from sources that are presumably trustworthy. The Latin text uses a version of this technique as well: Paulus Orosius often cites his sources when he draws on Livy or Augustine. However, the Old English translation of this reception refers not only to the literate Latin tradition of history but also to the more familiar figure of orality in Old English.[29] In short, it represents the textual portrayal of an oral tradition, in which *ic hierde* suggests a reliance upon nonwritten narrative transmission.

Ward Parks argues for the importance of distinguishing between the passive and active constructions of this form. When a narrator speaks in the active voice, he speaks as a direct hearer and transmitter of the story he tells. In the passive voice, he tells a story that has been heard but plays no part in the chain of transmission thereof.[30] This movement from first-person active to third-person passive is one way in which the Latin and the Old English texts are significantly different, despite the similarity of the concrete information conveyed. The use of the active voice in the Old English—even if it is only the act of hearing something said—presents the *Orosius*-narrator as an agent in the passing on of the narrative despite the past tense of the *cwæð*.

In the Latin *Historiae,* the equivalent section of the text uses the passive voice. Paulus Orosius notes the common knowledge of his time, but he does not play an active role in passing it on: "Sed—ut saepe dictum est semper Romanorum aut domesticam quietem extraneis bellis interpellatam aut externos prouentus morbis interioribus adgrauatos, tantum ut omnimodis ingentes animi undecumque premerentur" (III.21.90) [But—as has often been pointed out, the Romans' high hopes have always been completely checked from all

---

29. For a thorough consideration of orality in the *Orosius*, see VanderBilt, "Translation and Orality."

30. Parks, "'I Heard' Formulas," 52. The chain of transmission examined by Parks begins from a single point of departure: in a culture where orality is primary, "poems and stories are perceived not as things or objects but as events that occur in time" (52).

directions, either by having their harmony at home disrupted by war abroad or their foreign adventures made worse by plague at home (143.7)]. The passive construction (*saepe dictum est*) in the Latin suggests the transmission of received knowledge on the part of the historian. The difference between the two usages lies in the way in which authority—and thus the character of the narrator—is constructed.³¹ *Dictum est* is both passive and impersonal, suggesting that although other specific sources have been cited mere lines before in the text, this "truth" is generally accepted by all. The *sed* suggests a turn away from the authorities that have been mentioned thus far in the *Historiae*, such as Orosius's citation of Livy for specific figures about the loss of life in the battles between the Romans, the Samnites, and the Gauls, and toward a different kind of truth.³²

Where the passive voice of the *Historiae* suggests that Paulus Orosius relies on other authorities for his mandates and judgments, the *Orosius*-narrator in the Old English *Orosius* acts as an authority himself. The use of the first person in this section stands in for and amplifies the *cwæð* Orosius by directly citing the authorial figure: he reports that "Ic hierde to soþum secgan" [I heard it said as a truth]. The use of the pronoun *ic* establishes an immediate relationship between the *Orosius*-narrator and the knowledge he passes on. The difference between the two passages lies not in the factual information conveyed but in how each text characterizes its narrator. The Old English text invokes the poetic *ic hierde* construction as a way of "summoning [the] recollection [of things said] into [its] own telling."³³ The *Orosius* figures its narrator as part of the textual representation of an oral tradition—a tradition that, if not entirely foreign to the culture in which the *Historiae* was written, is certainly temporally and geographically distant. When combined with the presence of the *cwæð* construction, the first-person *ic hierde* of the *Orosius*-narrator claims the authority of a writer who is antiquated in early medieval England, as temporally remote from that context as the fifth-century Orosius was from his classical sources. In short, the voice represented in the *Orosius* as that of Paulus Orosius is out of its proper time, and the active role it plays in shaping the history contained in the text can be understood as both Latinate and Old English in origin.

---

31. Although the passive voice is easier to form in Latin, Old English is no stranger to it. Indeed, many of the examples of the passive voice in the Alfredian translations in Mitchell's *Old English Syntax* (307–8) are drawn from the *Orosius*.

32. He also notes that the triumphal procession was met with dead bodies of Roman plague victims (III.x, p. 75).

33. Parks, "'I Heard' Formulas," 53.

Only once in the Old English text is the *cwæð Orosius* used to make a truth-claim regarding faith, an issue one would expect an anti-pagan polemicist to approach with absolute authority. In Book II.i, the *Orosius*-narrator makes the following statement about the basic tenets of the Christian faith: "Ic wene, cwæð Orosius, þæt nan wis mon ne sie, buton he genoh geare wite þætte God þone ærestan monn ryhtne 7 godne gesceop, 7 eal monncynn mid him" (II.i, p. 35) [I believe, said Orosius, that no man be wise unless he knows clearly enough that God shaped the first man just and good, and all mankind with him]. This section prefaces a number of other statements of belief associated with Christianity, culminating in an explication of how divine power and temporal power interact:

> Nu we witon þæt ealle onwealdas from him sindon, we witon eac þæt ealle ricu sint from him, for þon ealle onwealdas of rice sindon. Nu he þara læssena rica reccend is, hu micle swiþor wene we þæt he ofer þa maran sie, þe on swa unmetlican onwealdun ricsedon. (II.i, p. 36)

> Now we know that all powers are from him; we also know that all kingdoms are from him, because all powers are of kingdoms. Now because he [God] is the governor of the lesser kingdoms, how much greater then do we believe [his power] to be over the greater, those who ruled with such unmeasured power.

In an elegant syllogism, the text makes clear the relationship of power and authority as they are connected to the shaping of the world. Because power is granted by God, and power is granted to kingdoms (*rice*), then all kingdoms must hold power from God. The subtext is that this truth holds regardless of whether the kingdom acknowledges the deity. As readers, we are asked to see a truth that might not be acknowledged by non-Christian actors in history. The narrator thus implies that the historian's knowledge is potentially applicable universally: the *Orosius*-narrator states a truth that is as much English as it is Roman. This knowledge binds together a Christian community that exists across time, which is signaled by the transition from first-person singular to first-person plural.

In this instance, *we witon* appears alongside both the *cwæð* construction and the first-person assertion *ic wene*. The movement from a statement of personal belief apparent in "ic wene, cwæð Orosius" to the statement of shared belief implied by *we witon* includes the *Orosius*-narrator with his Christian audience; it also introduces the volitional role associated with the narrator's authority to both shape and judge history. The *cwæð* construction occurs only five times in association with *ic wene* and this articulation of shared faith is the only instance in which it is stated in a positive sense. The other four instances of *cwæð Orosius* in this context occur in negative constructions: "ne wene ic, cwæð Orosius." Each time, it concerns the possibility of history being told in a different way—a way with which the *Orosius*-narrator does not agree. The *Orosius*-narrator thus makes an implicit claim that he is the purveyor of the authoritative version of history.[34]

SHAPING HISTORY

The authority wielded by the *Orosius*-narrator—either as a recorder of information widely known or as a second-hand witness to knowledge passed down from other sources—is complemented by the *Orosius*-narrator's ability to shape the writing of history and ultimately to judge those about whom he writes. Most often, this function relates to the question of how the books in the *Orosius* are arranged and which materials they include. An example in Book II marks the transition from one subject matter to another. The *Orosius*-narrator relates the story of the Laecademonians in their opposition to Persia. The scope of the text is reined in: "Nu we sculon eft, cwæð Orosius, hwierfan near Roma, þær we hit ær forleton" (II.v, p. 49) [Now we shall again, said Orosius, turn nearer to Rome, where we before left it].

Here, the *cwæð Orosius* translation effect indicates a decision, one that entails a measure of judgment. The *Orosius*-narrator suggests that his return to Roman matters is necessary for two reasons. First, he is unable to relate the number of evil deeds that were performed in this period of history.[35] Second, he emphasizes that he lacks the knowledge to speak authoritatively about all matters: "Ic eac ealles þises middangeardes na maran dæles ne angite buton ðætte on twam onwealdum gewearð, on þæm ærestan and on ðæm siþemestan: þæt sint Asirie and Romane" (II.v, p. 49) [I also of all of this middle earth do not understand the greater part, except for what happened in two empires, in the first and in the most recent: those are the Assyrians and the Romans].

---

34. The negative instances of the *ic wene* and the *cwæð* construction occur only in Books II and III. In Book II.viii, it accompanies the statement that the *Orosius*-narrator does not believe that anyone can relate the harm done by the Romans (52). Also in Book II.viii, it accompanies the decision to end Book II and move to Book III, a use I discuss below (53). The first use in Book III.i accompanies the assertion that no one fought more hardily than two specific leaders (54). Finally, in Book III.xi, the *Orosius*-narrator asserts the magnitude of death that accompanies a battle, claiming that no one could count the number of the slain (81).

35. "For þon ic ne mæg eal þa monigfealdan yfel emdenes areccean" (II.v, p. 49) [Because I cannot tell all of the manifold evils (they committed) without (any) exception].

This admitted limit to the *Orosius*-narrator's knowledge is not present in the Latin text. In the *Historiae,* only the overwhelming number of evils stops Paulus Orosius from cataloguing further events, and we are left with the impression that he moves on only because he needs to give each part of the world equal time.[36]

At other points in the text, the *cwæð* construction performs a textual marking of boundaries and makes clear how the *cwæð Orosius* muddles temporal distinctions between early medieval England and Late Antique Rome. Near the end of Book II, for example, the phrase arises in the context of where and why the *Orosius*-narrator chooses to end the book in question: "Ne wene ic, cwæð Orosius, nu ic longe spell hæbbe to secgenne, þæt ic hie on þisse bec geendian mæge. Ac ic oþere anginnan sceal" (II.viii, p. 53) [I do not believe, said Orosius, now that I have to tell a long story, that I may end it in this book; so I shall begin another one]. In this instance, the *Orosius*-narrator decides to end a book simply because there is too much material for one volume.

The Latin text also signals that the historian has reached the limits of what he can finish in a single book, but to an extent, defers his agency over the decision. Paulus Orosius states, "Et quoniam uber dicendi materia est, quae nequaquam hoc concludi libro potest, hic praesentis uoluminis finis sit, ut in subsequentibus cetera persequamur" (II.19.62) [Now since there is an abundance of material, which cannot in any way be dealt with definitively in this book, I have put an end here to this volume so that we may examine what is left in the ones that follow (108.16)]. The materials themselves are abundant and incapable of being confined to the current book. Whereas in the *Historiae,* Paulus Orosius seems to face a necessity, the *Orosius*-narrator actively chooses the moment at which he moves to a new book. He thus shapes the materials of the history he writes.

The use of the *cwæð Orosius* to mark authorial choice in the arrangement of the text is more significant than one might initially suspect. In fact, the use of the *cwæð* construction extends not only to the length and division of different sections of the text but also to the material included in those sections. In Book I.xi, the *Orosius*-narrator suggests that he omits certain materials because a further reading list is readily available:

> Hwa is þætte ariman mæge hwæt þær moncynnes forwearð on ægðere hand? Þæt Omarus se scop sweotelicost sægde. For þon nis me þæs þearf, cwæð Orosius, to secgenne, for þon hit longsum is 7 eac monegum cuð. (I.xi, p. 31–32)

---

36. See *Historiae,* II.12.49.

Who is there that may count how many men were lost on both sides, as Homer the *scop* has most clearly said. For that reason, it is not needful for me, said Orosius, to say, because it is long and also known to many.

The first part of this statement suggests that the narrator has a basic awareness of the contents of song and story that have gone before him—he even assimilates Homer to an Old English context by calling him a *scop*. The *Orosius*-narrator implies that because this part of history has already been recorded, what matters is the interpretation of the texts that have been handed down.

Such an assertion by the *Orosius*-narrator raises the question of whether or not English audiences could have had access to the stories in question. Although some of Paulus Orosius's sources were available in the period, there is virtually no possibility that a reader in early medieval England had access to the mythological stories of Homer.[37] What we hear at this point, rather, is the voice of a Latin historian breaking through the Old English prose. The *Orosius*-narrator asks his audience to learn of these stories on their own, even though there is no source from which they could do so. The expectation that the audience might learn these apparently well-known stories for themselves is one that comes quite literally from another time.

Because of the omission or loss of any translation of the preface to the Latin *Historiae* in the Old English *Orosius*, these moments that suggest an authorial presence (however narratively constructed) give our only glimpse of the translator's perception of the Latin *Historiae*'s goals in relating the history of the world.[38] In several places, the text speaks against those pagans who would attribute the fall of Rome in 410 CE to the acceptance of Christianity on the part of the Roman populace, which suggests the revisionist goals of the project. In a discussion of the content of Book III, the use of the *cwæð* construction suggests that there is, in fact, a remarkably clear vision of the history's purpose: "For þon ic wolde gesecgan, cwæð Orosius, hu Creca gewinn [angan], þe of Læcedemonia ðære byrg ærest onsteled wæs, and mid spell-

---

37. See Bately, *Old English Orosius*, 222n32/2. Bately's discussion of the Orosius's sources in her introduction is particularly helpful for determining what Latin texts were available to the *Orosius* translator (see especially lxi–lxiii). Additionally, see Bately, "Classics and Late Ninth-Century England," in Bernardo and Levin, *Classics in the Middle Ages*. Here, Bately argues that although the translator of the *Orosius* cites Homer as an authority, "his secondary Latin source, however, like Alfred's [in the *Boethius* translation] is probably ultimately Dares Frigius" (63). Lapidge casts doubt on Bately's source identifications, arguing that "for a number of these sources—Livy, Curtius Rufus, and Suetonius—there is no independent evidence of circulation in England before 1066" (*Anglo-Saxon Library*, 49n84).

38. This absence bears some resemblance to the Old English *Bede* as examined in Discenza, "Construction of Anglo-Saxon Authority." See also Davis, "National Writing."

cwidum gemearcian" (III.i, p. 55) [Therefore, I wish to say and mark with historical narratives, said Orosius, how the war of the Greeks began, which was first raised from the city of Læcedemonia]. In this instance of the *cwæð* construction, the *Orosius*-narrator tells his readers what the translator sees himself doing: in this history, he "wish[es] to say" [*wolde gesecgan*] and also "mark with historical narratives" [*mid spellcwidum gemearcian*] the events of the past. The Old English translator invokes the proper name of Orosius precisely at the moment in which his craft is most apparent.

Using the phrase *mid spellcwidum gemearcian,* the *Orosius* explicitly outlines part of its agenda, suggesting a specific interpretation and recording of the events in question. *Gemearcian* is a relatively common word in the corpus, occurring over four hundred times and having several separate but related meanings—"to mark, point out, describe, assign, appoint, determine."[39] Crucially, all of these meanings suggest the agency of the subject who performs them. The verb *gemearcian,* therefore, seems to indicate a very specific kind of shaping that is essential to the definition of its object. *Spellcwide,* on the other hand, is a *hapax legomenon* in the Old English corpus, defined in Bosworth-Toller as "historical narrative."[40] Both *spell* and *cwide* might well be interpreted with a certain homiletic or didactic quality, which suggests that the work done by the text is a kind of judgment of the past in specifically Christian terms. *Mid spellcwidum gemearcian* might therefore be translated best as "with historical interpretations [or judgments] mark the boundaries of" each of the societies and peoples in question. The result of this retranslation of the hapax *spellcwide* is the understanding that the project of the Old English *Orosius* is to write out *and* evaluate the stories of peoples present in the world history it translates.

---

39. Bosworth and Toller, "Anglo-Saxon Dictionary Online," s.v. *ge-mearcian*. This dictionary is hereafter cited as BT.

40. This definition is telling—both *spell* and *cwidan* have overtones of the idea of the modern "story," but a tracing of their semantic ranges suggests a far more meaningful interpretation in the context of the Old English world history. *Spell* is mostly used in the context of narratives or stories more generally, whether they are true or false. It has another meaning that occurs in overtly Christian contexts as a "message" or "announcement" with the intention that such news be spread—one such example is *Godspell,* the "good news" or modern "Gospel." *Cwide* similarly encodes ideas of storytelling, but with a slightly different overtone, including "wise utterance, saying" and "treatise or sermon." *Cwide* carries a semantic range that moves from thought more generally to religious homiletics and legal discourse—further strengthening the implication of the intellectual element of the work of the historian. See BT, s.v. *spell*; DOE, s.v. *cwide*; BT, s.v. *spell-cwide*.

JUDGING HISTORY

This evaluation most often positions the *Orosius*-narrator as judge of good and evil, assessor of what is shameful, and arbiter of what should and should not be preserved in the writing of history. However, the role played by the *Orosius*-narrator is complicated by the temporal heterogeneity of the translation and the judgment of the past rendered by the translated text. By judging not simply the morality of the past but its very right to be remembered, the *Orosius*-narrator alters the past as it is written: he changes the past (textually) by amending the translation. It is this final function indicated by the phrase *cwæð Orosius* that connects most clearly to the idea of the historian as one who "with historical interpretations [or judgments] marks the boundaries of" history. Textual authority becomes moral authority, identified by its ability to deliver the true message of events signified by Christian doctrine.

In his judgment of history, the key distinction that the *Orosius*-narrator makes is between the pre-Christian past and the Christian present and future. The text's agenda is to contrast the two by arguing that the world has distinctly improved since the Incarnation. Furthermore, by writing a Christian universal history, the *Orosius*-narrator claims authority over the interpretation of the past. The Old English *Orosius* accomplishes this by invoking Orosius's name. In Book IV, for example, the *Orosius*-narrator speaks directly to the false interpretation of history and, moreover, against the juxtaposition of the past and present that would cast the pre-Christian world favorably by comparison. The *cwæð* construction frames the interpretation of the years that the Romans wish to set against the catastrophes of their present: "Wiotodlice, cwæð Orosius, nu we sindon cumen to þæm godan tidun þe us Romane oþwitað, 7 to ðære genihtsumnisse þe hie us ealneg fore gielpað þæt ure ne sien ðæm gelican" (IV.vii, p. 97) [Truly, said Orosius, now we are come to those good times with which the Romans reproach us, and to the plenty with which they always boast before us, that (our times) are not like theirs]. This assertion comes in a passage concerning a temporary peace that occurred during the Punic Wars. Yet in claiming these kinds of "good times," the Christians' detractors seem unaware of basic arithmetic. The wars had gone on for four hundred years, and peace lasted only a single year. Clearly, then, the "good times" of the Romans are not *really* good times at all.[41] Their interpretation of history, therefore, only proves that the Romans' view is simply not large enough. It

---

41. For an alternative analysis of the idea of *cristendom* as an interpretive paradigm in the Old English *Orosius* and other Alfredian translations, see Harris, *Race and Ethnicity in Anglo-Saxon Literature*, 83–106.

does not consider the long history of warfare, violence, and evil in which this momentary peace was situated.[42]

The division of Christian and pre-Christian times also arises in another passage related to the Punic Wars: the moment when a series of rainstorms prevents Hannibal from engaging the Romans in what would presumably have been a decisive defeat for them. On the third return of the storm, the Old English text relates the Carthaginian leader's interpretation of the rains: "Þa angeat Hannibal, and him self sæde, ðeh ðe he wilniende wære 7 wenende Romana anwealdes, þæt hit God ne geþafode" (IV.x, p. 103) [Then Hannibal understood, and said to himself, that though he was desiring and hoping for power over the Romans, God did not permit it]. Hannibal recognizes in the event the proper interpretation of history despite his cultural background and lack of Christian faith.

Given that the non-Christian Hannibal was able to understand the meaning of the storms, the *Orosius*-narrator asks the "Romans" to account for their lack of insight and suggests that their Christian future preserved them during their non-Christian past:

Gesecgað me nu Romane, cwæð Orosius, hwonne þæt gewurde oþþe hwara, ær ðæm cristendome, [þæt] oþþe ge oþþe oðere æt ænegum godum mehten ren abiddan, swa mon siþþan mehte siþþan se cristendom wæs, 7 nugiet magon monege gode æt urum Hælendum Criste, þonne him þearf bið. Hit wæs þeh swiþe sweotol þæt se ilca Crist se þe hie eft to cristendome onwende, þæt se him þone ren to gescildnisse onsende, þeh hie þæs wyrþe næron, to þon þæt hie selfe, 7 eac monege oþere þurh [h]ie, to ðæm cristendome 7 to ðæm soþan geleafan become. (IV.x, p. 103–4)

Tell me now, Romans, said Orosius, when or where was it that it happened, before Christendom, that any (of) you or any others could have rain by praying to the gods, as you now might, now that Christendom exists, and may now have so many good things from your Saviour, Christ, when there is need of him. It was, however, clearly evident that the same Christ, he who after turned [the Romans] to Christianity, sent to them that rain as a shield,

---

42. Although the Latin version of this part of the history is far longer in its lamentation of the short memory of the Roman historians, it makes a similar point to the Old English and in fact strengthens it, with this assertion of Paulus Orosius (in the first person, a far more frequent occurrence in the Latin): "ei mihi, cognouisse haec et denudasse quam etiam me pudet!" (IV.12.120) [Woe is me! How it shames me to have come to know about and uncovered these events! (179.8)].

though they were not worthy of it, so that they themselves and also many others through them, might come to Christianity and to the true belief.

The implications of the reading proffered by the *Orosius*-narrator do not stem from any difference with the Latin, although the material included is quite abridged. Rather, the *Orosius*-narrator is aware of a basic truth of Christian historical interpretation of which the Romans are ignorant. The narrator has learned from history and is able to understand it correctly. The Romans can be written into a version of historical events that interprets them from a hermeneutic position that reads all things as having a divine "message" encoded within them. The Romans were not saved for past merits. They were saved in the past so that the city of Rome might one day be Christian and so that other peoples might be converted through reading their history.

The *Orosius*-narrator takes a point of view that is greater than that of humans—he interprets history in the nonlinear terms of God's providence. In the *Orosius,* the future always conditions (and reveals) the past because for God, time is not chronological but exists in an eternal present. Human interpretation, by contrast, is limited to the historical unfolding of events and therefore cannot see how they demonstrate the truth of God's power. The past cannot be fully understood without the understanding of the future toward which it moves, a privileged position occupied by the *Orosius*-narrator.

This larger temporal scale allows the *Orosius*-narrator to stand as the judge of that which is shameful in historical narratives: he can choose what counts as proper history based on its moral righteousness. The relationship between that which is shameful and that which ought not be written into history is direct and has numerous implications for the temporal status of the Old English text. One of the very first examples of his historical judgment, his account of the Amazons, makes a firm distinction between the Amazons themselves and the writing of their history: "Hit is scondlic, cwæð Orosius, ymb swelc to sprecanne hwelc hit þa wæs" (I.x, p. 30) [It is shameful, said Orosius, to speak about such (things) as were then]. These deeds have been written about by other historians in other texts: those who wish to learn of the misdeeds of the past may easily do so elsewhere. In the *Orosius*-narrator's view, however, passing on the stories through historical writing is itself an offensive act.[43] Moreover, the *Orosius*-narrator judges what can be considered part of a

---

43. A similar moment in which history is judged to be shameful, and therefore to be elided, occurs in Bede's *Ecclesiastical History,* in which Bede claims that the kings after Edwin—who lapsed in their Christian faith—were expunged from the historical record. See *HE* III.2.214.

Roman conception of history and those who are—and ought to be—left out.[44] Intrinsic to these judgments is a sense of the power the past can hold over the future. In bringing the Latin text into the Old English language, the authority of the *Orosius*-narrator's proper name marks the moment where this influence might be felt most profoundly: when he gives his reasons for abridgment.

The task of writing about the evils of the past is profoundly difficult, as both the Latin and Old English texts note. The complexity and length of events justify the use of abbreviation and summary; however, the two versions give different reasons for why narration is problematic. Paulus Orosius avers that his choice to shorten certain stories in the *Historiae* results from an obligation to the work he has yet to do:

> At ego nunc cogor fateri, me prospiciendi finis commodo de tanta malorum saeculi circumstantia praeterire plurima, cuncta breuiare. nequaquam enim tam densam aliquando siluam praetergredi possem, nisi etiam crebris interdum saltibus subuolarem. (I.12.25)

> But now I am forced to confess that the goal of bringing to its end an account of the great evils of this time compels me to pass over many more events and to shorten my account of all of them. Indeed, I would be unable to pass through such a thick forest, unless I were to fly forward from time to time by leaps and bounds. (61–2.1)

Paulus Orosius's inability to pass through the "thick forest" conditions his approach to writing. Moreover, he observes a need to move on to the more recent past, "praesertim cum et Graecorum praetereunda non sint et Romanorum uel maxime recensenda sint" (I.12.25) [this is all the more true as we must not pass over the history of the Greeks and must give special attention to the Romans (62.3)]. The interests of the future—and particularly the Christian present and immediate past to which Orosius writes—condition the pace at which he must move through the more distant, mythological past.

In the Old English, the *Orosius*-narrator similarly observes a need to edit out material. The narrator emphasizes the number of evils committed in the past, but questions the ability of anyone to tell the full story: "Hwa is þæt þe eall ða yfel þe hi donde wæron asecgean mæge oððe areccean?" (I.viii, p. 27) [Who is there that could tell or narrate all of the evil that they were doing?]

---

44. See Geary, who argues that "the very process of writing a history that included [non-Christian] peoples meant an attempt to incorporate them into 'history'; that is, universal history, which for [medieval historians] could only mean the history of Rome" (*Myth of Nations*, 171).

The use of both *asecgean* and *areccean* to describe the impossible tasks of which the *Orosius*-narrator speaks indicates that the writing of these texts—and the telling of these stories—defies the narrative ability of the historian.[45] It is also clear that the two words are somehow equivalent: to speak is in fact to tell, and the narrative that the *Orosius*-narrator wishes to tell is not simply of the evil of men but of the implications of that evil for future generations who might learn from it.

The cosmological world itself is affected by the moral status of these evil men and their stories. The sentence that closes this section of the Latin text's consideration of the evil nature of former times focuses on the survival of humanity in spite of its own destructive tendencies and immoral ways: "Conici datur, qualiter homines sustinuerint, quod etiam astra fugisse dicuntur" (I.12.26) [We might wonder how men could endure that from which they say even the stars fled. (63.10)]. Whatever else may be said about this passage, the stars take on an active—if fugitive—role in indicating the evil of past actions, as well as in the judgment thereof. The Old English translation, by contrast, adds a layer of narrative to the general statement of the Latin text: "On þæm dagum wæron swa u[n]gemetlica yfel þæt þa men sylf sædon þæt hefones tungul hiora yfel flugon" (I.viii, p. 28) [In those days there were such unmeasurable evils that men said (themselves) that the stars of the heavens flew from their evil]. If the reasoning behind the *Historiae* is to relate the former wickedness of men in order to downplay more current calamities, then the Old English alteration to this line is significant because it posits a past awareness of these evils—*men sylf sædon* [men said themselves] that the stories are true. History, then, and the historians who write it, make the same choice as the stars do when they flee from retelling these stories.

The work of the historian involves volition, including the choice to leave out that which is not worthy of record. In the Old English text, these moments are attributed to the *Orosius*-narrator. Both the wish to silence these stories and the judgment such silencing invokes suggest that the *cwæð Orosius* construction dissociates the Old English translator from the desire to silence history. The moments at which the *cwæð* construction suggests that the narrating voice makes both a distinction and a judgment between a Christian and a non-Christian world are also the points in the narrative at which the *Orosius* makes a specific claim as to the authority of the narrator over his work.

---

45. *Asecgan* can carry connotations of speaking or saying as well as recounting or telling a story (see DOE, s.v. *asecgan*); *areccan* can carry connotations of "to set forth, express; recount, tell, narrate; explain" (DOE, s.v. *areccan*).

AUDIENCE, TEXTUAL COMMUNITY, AND THE "NOW"

By creating an *Orosius*-narrator who relates the words of a fifth-century Roman historian while also speaking from a vantage point that can see and understand history as a whole, the Old English *Orosius* draws attention to itself as a translation. After all, there would be no need to assert that "Orosius said" anything if the authority in question was not fragile, subject to breaking under the weight of the history it purveys. The presence of the *cwæð Orosius* translation effect, however, also calls attention to the kind of textual community the translation seeks to create, demonstrating through its anachronism the kind of temporal heterogeneity that is integral to these imagined groups.[46] By virtue of its address to an audience that will notice and respond to its presence, the translation effect of the *cwæð Orosius* suggests the historical perspective of the audience in question. The audience must know that the text is a translation in order to recognize that it calls attention to itself as such. In certain cases of the *cwæð* construction, it not only invokes the presence of that audience but also addresses it directly, through the use of a series of (usually contentious) questions to the audience. Even though the materials and the approach, as Discenza and Godden observe, are altered for the new historical period, the Roman context persists in these moments of address.[47] The translation is meant for a ninth-century Old English audience, but it does not always speak to that audience on or in its own terms. Rather, the *Orosius*-narrator often retains the implication or even direct assertion that his address is meant for the Romans who provoked Paulus Orosius's *Historiae* in the first place. The Old English *Orosius* thus imagines a textual community that is Roman and Christian, but also linguistically identifiable as readers of Old English. This textual community must thus be composed of people drawn from multiple time periods.

At several points in the *Orosius*, the narrator addresses an implied audience directly, and seven of these instances address that audience either about specifically Roman concerns or as Romans themselves. As a result, the *Orosius* both creates its audience and endows it with an identity and a capacity for response. The questions the *Orosius*-narrator poses to these *Romane* ask his audience to understand history the way that he does. As a result, the audience is asked to take on the broader view of multiple time periods that fall within the purview of the historian. This greater, more extensive knowledge

---

46. For the literary productivity of anachronism in medieval literature, see Dinshaw, *How Soon Is Now?* Temporal heterogeneity stands in contrast to "homogeneous, empty time" (261), a distinction made by Benjamin's "Theses on the Philosophy of History."

47. See Godden, "Rewriting the Sack of Rome"; Discenza, *King's English*.

must then be used to judge their own—putatively Roman—understanding of history. One such instance speaks of the Punic Wars and the many casualties thereof, showcasing the *Orosius*-narrator's requirement that his audience undertake a comparison:

> Hu magon nu Romane, cwæð Orosius, to soþe gesecgean þæt hie þa hæfden beteran tida þonne hie nu hæbben, þa hie swa monega gewin hæfdon emdenes underfongen? (IV.ix, p. 102–3)

> How may the Romans now, said Orosius, truly say that they had better times then than they now have, when they had so many battles undertaken simultaneously?

Here the audience of the Old English *Orosius* must judge history, just as the historian does. On its surface, the question seems rhetorical, because the Romans cannot seriously claim these things. What matters to my argument, however, is not the rhetorical nature of the question but rather the time in which these Romans make their claim: they say that the past was better than *now*. The use of *nu* to make this assertion opens the possibility of an audience that must contest these assertions in their *own* now, against the claims of present Romans.[48]

The *Orosius*-narrator imagines his audience as Romans who could still exist in the present of the Old English *Orosius*. This identification might initially seem incommensurate with the inclusion of the past tense of "Orosius said"—yet it becomes clearer in his argumentative questioning of the Romans themselves. As examined above, during his narration of the Punic Wars the *Orosius*-narrator relates that Hannibal interprets the rain that prevents his attack on the Romans as a sign that he will not have dominion over the them because God does not will it. The *Orosius*-narrator then addresses his audience directly:

> Gesecgað me nu, Romane, cwæð Orosius, hwonne þæt gewurde oþþe hwara, ær ðæm cristendome, [þæt] oþþe ge oþþe oðere æt ænegum godum mehten ren abiddan, swa mon siþþan mehte siþþan se cristendom wæs, 7 nugiet magon monege gode æt urum Hælendum Criste, þonne him þearf bið. (IV.x, p. 103–4)

---

48. See BT, s.v. *nu*. See also Fafinski, "Faraway, So Close."

> Tell me now, Romans, said Orosius, when or where was it that it happened, before Christendom, that any [of] you or any others could have rain by praying to the gods, as you now might, now that Christendom exists, and may now have so many good things from your Saviour, Christ, when there is need of him.

This particular invocation of the Romans serves a dual purpose. The *Orosius*-narrator both establishes an historical event for interpretation and interprets that historical event for his audience. The reading the *Orosius*-narrator gives—that the rain was sent to save non-Christian Rome so it could become Christian—offers an explicit rendering of how a future people might read the past.

Here, the *Orosius*-narrator addresses Christian Romans. These Romans are presumably the direct descendants of the non-Christians saved by the rains in the battle with Hannibal. The audience, thus assumed to be both Roman and Christian, is expected to share the narrator's longer, divinely aligned, view of events. The work done by the narrator's understanding of providential history can rewrite secular, imperial history to make Hannibal's knowledge of God's will entirely consistent with subsequent events and their interpretation. The community to whom the *Orosius*-narrator speaks, despite being located in early medieval England, is nevertheless called together as a distinctly Roman audience. This audience is not asked to be Roman in the sense of a national identity, but rather to be Roman in its reading practices and therefore to acknowledge the truth of the *Orosius*-narrator's understanding of history.

Yet the contentious questions of the Old English *Orosius* are not restricted to addressing an audience specifically *as Romans*. Rather, the *cwæð* construction can also address an audience in general, an audience that could exist both in the past and in the present of the translation's composition. In the first book of the *Orosius*, a collocation of the first person, the *cwæð* construction, and the word *nu* demonstrates the multivalent temporalities that attend the work of translation in the text:

> Ic wolde nu, cwæð Orosius, þæt me ða geandwyrdan þa þe secgað þæt þeos world sy nu wyrse on ðysan cristendome þonne hio ær on þæm hæþenscype wære, þonne hi swylc geblot 7 swylc morð donde wæron swylc her ær beforan sæde. Hwær is nu on ænigan cristendome betuh him sylfum þæt mon him þurfe swilc ondrædan, þæt hine mon ænigum godum blote? oððe hwær sindon ure godas þe swylcra mana gyrnen swilce hiora wæron? (I.viii, p. 27)

> I now wish, said Orosius, that those might answer me, those who say that this world is now worse in this Christendom than it was before, in the hea-

then times, when they were doing such sacrifices and such murders, as I have said above. Where is there now, in any part of Christendom, that among themselves men need to have such dread, that anyone would sacrifice them to gods? Or where are our gods who such atrocities desire as those were?

The repetition of the term *nu* here alongside a demand for an answer to the *Orosius*-narrator's questions creates a very specific temporal function for the translation effect. By invoking the proper name of the Orosius in the *cwæð* construction, this passage appears as a kind of reported speech—indeed, as a kind of translation. At the same time, however, the contentious demand for an answer now, *in Old English,* presents a dual view of this particular temporal present. On the one hand, it is clearly the now of Paulus Orosius, who demands an answer from his contemporaries as to why they think their own time is worse than the times in which humans were sacrificed to gods. On the other hand, it simultaneously assumes an Old English audience, who should also provide answers to these questions.[49]

In essence, this passage's use of *nu* is not univocal: each "now" that it asserts refers to a different moment. In the first instance, "Ic wolde nu, cwæð Orosius" [I now wish, said Orosius] refers to a past legible both in the implication of the *cwæð* construction and its verb tense: this is the past of Paulus Orosius, the past in which he wrote the *Historiae*. This past of writing is complemented by the second two uses of *nu* in the passage, first that "þeos world sy nu wyrse" [this world is now worse] and second in the question "hwær is nu" [where is there now] anyone who could fear being sacrificed to gods. These instances of *nu* are more capacious than the first: it could apply in the time that Paulus Orosius wrote the *Historiae,* but its appearance in the Old English version of the *Orosius* suggests that this question is just as applicable "now" in the ninth century as it would have been in the fifth.

In fact, there are at least three distinct kinds of time implied by the nearly one hundred uses of *nu* in the Old English *Orosius*: the present of Paulus Orosius, the present of the Old English text, and the present of reported speech (which, of course, can encompass multiple different times).[50] Moreover, approximately six occurrences of the term *nu* are in conjunction with *giet* (yet), suggesting that the time in question extends into the present of the text's reception in Old English. This suggestion, as the passage above demonstrates, is far from straightforward.

---

49. For a similar analysis of a multivalent "now," in an Old French Text, see Campbell, "Time of Translation."

50. Holdsworth's essay on time frames in *The Dream of the Rood* offers a compelling reading of the different times and functions of narration in Old English. See Holdsworth, "Frames."

An example from the final book of the *Orosius* shows how complex the time indicated by *nugiet* becomes when used in conjunction with the *cwæð* construction: "Feng Archadius to anwalde, to þæm eastdæle, 7 hine hæfde xii ger, 7 Onorius to þæm wæstdæle 7 nugiet hæfð, cwæð Orosius" (VI.xxxvii, p. 155) [Archadius took power over the eastern part (of the empire) and had it for twelve years and Honorius over the western part, and (he) now yet has it, said Orosius]. This segment may well seem like an anachronism at best and a mistake at worst. The translator has clearly not altered his source sufficiently to avoid the impossible statement that Honorius *nugiet hæfð* [now yet has] power over the western part of the realm, some four hundred years later.[51] This reading of the passage, however, dismisses the temporal work that the *nugiet* can do in this context. Here, we can see more than just the past times invoked in the work of a translator. Rather, the temporally expansive use of *nugiet* suggests that the time of the *Orosius*-narrator, who speaks through the invocation of the *cwæð* construction, can encompass the present of ninth-century readers of the text.

The temporalities that cohabit the *Orosius* can finally be located in terms of a single word: the *nu*, or "now," of the text and its audience. In an earlier example, Orosius "wolde nu [. . .] þæt me ða geandwyrdan" [I now wish (. . .) that those might answer me]. In the opening of the narrator's direct address to the Romans, he requires that they "gesæcgað me nu Romane" [tell me now, Romans]. The *Orosius*-narrator asks for an answer "now," which suggests that the text anticipates such questions on the part of an early medieval English audience who might identify with a Roman past in order to interpret these events. The "now" is a restatement or repetition of Paulus Orosius's question, written into the time of ninth-century England.

Textually at least, the *cwæð Orosius* constructs a community of those who successfully understand and are changed by the past. The result is the creation of a textual space cohabited by fifth-century Rome and ninth-century England. Audiences both past and future are required to read of and learn from history's lessons. The very assumption of the translatability of the text suggests that the *Orosius*-narrator speaks to his Old English audience in their own time, mingling the temporalities of discrete periods in history.

---

51. Indeed, Godden argues that such moments "are a forceful reminder, and presumably a deliberate one, that the polemical, optimistic perspective of the work, even in its Old English form, is that of the early-fifth-century Orosius speaking to Romans, both unaware that Rome was shortly to lose its power" ("Rewriting the Sack of Rome," 61).

CONCLUSION

In this chapter, I have outlined how the Old English *Orosius*, using the *cwæð Orosius* translation effect, creates both a narrator and an audience that are not easily limited to either fifth-century Rome or ninth-century England. The address of the *Orosius*-narrator asks his future audience to identify as one that is Christian, Roman, and discontent with its present circumstances. By assuming this audience, the *Orosius* anticipates a response that it both summons and represents in its own present. The "now" to which it speaks is a heterogeneous one, suggesting the complexity of both the task of translation and its reception.[52] The text attempts to dissuade not only those who argue that the fall of Rome is occasioned by the conversion of the Empire to Christianity but also those who will do so in the future. In short, it responds to what was articulated in Paulus Orosius's time, as well as to what could not yet have been articulated: the Old English reception of the *Historiae*.[53]

When the *Historiarum adversum paganos libri septem* was translated into Old English, a future audience became the addressee of its message of Christian interpretation of the past. An Old English audience was asked to respond to the same question that Paulus Orosius asked his fifth-century audience in the Latin text: why was the past more evil than the present? The assumption made in the *Orosius* is the continuing need to defend the answer: the present is Christian. The *Orosius*-narrator, then, asks his audience to imagine themselves as unhappy Romans—to identify with elements of the past that are no longer applicable to their society and some of which are even anachronistic. These include the "now" that refers to a period four hundred years earlier, as well as a "Roman" identity articulated in a language of the British Isles. Using the *nu* and the *Romane*, the *Orosius*-narrator creates a "now" that is fundamentally extended in time.

The preceding reading of the Old English *Orosius* demonstrates how the analysis of translation effects reveals the complexity of the temporalities associated with translation. Moreover, it shows that the textual communi-

---

52. See Benjamin, "Theses on the Philosophy of History."
53. This understanding of the Old English *Orosius* bears some resemblance to Mikhail Bakhtin's theories of the dialogic in *The Dialogic Imagination*. Bakhtin argues that "every word is directed toward an *answer* and cannot escape the profound influence of the answering word that it anticipates" (280). This directionality of the word—toward the answer it will encounter but has not yet encountered—is part of its heterogeneous temporality; even at its inception, a future *reception* is always already implicated. Drawing on the past yet already conditioned by what it will encounter in its reception, a model of translation as a "living word" allows an understanding of texts wherein any given narrative already anticipates a future reception and response (276).

ties brought into being by translation are fundamentally different from those formed around other texts. By systematically tracing the operation of the *cwæð* construction in the *Orosius,* as well as that of the author-figure and audience it creates, a new vision of the Alfredian project of translation and its associated texts comes to light. Aimed at galvanizing historical communities that were already extant, if failing, the imagined textual communities within these translations evoke more than a ninth-century English identity. Their translation effects create a conception of time that is both forward-looking and retrospective, through which the Old English *Orosius* proffers a history that its audience might need, in the hopes of rendering that audience, its authors, and their communities immortal.

CHAPTER 2

Sanctity and Soil
Ælfric's *Life of Oswald, King and Martyr*

AT THE END of the *Life of Saint Edmund, King and Martyr*, Ælfric of Eynsham stakes a claim for the presence of holy saints in England:

> Nis angel-cynn bedæled drihtnes halgena .
> þonne on engla-landa licgaþ swilce halgan
> swylce þæs halga cyning is and cuþberht se eadiga .
> and sancte æþeldryð on elig . and eac hire swustor
> ansunde on lichaman geleafan to trymminge .
> Synd eac fela oðre on angel-cynne halgan
> þe fela wundra wyrcað . swa swa hit wide is cuð
> þam ælmihtigan to lofe . þe hi on gelyfdon .
> (32.259–66)[1]

Nor are the English kind bereft of the Lord's saints, because in England there lie such saints as the holy king [Edmund] is, and Cuthbert the blessed, and Saint Æthelthryth in Ely, and also her sister, entire in body to strengthen faith. And also there are many other holy [people] among the English, who work many wonders as it is widely known, to the praise of the Almighty, in whom they believed.

---

1. Old English text from the *Lives of the Saints* is drawn from Skeat, *Ælfric's Lives of the Saints*.

In this passage, Ælfric stresses that these holy saints are present among the "English kind"[2] and in England. The dual emphasis suggests a focus on England's holiness, which is derived from the holiness of specific English saints about whom he has written.[3] "The holy king" refers quite clearly to Edmund, in whose *Life* the catalogue occurs. "Cuthbert the blessed" means the bishop Cuthbert, about whom Ælfric wrote in his *Catholic Homilies*.[4] "Holy Æthelthryth" appears in the same collection of saints' lives as Edmund, but by calling her "Saint Æthelthryth in Ely," Ælfric clearly emphasizes the English origins of the virgin saint and her sister. These lines establish Ælfric's interest in a genealogy of holiness proper to England—one that persists beyond the days of the saints and into the present, and "assures the English [. . .] that God's blessing is still in place for contemporary England."[5]

Long before this assertion, however, Ælfric establishes a genealogy of knowledge that outlines the provenance of Edmund's story. It is a narrative passed down through multiple retellings:

> Sum swyðe gelæred munuc com suþan ofer sæ fram sancte benedictes stowe on æþelredes cynincges dæge to dunstane ærce-bisceope þrim gearum ær he forðferde . and se munuc hatte abbo . þa wurdon hi æt spræce oþþæt dunstan rehte be sancte eadmunde . swa swa eadmundes swurd-bora hit rehte æþelstane cynincge þa þa dunstan iung man wæs . and se swurd-bora wæs forealdod man . (32.1–7)

> A certain very learned monk came from the south, over the sea, from the Saint Benedict's place, in the days of King Æthelred, to the archbishop Dunstan three years before he died, and the monk was called Abbo. Then they were in conversation until Dunstan told (him) about Saint Edmund, just as Saint Edmund's sword-bearer told it to King Æthelstan when Dunstan was a young man and the sword-bearer was an old man.

This narrative links the time of Abbo's retelling of Edmund's story directly back to the time of Edmund himself.[6] In this account, Ælfric draws attention to translation and how it preserves Edmund's story by describing how he

---

2. See Foot, "Making of *Angelcynn*."
3. Thacker, "*Membra Disjecta*" in Cambridge and Stancliffe, *Oswald*.
4. See Godden, *Ælfric's Catholic Homilies*.
5. Sklar, "Ælfric's *Life of Saint Edmund*," 135. See also Davis, "National Writing"; Harris, *Race and Ethnicity in Anglo-Saxon Literature*; Foot, "Making of *Angelcynn*."
6. For a full account of Abbo's interventions into the transmission history of the passion of Saint Edmund, see Pinner, *Cult of Saint Edmund*, 33–47; see also Jordan, "Holiness and Hopefulness."

came to translate it: "Þa gesette se munuc ealle þa gereccednysse on anre bec . and eft ða þa seo boc com to us binnan feawum gearum þa awende we hit on englisc . swa swa hit her-æfter stent" (32.7–10) [Then the monk set down all of this story into a book, and after, when the book had come to us, in a few years we translated it into English, as it follows hereafter]. Ælfric takes the *Life* that Abbo presumably wrote in Latin and translates (*awendan*) it to English. This description emphasizes the chain of transmission that allows the narrative to become part of the *Lives of the Saints*. By using the typically Alfredian *awendan* to describe his translation activity, Ælfric leaves no doubt as to the role he plays in the history of the story, nor of the tradition of translation on which he draws. He is a translator.[7]

The descriptive function of Ælfric's preface to the *Life of Edmund* constitutes a translation effect of a different kind than those explored in my first chapter: it demonstrates the intellectual work that the very *concept* of translation performs in the corpus. More generally, the translation effects in the *Lives of the Saints* establish the importance of translation in community formation. They signal the creation of a tradition, drawing together an imagined textual community across time by retelling shared narratives from a Christian tradition. Where often the *cwæð Orosius* construction indicates a passage that does not necessarily hail directly from the text's Latin version—and thus expands the time of translation to a heterogeneous "now"—the translation effects in Ælfric's *Lives of the Saints* demonstrate a related but separate use. Translation effects in Ælfric's work also expand the imagined textual community of his narratives across time. However, they further expand such communities to include multiple geographies as well, as part of his larger agenda to highlight the importance of English saints to both their local communities and the larger Christian world. In the case of Edmund, the narrative transmission of the saint's life asserts a multilingual provenance for the narrative alongside Ælfric's own work in translating it. In turn, it extends the transmission history of the work to include the audience for whom Ælfric records Edmund's life. It thus implicitly suggests the potential for future retellings and translations that might broaden its textual community beyond England and the continent.

In this chapter, I examine how translation effects draw attention to moments of narrative transmission and therefore shape an imagined textual community that exists across both time and geographical space. I begin by

---

7. For a full analysis of *awendan* (including its distinction from *areccean*), see Davis, "Performance of Translation Theory," in Boenig and Davis, *Manuscript, Narrative, Lexicon*. For more detail on Ælfric's approach to translating the *Life of Edmund*, see Lazzari, "Kingship and Sainthood," in Lazzari et al., *Hagiography in Anglo-Saxon England*; Waterhouse, "Discourse and Hypersignification," in Szarmach, *Holy Men and Holy Women*.

comparing the temporality of translation in the Old English preface to that of the Latin preface of *Lives of the Saints*. I then survey the methods by which Ælfric locates the saints of his collection in both space and historical time, demonstrating his special interest in the English saints and the transmission of their hagiographies. Finally, I turn to translation effects in the *Life of Oswald, King and Martyr*. These take forms such as references to language as well as to the distribution of holy relics. As this chapter shows, attending to translation effects reveals how Ælfric reshapes his source text—Bede's *Historia Ecclesiastica*—in order to mask the inter-kingdom conflicts that, Ælfric implies, a transtemporal and transgeographical Christian community supersedes. Collectively, the translation effects Ælfric deploys in the *Lives of the Saints* serve as a case study of how a particular author can use such effects to specific narrative ends: in this case, inscribing England into a transtemporal community of Christians.

PREFACING TRANSLATION

Saints and their stories are not necessarily separable: the survival of stories of such "drihtnes halgena" (32.259) [the Lord's saints] in Ælfric's era stake a claim for the place of England among other Christian kingdoms. Without the translation of these stories into the common vernacular, the status of the *Angelcynn* would be diminished. Yet Ælfric does not undertake this work without trepidation. He makes his ambivalence about translation exceedingly clear in the prefaces to the *Lives of the Saints* collection. These prefaces highlight the difficulties that result from translation's multiple temporalities.

Ælfric's *Lives of the Saints* juxtaposes a Latin-language preface with an English-language one, each of which frames his work quite differently. Ælfric's Latin preface begins with a simple statement of his aims: "Hunc quoque codicem transtulimus de latinitate ad usitatam Anglicam sermocinationem, studentes aliis prodesse edificando ad fidem lectione huius narrationis" (*Preface* 1.1–3) [I have also translated this book from Latin to the common English speech, desiring to profit others by improving them in the faith through the reading of this story].[8] Ælfric describes his work using the verb *transferre*, meaning "to put, transfer, or render into another language, translate."[9] Putatively, his goal is to teach: to allow those who wish to learn to have access

---

8. Latin translations from Ælfric's *Lives of the Saints* throughout this chapter are my own, following Skeat. Latin and English translations from Bede's *Ecclesiastical History* are from Colgrave and Mynors, *Bede's Ecclesiastical History*. For a full discussion of Ælfric's approach to these prefaces, see Dearnley, *Translators and Their Prologues*.

9. DMLBS, s.v. *transferre*[6].

to the materials at hand in "usitatam Anglicam sermocinationem" [common English speech]. Ælfric is not, however, insensitive to the difficulty of performing translation. In a detail notably absent in the Old English preface, Ælfric describes both his alterations to the Latin text and his reasons for making them:

> Quod nollem alicubi ponere duos imperatores siue cesares in hac narratione simul, sicut in latinitate legimus; sed unum imperatorem in persecutione martyrum ponimus ubique; Sicut gens nostra uni regi subditur, et usitata est de uno rege non de duobus loqui. (*Preface* 2–4.17–21)

> Insofar as I did not wish to put anywhere two emperors or caesars in this story at the same time, as we read in the Latin; but I put everywhere one emperor with regard to the persecution of martyrs; just as our people are placed under one king, and are accustomed to speak of one king not of two.

Here, Ælfric acknowledges that he has altered—or, as modern translation theory would have it, *domesticated*[10]—the materials that he translates. Where the Latin source speaks of two emperors, he has changed it to refer to only one. He does so because English sensibilities demand the change.[11] This moment in the Latin preface constitutes a translation effect, not because it is itself a moment of translation but because it draws attention to translation as an interpretive problem in Ælfric's oeuvre. In order for Ælfric to make these stories accessible to a new community, temporal distance—and the differences that such distance imposes—must be erased. The Latin asks, "Non mihi inputetur quod diuinam scripturam nostrae lingue infero, quia arguet me praecatus multorum fidelium et maxime æþelwerdi ducis et æðelmeri nostri, qui ardentissime nostras interpretationes amplectuntur lectitando" (*Preface* 4.29–32) [Let me not be (negatively) charged with bringing the divine scriptures into our language, because the entreaty of many of the faithful will prove me, and especially com-

---

10. Venuti defines domesticating and foreignizing as "ethical effects whereby translation establishes a performative relation both to the source text and to the receiving situation" (*Translator's Invisibility*, xiv). See also Schliermacher, "On the Different Methods of Translation" in Venuti, *Translation Studies Reader*. It is important to note that this term describes not specific translation choices but rather "the ethical effects of translated texts that depend for their force and recognition on the receiving culture" (Venuti, *Translator's Invisibility*, xiii). In this case, the ethical dimension of Ælfric's translation practice—that he consciously and avowedly alters his work for reception into Old English cultural norms—is undertaken with trepidation: that is, Ælfric knows his alterations might disrupt the understanding of the texts he translates.

11. See Rossi-Reder, "Embodying Christ, Embodying Nation," in Calder et al., *Sex and Sexuality*. Rossi-Reder avers that this section of the text betrays a sense of Ælfric's focus on Englishness, and "relates to his religious and nationalist attitudes" (197).

mander Æthelweard and our Æthelmær, who embrace our interpretations by their most eager repeated readings]. Here, Ælfric is almost defensive: he wants to preclude being "charged" with translation, even though important political figures have found his translations useful—or at least, he claims, have eagerly and repeatedly read them.

In contrast, the Old English preface begins with a slightly different approach, addressing those patrons directly: "Ælfric gret eadmodlice æðelwerd ealdorman and ic secge þe leof . þæt ic hæbbe nu gegaderod on þyssere bec þæra halgena þrowunga þe me to onhagode on englisc to awendene . for þan þe ðu leof swiðost and æðelmær swylcera gewrita me bædon" (*Preface* 4.35–39) [Ælfric humbly greets *ealdormann* Æthelweard, and I say to you, beloved, that I have now gathered in this book the passions of the saints that were within my power to translate into English, because you, beloved, and Æthelmær also most eagerly asked me for such writings]. In the Old English, Ælfric seems less defensive in part because he gives less detail with regard to his process: he was asked to translate these texts by his patrons, and so he did.[12] Moreover, the Old English preface addresses his patrons directly, whereas the Latin seems addressed to a literate but unspecific audience—one who might question either Ælfric's motives or his methods.

The Old English preface also focuses in a detailed way on the relationship between Ælfric's translation and his sources. He avers that his work hews closely to the original source material he translates: "Ne secge we nan þincg niwes on þissere gesetnysse . / forþan ðe hit stod gefyrn awriten / on ledenbocum þeah þe þa læwedan men þæt nyston" (*Preface* 4.46–48) [We do not say anything new in this book because it stood written of old in Latin books, although laymen did not know it]. Ælfric's avowed interest in the provenance of his materials—the fact that they existed in the past even if people outside the clergy did not know them—is mirrored by his concern at the ending of the Old English preface with the future of his translations.[13] He cautions future scribes to stay within the bounds of his text: "Ic bidde nu on godes naman gif hwa þas boc awritan wille . / þæt he hi wel gerihte be þære bysne . and þær namare betwux / ne sette þonne we awendon" (*Preface*, 6.74–76) [I pray now

---

12. These works were meant for Æðelweard and Æðelmær, who were ealdormen in the court of Æðelræd from 990–1005. See Cubitt, "Ælfric's Lay Patrons," in Magennis and Swan, *Companion to Ælfric*.

13. It is worth noting that this kind of understanding and concern had a precedent, to a degree, in Alfred's *Preface* to the *Pastoral Care*, in which he expressed his concern that Latin learning was no longer as rigorous. See Sweet, *King Alfred's West-Saxon Version of the Pastoral Care*. For further analysis of Ælfric's disavowal of originality, see Treharne, "Literature of Reform and Reward," in Balzaretti and Tyler, *Narrative and History*.

in God's name that if anyone wishes to copy this book, that he correct it carefully according to this copy, and include within it no more than we have translated]. Complementing his concern for the past and the *ledenbec* [Latin books] from which he translated the materials in the current volume, Ælfric looks to the future by asking that the copyists who might wish to write down his work avoid any alteration to it. This moment, too, comprises a translation effect: Ælfric not only draws attention to the presence and necessity of translation in his *Lives of the Saints* but also highlights the multiple temporalities of the communities that his translation will bring together and the possible threats inherent in bringing together such groups. Future copyists could impugn his good name by changing the work. Ælfric attempts to circumscribe the temporally expansive community that will encounter his work by explicitly drawing attention to these vicissitudes of translation.

Both Ælfric's insistence on his fidelity to his sources and his request that others be faithful to his work demonstrate the extension of translation in time. The temporality of translation is longer than that of an untranslated text and relies on a past work that a present writer transmits to future audiences.[14] Each step threatens to introduce changes and infelicities. Ælfric's address to his future copyists emphasizes that translation bears with it a commitment to these extended temporalities and the authority of the written word.[15] Intriguingly then—though not surprisingly—the Latin and the Old English prefaces perform markedly different functions. In the Latin, Ælfric emphasizes how he intervenes in the texts he translates for an audience that could appreciate his work. His approach alternates between word-for-word and sense-for-sense, and he domesticates the works he translates to make them more appropriate for an English context. The Old English emphasizes his fidelity to the works that he translates and his hope that such fidelity will be maintained by later writers. The future must safeguard the work of the past. Ælfric's Latin preface speaks to those who understand translation and its vicissitudes; the English one admonishes those who would ruin his careful work. In both cases, they reveal the multiple times and audiences Ælfric addresses.

LOCATING THE ENGLISH SAINTS

Ælfric complements his focus on the temporality of translation in the prefaces to *Lives of the Saints* with careful attention to where his saints hail from

---

14. See Bassnett, *Translation*, 81–103.
15. See Griffin, "Time of the Translator."

in historical time and geographical space. The opening of each *vita* in Ælfric's *Lives* points to specific geographical and temporal locations of the subjects of his hagiography, demonstrating an ongoing concern with the particulars of the community to which each saint belongs. Ælfric's method of identifying the saints at the outset of their lives does vary widely across the collection. Yet from these variations a pattern emerges. As will be seen below, the English saints are distinguished by the detail and certitude with which Ælfric identifies their locations and eras, whereas the Late Antique saints tend to be less definitively described. Put another way, Ælfric simply seems less interested in the places and moments from which the Late Antique saints hail.[16] For example, in the *Life of Saint Cecilia*, Ælfric begins with a succinct description of Cecilia's time period:

> Iu on ealdum dagum wæs sum æðele mæden
> cecilia gehaten fram cild-hade cristen
> on romana rice þa þa seo reðe ehtnys stod
> on þæra casera dagum þe cristes ne gymdon .
> (34.1–4)

> Long ago in old days there was a noble maiden called Cecilia, [who was] Christian from childhood, in the kingdom of the Romans when the just withstood persecution in the days of the emperors who did not heed Christ.

Ælfric outlines key points about Cecilia: she is noble, a Christian from her childhood, and born in Rome during a time when Christians were persecuted. The general reference to emperors and an expansive location in the Roman Empire does not make Cecilia's origin as a noble woman terribly precise. Many such emperors existed and the Romans controlled extensive amounts of land. Similarly, in the *Life of Saint Basil*, the main points conveyed about Basil are quite simple: he is a *halig biscop* (3.1) [holy bishop] whose holiness was evident "þeah þe he to longum fyrste ungefullod wære" (3.3) [even though he was unbaptized for a long time]. Similarly general openings are found in many of the *Lives of the Saints*.[17]

One method Ælfric does use to locate his Late Antique saints is through their connection to other holy men and women, thus constructing a tradition

---

16. For an analysis of the political ramifications of Ælfric's approach to translating Latin, see Stephenson, *Politics of Language*, 158–87.

17. See Eugenia, Julian and Basilissa, Sebastian, Agatha, Lucy, the Forty Soldiers, Mark, Alban, the Seven Sleepers, Mary of Egypt, Abdon and Sennes, Maccabees, Saint Maurice, Saint Eustace, Saint Euphrosyne, Chrysanthus and Daria, and Vincentius.

of holiness in which these saints participate.[18] These connections form a textual community that links the writers and readers of the saints' lives with the communities that venerated the saints as well as with the saints themselves. Thus the writing of hagiography connects the local community that uses the *Lives of the Saints* to the larger Christian community of which the saints form an integral part. This narrative transmission indicates another kind of translation effect: they remind Ælfric's audience that these stories are part of a larger narrative background, and in so doing, remind the reader or listener that such stories are, like the entire collection, translations.[19] Put another way: despite Ælfric's avowed concern about the infelicities that translation can introduce, translation effects have an explicitly community-forming function for him. They mark the *Lives of the Saints* as inherited or received narratives and therefore draw together past and future readers within a single temporally and geographically expansive textual community.[20]

The *Life of Saint Agnes* provides a useful example of this phenomenon by connecting Ælfric's version of Agnes's story to St. Ambrose. Here, the overlap is especially meaningful, because it establishes a holy provenance for the story Ælfric relates:

Ambrosius bisceop . binnan Mediolana
afunde on ealdum bocum . be ðære eadigan agne .
hu heo on rome byrig reðe ehtnysse acom .
and on mægðhade martyr-dom ðrowode .
Ða awrat ambrosius . be þam mædene ðus .
(7.1–5)

Ambrosius the bishop, in Milan, found [out] in old books about the blessed Agnes, how she in the city of Rome bore cruel persecutions, and [how] in maidenhood she suffered martyrdom. Then Ambrosius wrote of the maiden thus.

The opening of the *Life* establishes its narrative tradition: Ambrose finds Agnes's story in old books and becomes her first formal hagiographer—and, potentially, her story's first translator. Ælfric creates a precedent for his *Life* by framing his writing as a transmission of Ambrose's text. Moreover, he creates a sense of temporal heterogeneity through his use of *ðus*: Ambrose would

---

18. See Brown, *Cult of the Saints*, 69–85.
19. For further analysis of Ælfric's translation style, see Minkoff, "Example of Latin Influence," and "Consequences of Ælfric's Theory of Translation"; Wilcox, "Ælfric and Maccabees."
20. The *Lives* for which Ælfric includes this narrative tradition include Maur, Agnes, Apollinaria, Martin, and Thomas.

have written in Latin but the transmission of "his" version of this story is very much in Old English.

Ælfric also self-consciously positions himself as a translator and disseminator of the holy *Lives* in the *Life of Saint Thomas*. In this case, Ælfric's interest in his own narrative tradition stems from a putative concern about authenticity. Written in Latin rather than Old English, the opening lines of the preface to the *Life of Saint Thomas* implicitly claim a specific type of authority that serves to legitimize Ælfric's inclusion of the *Life* in his collection. However, Ælfric deploys this authority negatively by outlining both his concerns as to whether or not it should be passed down and the reasons that ultimately recommend its inclusion. Ælfric first claims to doubt whether he should translate the story at all (36.1–2). His concern stems from Augustine, who also found part of the narrative to be suspect (36.2–6). By connecting his trepidation to Augustine's, Ælfric places himself in a community of Christian writers who can judge the fitness of stories for the edification and instruction of other Christians. Ælfric ultimately decides to include the story because of his patron's intervention: "Et ideo uolo hoc pretermittere et cetera interpretari que in eius passione habentur sicut æþelwerdus uenerabilis dux obnixe nos praecatus est" (36.10–12) [And therefore I wish to omit (the offending materials) and translate the rest (of the materials) in the passion just as the venerable lord Æthelweard has resolutely asked of us]. The preface connects Ælfric's translation to his sources of authority: Augustine and Æthelweard. Ælfric thus positions himself both as a learned Christian who doubts part of the work—like Augustine—but also as a writer with a learned Christian patron who wishes for the modified text to be included in the collection he has commissioned. Writers, readers, and translators are all brought into the textual community that Ælfric's preface imagines. Moreover, through the process of translation, that textual community extends to both late Antique versions of the story and Ælfric's contemporary locus of power.

The *Lives* of the English saints deploy similar formulae as those of the Late Antique saints—they hail from various locales and times, and are part of various textual genealogies of holiness—but the ideological work performed by these openings differs significantly. By establishing a parallel between Late Antique and early medieval English saints, Ælfric claims for his own people traditions that are as much universally Christian as they are local and specific to England. More than simply aligning the saints themselves, this narrative choice suggests equivalences between early medieval England and the Late Antique locales that gave rise to the other saints in the collection. Implicitly, this positions the English communities about which—and for whom—Ælfric wrote as sites of holiness.

The paradigmatic example of this impulse is the *Life of Edmund*, examined above. In its opening lines, Ælfric includes the traditional provenance of the story that he is about to tell, connecting the narrative of Edmund's *Life* to other holy men who have written or told various versions of it. By including this tradition, Ælfric establishes a direct link between King Edmund himself and the writers and readers of his holy life. The result is a saint—and a *Life*—connected to several crucial early medieval English nobles and holy men, including archbishop Dunstan and King Æthelstan. The inclusion of Abbo of Fleury, the French Benedictine abbot, as one of the other authorities on whom Ælfric relies for the story of Edmund, situates the narrative at a particular time and place: one in which England was a source of learning as well as narratives about holy saints.[21]

However, this continental connection also implies that English holiness and English saints participate in a larger Christian community made possible through Benedictine spirituality, signified by the inclusion of the French Abbo's writing of the English Edmund's hagiography. This association of the holy English king with the French abbot from "Saint Benedict's Place" (32.1) puts Edmund on par with continental saints while it concomitantly suggests that continental authorities can and do learn about holiness from England.[22] The figures to whom Ælfric refers in the *Life of Edmund* emphasize the narrative's ties to both earthly and spiritual hierarchies. Ælfric begins with Abbo himself, then identifies Dunstan—a major figure of the Benedictine reform movement and the teacher of Ælfric's own teacher, Æthelwold[23]—as the source of the story of Edmund. This connection further solidifies the unifying nature of the Benedictine rule and its ability to call together a spiritual community alongside a secular one. And of course, this tradition is also multilingual: the English Dunstan relates a received narrative to the French Abbo who presumably writes it down in Latin (32.6–7).

These associations emphasize the interconnection of the earthly and spiritual realms in the text. The seat of spiritual power is represented by monastic authorities: Dunstan, Abbo, and by extension, Ælfric himself. Earthly power is represented by King Æthelstan, the sword-bearer, and Saint Edmund the king. This alliance of earthly and spiritual authority strengthens the claims that Ælfric makes both for the holiness and the efficacy of the king and mar-

---

21. This is, of course, a time that Alfred refers to in his *Preface* to the *Pastoral Care*.
22. On the relationship between this preface, English identity, and restoration, see Sklar, "Ælfric's *Life of Saint Edmund*," 133–34.
23. See Hall, "Ælfric as Pedagogue," in Swan and Magennis, *Companion to Ælfric*; for Ælfric's devotion to Æthelwold, see Stephenson, *Politics of Language*, 136–37.

tyr.[24] Moreover, it inscribes Ælfric into a tradition that connects his translation of the text—"And eft ða þa seo boc com to us binnan feawum gearum þa awende we hit on englisc . swa swa hit her-æfter stent" (32.8–10) [And after, when the book had come to us, in a few years we translated it into English, as it follows hereafter]—directly to the saint himself via transmitted narratives. The preface to the *Life of Edmund* creates a community of authorities who are closely connected to the text. This authoritative community grants weight to the story the homily relates as it demonstrates the power of God made manifest in the life of a pious king.[25] Moreover, the recounting of the chain of transmission—which, as a translation effect, draws attention to the narrative *being a translation*—emphasizes the multilinguality of this group of interlocutors who expand this textual community in time.

That the traditions Ælfric draws on include the earthly power of pre-Conquest English kings is unsurprising. Given that Saint Edmund was himself a king, the holiness of such monarchs was, in certain cases at least, beyond question.[26] Ælfric's interest in a specifically English holiness, however, also extends to the bishops and ecclesiastical hierarchy of the island. The thematic similarity between the opening lines of the *Life of Swithun* and the *Life of Edmund* creates a telling comparison. Ælfric uses the opening of the *Life of Edmund* to establish Edmund's exemplarity and his identification with the Christian community in England, signaled by the list of kings, learned monks, and soldiers he mentions. In the *Life of Swithun,* a similar lineage of holy men and powerful kings specifies Swithun's time period and pinpoints the English location, Winchester, where he lived. As in the case of Edmund, where the relationship between Edmund's story and Ælfric's writing is established through Ælfric's links to Dunstan, Ælfric manufactures a direct line between the Winchester of his own time and the Winchester of Swithun's *inventio*.[27] He begins with the invocation of a king, one who was particularly well known and revered: "On eadgares dagum ðæs æðelan cynincges . þaða se cristendom wæs wel ðeonde þurh god on angelcynne" (21.1–3) [In the days of Edgar, the noble King, when Christendom was well thriving among the *Anglecynn*

---

24. For a consideration of the educative and political purposes of the *Life of Edmund*, see Jordan, "Holiness and Hopefulness," 8.

25. Ælfric further solidifies Edmund's role in the community through his "acknowledgement of popular stories of the saints" throughout his work (Faulkner, "Ælfric, St. Edmund, and St. Edwold," 4).

26. This is true even if their explicit sanctity as martyrs *and* kings can be disputed. See Gunn, "Bede and the Martyrdom of St. Oswald," in Wood, *Martyrs and Martyrologies*.

27. Lorden notes that "[Ælfric] asserts his connection to Winchester as an alum of the Old Minster, and his account valorizes the time and place of Swithun's revelation as not only distant but past" ("Landscapes of Devotion," 303). See also Stephenson, *Politics of Language*.

because of God]. King Edgar was widely considered to be a good Christian king and a holy man, which is particularly important because Swithun himself is all but forgotten. During the reign of Edgar, however, "þa geswutelode god þone sanct swyðun / mid manegum wundrum . þæt he mære is" (21.4–5) [God made known Saint Swithun, through many miracles, [revealing] that he is great].[28]

Because Swithun comes from Winchester, his lineage is particularly important for Ælfric. Ælfric recounts that lineage in detail, describing where Swithun falls in the order of bishops. This specificity is necessary because Swithun was, before his *inventio,* completely unknown. Ælfric notes, "His dæda næron cuðe ærðan hi god sylf cydde" (21.6) [His deeds were unknown before God himself made them known], and "ne we ne fundon on bocum hu se bisceop leofode" (21.7) [nor have we found [anything] in books about how this bishop lived].[29] Swithun's position in the community of saints is thus somewhat different than the saints that Ælfric mentions at the conclusion of the *Life of Edmund.* His works are confined to the miracles that took place through his power long after his death, in contrast to the holiness other saints display while still alive or (at most) shortly after death. Accordingly, Swithun's miracles often take place at his tomb. Importantly, Ælfric most distinctly values not the place of Winchester but what it represents in the life: its "ideals."[30] Moreover, Ælfric's insistence on the lack of books to maintain Swithun's legacy offers a strange contrast with the translation effects used in the story of Edmund. Here the authenticity of the saint is attested to not through learned authority, but through the miracles that can be ascribed to him and subsequently inscribed in his hagiography. Miracles, and the stories people tell about them, stand in for the stories of the saint himself.

---

28. Treharne has argued that the reference to Edgar not only provides a "specific historical and cultural context," but also positions Swithun's *inventio* as a kind of "reward" for the Christian leadership of Edgar ("Literature of Reform and Reward," in Balzaretti and Tyler, *Narrative and History,* 180).

29. See Lapidge, *Cult of Saint Swithun.* As Lapidge highlights, the anonymous author of the *Vita Sancti Swiðuni* portrayed the saint as "exceedingly humble; and that as a reflex of this humility he asked to be buried outside the church in an inconspicuous grave"—even though Swithun was actually buried in a rather large grave right near the church (7). Despite its inauthenticity, however, the story of the *inventio* gives him a more powerful presence as a saint "newly revealed." Extant evidence of his reign is limited to knowledge of the time of his episcopacy (852–63), an episcopal profession of faith written in extremely erudite Latin, and a land charter (4–6). For further analysis of Latin and vernacular lives of Swithun, see Lorden, "Landscapes of Devotion"; and Stephenson, *The Politics of Language.*

30. Lorden argues that Ælfric "concerns himself with advocating the ideals of the Winchester that educated him," a contrast to Wulfstan and Lantfred ("Landscapes of Devotion," 304).

As with Swithun and Edmund, the opening of the *Life of Saint Æthelthryth* also refers to a kind of holiness that exists in a specifically English community. In this case, narrative transmission is not an explicit topic. However, Ælfric's ongoing interest in a distinct kind of community connects Æthelthryth to the larger agenda that includes the lives of Edmund and Swithun. Ælfric uses *englisc* [English][31] as a modifier to describe Æthelthryth. This modifier indicates cultural provenance and a common language associated with a specific place, but it also creates a subtle alliance between being *englisc* and being holy. Ælfric begins, "We wyllað nu awritan þeah ðe hit wundorlic sy / be ðære halgan sancte æðeldryðe þam engliscan mædene" (20.1–2) [We now wish to write, although it is wonderful, about the holy saint Æthelthryth, the English maiden]. This amalgamation of culture, language, religion, and place creates a sense of shared identity in a time before nations as such existed.[32]

While Æthelthryth is only described as the "English maiden," the biographical details that Ælfric goes on to include make it clear that this choice had nothing to do with ignorance of more specific information. Æthelthryth comes from a very specific lineage: "Anna hatta (*sic*) hyre fæder east engla cynincg . / swyðe cristen man swa swa he cydde mid weorcum . / and eall his team wearð gewurðod þurh god" (20.5–7) [Her father was called Anna, King of the East Angles, a very Christian man as he showed with his works, and all his family became honored by God]. Here we can note the contrast between Æthelthryth and Cecilia, who was simply described as a Christian long ago in Roman lands.[33] Ælfric identifies Æthelthryth by her time period, by her location, *and* by her father's name—which is notable because it is royal and Christian. By identifying Æthelthryth's father as a Christian King, Ælfric makes her holiness something that seems inherited.

The opening lines of the *Life of Alban* share the specificity of the preceding examples but further designate a local Christian community in England. Ælfric highlights a specific Roman emperor—Diocletian—and the precise year in which he began his cruel reign, "æfter cristes acennednysse twam hund

---

31. The term *Engla-land* is used in a number of different moments in the *Lives*: in Alban, lines 11, 17, and 135; Swithun 193; Oswald 1; Edmund 260; and Thomas 100.

32. See Hastings, *Construction of Nationhood*; Davis, "National Writing." Davis argues that although the medieval nation is not the "same as the modern nation," the possibility of "imagining national identity is not restricted to one set of historically specific conditions such as print culture, democracy, capitalism, and secularization" (613). Lazzari argues that the inclusion of Æthelthryth and Swithun in *The Lives of the Saints* can be "attributed to the connection of Ælfric with Æthelwold" ("Kingship and Sainthood," in Lazzari et al., *Hagiography in Anglo-Saxon England*, 38).

33. A similar contrast emerges between Swithun and Basil—both are bishops, but Ælfric describes the English bishop more specifically.

gearum / and syx and hunt-eahtatigum" (19.3-4) [two hundred and eighty-six years after Christ's birth]. Ælfric further notes that, after ten years of his reign, Diocletian brings persecution all over the world, "oðþæt heo to engla lande swylce becom" (19.11) [until it also came even to England]. Again, Ælfric's interest in the persecutions seems to be due to the fact that Diocletian brings them, after ten years, to England itself.

The most obvious moment when Ælfric focuses on a Christian community, however, is highlighted in the questioning of Alban by a judge later in the narrative. The judge demands to know not only who Alban is, but from what family he originates: "Þa axode se dema ardlice and cwæð . / Hwylcere mægðe eart þu . oððe hwylcere manna" (19.53–54) [Then the judge quickly asked and said, "Which family are you from, or what (kind of) man?"] Alban's answer to this question—which, significantly, asks him to identify himself by his kinsmen or by what kind of man he is[34]—is perhaps most indicative of Ælfric's agenda in the *Life of Alban*:

Ða andwyrde albanus þam arleasan þus .
Hwæt belympð to þe hwylcere mægðe ic sy .
ac gif ðu soð wylt gehyran ic þe secge hraðe .
þæt ic cristen eom and crist æfre wurðige .
(19.55-8)

Then Alban answered the wicked man thus: "What does it concern you what family I am from? But if you will hear the truth, I say [it] to you quickly, that I am Christian and always worship Christ."

Alban's answer transposes the question of his secular lineage into one about his spiritual lineage. What matters is not his family of origin, so to speak, but rather his community of faith. His family is that of all Christians, and his function in that society—his rank—is to worship Christ. Rather than focusing on what he *is*, Alban's answer here focuses on what he *does* that makes him part of a Christian community—one with expansive and enduring temporal dimensions, indicated by his avowal that he will "always" [*æfre*] worship Christ. In this example, Alban highlights not the specificity of his English origin but the way in which his faith extends an English community into a larger Christian one.

---

34. Skeat here translates *manna* as "rank," which I have construed as "kind of man."

OSWALD, WARRIOR KING

Each of the English saints that I have surveyed here shares a direct connection to the people of what Ælfric called *Engla land,* England. His transmission of their stories suggests an investment in a sense of specifically English Christianity—an Englishness that Ælfric himself was a vital part of creating. Ælfric's *Life of Oswald, King and Martyr* reworks a version of the king's life found in Bede's *Historia Ecclesiastica*.[35] His alterations to Bede's narrative demonstrate an investment not only in tying English Christianity to the Late Antique precursors he finds with other saints but also in creating a link between the lineage of the saints and the land that, in some cases, they died to defend. In the case of Oswald, this association is made astonishingly literal in the figure of holy dust, which connects the saint to the people he protects. As with Edmund, Oswald's dual status as both king and saint associates the hierarchy of early medieval English rulers with the Christian community of which such rulers were a part. Moreover, his sanctification of the soil links his holiness directly to the land itself and raises the possibility of a Christian community that is partially defined by its distinct geographical location.

The majority of critical attention to Oswald focuses on the version in Bede[36] and, moreover, takes an historical rather than a literary perspective on the cult of Oswald in England and on the continent.[37] That is, scholarly treatments generally examine either the character of the cult that surrounded Oswald and his relics or the genesis of that cult, from both Christian and non-Christian sources and perspectives.[38] Although a number of scholars note the emphasis on the holy soil that is created by Oswald's intercession and death,

---

35. Although Ælfric does not explicitly cite Bede as the source for his version of Oswald's *Life,* the story of Oswald has only three redactions in early medieval English literature. The first occurs in the *Historia Ecclesiastica,* the second in Alcuin's "Bishops, Kings, and Saints of York," and the third in Ælfric's *Lives of the Saints.* Bede's *Historia Ecclesiastica* is commonly considered as the primary source of Ælfric's version. See Hare, "Heroes, Saints and Martyrs." See also Donoghue, *Old English Literature,* 81; Hurt, "Ælfric and the English Saints." For Alcuin's version, see *Alcuin,* ed. and trans. Godman. For Bede, see Colgrave and Mynors, *Bede's Ecclesiastical History.* For an exploration of Bede as an authority in Ælfric's *Catholic Homilies,* see Hill, "Ælfric and the Authority of Bede."

36. See Chenard, "King Oswald's Holy Hands."

37. See Cubitt, "Sites and Sanctity"; Hare, "Heroes, Saints and Martyrs."

38. See Cubitt, "Universal and Local Saints" in Thacker and Sharpe, *Local Saints and Local Churches*; Niles, "Pagan Survivals," in Godden and Lapidge, *Cambridge Companion to Old English.*

literary perspectives on the *Life* usually focus more closely on the power of the saint's bodily relics: the hand and head of the warrior-king.[39]

By contrast, I argue that the significance of Oswald's holiness is also located in the dust that he sanctifies. The dust comes to stand in for and replicate the effects of the narrative of his life: both dust and story circulate, and so propagate the formation of community via their holiness. By examining Ælfric's alterations to Bede's narrative of Oswald's life, I demonstrate that the divergences between the two portrayals indicate different attitudes to both cultural identity and saintly exemplarity. Ælfric's version of the text creates a vision of Christian community that downplays the difficulty of uniting separate kingdoms in pre-Conquest England by ignoring or marginalizing interkingdom conflict, whereas Bede's text emphasizes the distinctions between such groups. Moreover, Ælfric's association of Oswald with specific holy places creates a clearer propagandistic effect in the narrative of the martyr-king.

Oswald's connection to the soil he both ruled and sanctified highlights how his function as an English martyr-king grants an exceptional status to both the saint and the land with which he is associated—land Ælfric consistently identifies as *English* because of Oswald's various battles to protect it from invaders. In order to understand how the translation effects reinforce this purpose, one must first demonstrate how Ælfric's idea of religious community manifests in his version of the story. Ælfric makes careful temporal and geographical claims in order to shore up an English Christian community. These claims help reveal the pervasive work of translation effects in the *Life*.

Ælfric's *Life of Oswald, King and Martyr* centers on three events in the Northumbrian's life: his battle against Cadwalla at Heavenfield, the works of Bishop Aidan, and a final battle against Penda at Maserfeld. Ælfric begins with Oswald's childhood, relating that he is converted to Christianity while exiled in Ireland. Upon his return to England, Oswald wins a battle against the forces of the heathen king Cadwalla, who killed Oswald's holy uncle, King Edwin of Northumbria. At the battle at Heavenfield, Oswald commands his followers to erect a cross, which later promotes healing for those who either visit it or receive the moss that grows upon it. As king, Oswald turns his energy to converting his people, inviting Bishop Aidan from Ireland to help in the matter. Finally, Ælfric relates the story of Oswald's defeat at Maserfeld by Penda, a Mercian king who had been allied with Cadwalla in the Heavenfield battle. Throughout the *Life*, Ælfric focuses on the miracles that surround Oswald and

---

39. See Christie, "Self-Mastery and Submission," in Cullum and Lewis, *Holiness and Masculinity*; Hill, "Sacrificial Synecdoche," in Wilcox and Withers, *Naked before God*; Damon, "*Desecto Capite Perfido.*"

the sites of his battles, including several instances of miracles taking place as a result of soil that becomes holy by his intervention.[40]

The theme of sanctifying and protecting English land that suffuses Oswald's story is a very timely one, given the historical situation of Ælfric's own period (most particularly, the second Viking invasion).[41] Indeed, "the relationship between warfare and sanctity"[42] is a prominent concern for both Bede and Ælfric, and the source of a telling difference between them. Ideas about kingship were in flux during the period in which Bede writes:[43] as Clare Stancliffe observes, Bede's "portrayal of Oswald is a deliberate construct, put together to record those aspects of Oswald's achievements and character which Bede wished to bring to the notice of his own contemporaries and future generations—not least, kings."[44] Bede specifically uses Oswald to create a sense of "Northumbrian identity" that would have been unrecognizable to the historical king. Ælfric takes a contrasting approach,[45] investing his *Life* more fully in the holiness of the king and less in the historical particulars of his reign. Bede does not emphasize the holiness of the king; rather, his work "centers on what Oswald achieved during his life and then the power he had follow-

---

40. Ælfric displays a keen interest in using saints' lives for what some critics term "protonationalist" purposes elsewhere in his oeuvre, especially in his *Life of Saint Gregory*. See Lavezzo, *Angels on the Edge of the World*; Lees, "Vigilance and Nation," in Magennis and Swan, *A Companion to Ælfric*, 285.

41. Although Ælfric's protonationalism is not my main concern here, understanding its operation allows for a more thorough understanding of the character of the imagined textual communities of *Lives of the Saints*. The conflation of English and Northumbrian Christianity in particular illuminates how the story of Oswald creates an imagined identity for its readership. Ælfric's choice of Oswald in itself suggests the nationalistic thinking that is latent in the project. Contrastingly, Gretsch argues that in a newly emergent "Kingdom of the English," the earlier Æthelstan sought to identify what she terms a "pan-English" saint. This impulse emerged as part of a need "to form what in modern jargon would be called a 'corporate identity'" (*Ælfric and the Cult of the Saints*, 96). Cuthbert, Gretsch claims, made a better choice than Edmund or Oswald because of his lack of political implications. By Ælfric's period, however, Oswald's *Life* fulfilled a need for a pan-English saint who could galvanize a people against invading forces. As a king who fought non-Christian invaders, Oswald's hagiography creates possibilities for not only the protection of English land but also for its sanctification. For the relationship between gender and landscape, albeit in a very different context, see Stodnick, "Bodies of the Land," in Szarmach, *Writing Women Saints*. For an exploration of the relationship between Oswald and the Viking invasions, see Lazzari, "Kingship and Sainthood," in Lazzari et al., *Hagiography in Anglo-Saxon England*, 39.

42. Damon, *Soldier Saints and Holy Warriors*, 195.

43. Stancliffe argues that "Oswald is Bede's most convincing example of an Anglo-Saxon king who took his Christianity seriously, but at the same time remained a king, and indeed a successful king" ("Oswald, 'Most Holy and Victorious,'" in Cambridge and Stancliffe, *Oswald*, 46).

44. Stancliffe, 46.

45. Chase, "Saints' Lives, Royal Lives," in Chase, *Dating of Beowulf*, 163.

ing his death."[46] These divergent goals play out in the way the two accounts of Oswald's life reckon with his legacy as both a political and religious figure. Such investments become particularly apparent when questions of community and identity are at stake.[47]

One striking difference between Bede and Ælfric lies in their treatment of Oswald's uncle, the Christian King Edwin. Like Oswald, Edwin was a Northumbrian king linked to conversion, albeit a conversion that does not last. Edwin's story is perhaps most familiar from Bede's *Historia Ecclesiastica*, where the king's careful deliberation of whether or not to accept the Christian faith culminates first in his own conversion and then in the conversion of his people.[48] Oswald's holiness, by contrast, becomes most clear on the battlefield, where he triumphs in war as a result of his faith. In the *Historia Ecclesiastica*, Bede makes a distinction between earthly allegiances and heavenly ones. In his description of the kings between Edwin's reign and Oswald's, Bede states, "Qui uterque rex, ut terreni regni infulas sortitus est, sacramenta regni caelestis, quibus initiatus erat, anathematizando prodidit, ac se priscis idolatriae sordibus polluendum perdendumque restituit" (III.1.212) [No sooner had these two kings gained the scepters of their earthly kingdom than they abjured and betrayed the mysteries of the heavenly kingdom to which they had been admitted and reverted to the filth of their former idolatry, thereby to be polluted and destroyed (213)].[49] The Christian community that Edwin sought to establish by his conversion amounts to almost nothing for Bede. The intervening kings pollute themselves and their kingdom by their return to idolatry. As a result, Edwin's line—and by extension, his kingdom—is broken. In Ælfric's *Life of Oswald*, the relationship between the two kings is one

---

46. Gunn, "Bede and the Martyrdom of Saint Oswald," in Wood, *Martyrs and Martyrologies*, 59. As Gunn suggests, Ælfric might not have seen Oswald as a martyr, either.

47. As Hare observes, Bede struggled "to dissociate *Saint* Oswald from *King* Oswald's wars," a position reversed by Ælfric's later "account of Oswald that skillfully reorganized Bede's material to reassert elements of heroic tradition present in the saintly king's life and death." Hare notes the parallels and divergences in the text that surround Ælfric's treatment of the heroic king (Hare, "Heroes, Saints and Martyrs," § 22). See also Chase, "Saints' Lives, Royal Lives," in Chase, *Dating of Beowulf*, 161–71. Alternatively, Stancliffe thinks that Bede's portrayal of Oswald is actually quite successful in intermingling the saint and the king. See Stancliffe, "Oswald, 'Most Holy and Victorious,'" in Cambridge and Stancliffe, *Oswald*. See also Magennis, "Warrior Saints."

48. Cf. *HE* II.12.175–II.13.187. See also Hurt, "Ælfric and the English Saints," 91: "To an even greater extent than in the life of Cuthbert, Ælfric has taken Bede's work apart and reassembled it in his own way, producing a new version, rather than merely a simple translation or adaptation."

49. The Old English *Bede* is a bit harsher in its evaluation, noting that "hi sylfe þurh þæt forluran" (III.1.152) [through that [devil-worship] they damned themselves]. Old English text from Miller, *Old English Version of Bede's Ecclesiastical History*.

defined by both secular and spiritual lineages. The association is strengthened early in the story. In fact, the text narrates Edwin's death in the same lines as Oswald's conversion in Ireland:

> Se ferde on his iugoðe fram freondum and magum
> to scot-lande on sæ . and þær sona wearð gefullod
> and his geferan samod þe mid him siþedon .
> Betwux þam wearð ofslagen eadwine his eam
> norðhymbra cynincg on crist ge-lyfed .
> fram brytta cyninge ceadwalla geciged .
> (26.4–9)

> He travelled in his youth from his friends and kinsmen to Ireland by sea, and there he soon became baptized, with his companions who traveled together with him. In the meanwhile, Edwin his uncle was slain, the King of the Northumbrians who believed in Christ, by the British king named Cadwalla.

Edwin is designated as both the king of the Northumbrians—a title Oswald would share—and as a king "who believed in Christ." His death precipitates not miracles but a return to non-Christian darkness. It marks a moment where Christianity in England is lost, and so his belief is still worthy of remark. In Ælfric's narrative, Oswald's role as the king of Northumbria creates spiritual and narrative links between the monarch and his uncle, Edwin, that obfuscate a fissure in Northumbrian Christianity. Ælfric thus posits more continuity in Christian belief and community than does Bede.[50]

In the *Life of Oswald*, Ælfric rewrites Edwin's death to emphasize continuity rather than fissure. Rather than relate the story of these kings and their apostasy, Ælfric merely mentions that they came to their deaths in battle with Cadwalla: he killed "twegen his æftergengan binnan twam gearum" (26.10) [two of his successors in two years]. This observation provides a starting point for the discussion of Oswald's holy victory at Heavenfield. Ælfric's omission of these kings is, by itself, unremarkable. But read in tandem with Bede's version, a connection emerges. Bede writes, "Vnde cunctis placuit regum tempora computantibus ut, ablata de medio regum perfidorum memoria, idem annus sequentis regis, id est Osualdi uiri Deo dilecti, regno adsignaretur" (III.1.214) [So all those who compute the dates of kings have decided to abolish the memory of those perfidious kings and to assign this year to their successor

---

50. For a more complete account of Ælfric's translation activities, including his incorporation of different sources, see Lazzari, "Kingship and Sainthood," in Lazzari et al., *Hagiography in Anglo-Saxon England*, 50.

Oswald, a man beloved of God (215)].[51] Ælfric's glancing reference to the two kings effectively fulfills Bede's vision by omitting these kings' apostasy.[52] It also creates an artificial continuity in the Northumbrian Christian community. Ælfric thus closes the gap in time between Edwin and Oswald, creating less apparent temporal distance between two key moments in Northumbrian Christianity.

Language and translation become part of Oswald's story when the Bishop Aidan is summoned from Ireland to help reconvert Oswald's people. Scholars often focus on Aidan's role in creating Oswald's physical relics; he blesses the king's right hand, and it becomes incorruptible.[53] Yet when Oswald first sends for Aidan, we also see that translation plays a crucial role in how Oswald's narrative imagines community across time. Language at first poses an obstacle to the expansion of Christian community because Aidan is not able "gebigan his spræce / to norðhymbriscum gereorde swa hraþa þa git" (26.68–69) [to change his speech to the Northumbrian language quickly enough yet]. However, Oswald can already speak Irish fluently and so acts as interpreter. This moment in the narrative serves as a translation effect: despite the absence of Oswald's actual translations of Aidan's words, the narrative draws attention to the necessity of linguistic mediation and thus highlights the centrality of translation to conversion. Translation, that is, makes a Northumbrian Christian community possible. Oswald's linguistic ability—gained in his youthful exile in Ireland—allows him to become an intermediary between his people and the Christian faith.

Bede's version of the narrative omits the king's linguistic prowess and therefore also omits any sense of translation's importance to conversion:

> Ferunt autem quia, cum de prouincia Scottorum / rex Osuald postulasset antistitem, qui sibi suaeque genti uerbum fidei ministraret, missus fuerit primo alius austerioris animi uir, qui, cum aliquandiu genti Anglorum praedicans nihil proficeret nec libenter a populo audiretur, redierit patriam atque in conuentu seniorum rettulerit, quia nihil prodesse docendo genti, ad quam missus erat, potuisset, eo quod essent homines indomabiles et durae ac barbare mentis (III.5.228)

---

51. For the Old English *Bede's* version of the same lines, see III.1.154. Davis takes a more expansive view of Bede's relegation of these kings to oblivion: "Osric and Eanfrith must be *made* to be without history, precisely because historical time is a political argument, not an eschatological given" in Bede's text (*Periodization and Sovereignty*, 128).

52. For the idea that Ælfric "followed Bede's suggestion to eliminate the memory of these two traitor kings," see Lazzari, "Kingship and Sainthood," in Lazzari et al., *Hagiography in Anglo-Saxon England*, 51.

53. See Skeat, *Ælfric's Lives of the Saints*, 26.101–3; also *HE* III.6.230.

> The story goes that when King Oswald asked the Irish for a bishop to minister the word of faith to him and his people, another man of harsher disposition was first sent. But he preached to the English for some time unsuccessfully, and seeing that the people were unwilling to listen to him, he returned to his own land. At a meeting of the elders, he reported that he had made no headway in the instruction of the people to whom he had been sent, because they were intractable, obstinate, and uncivilized. (229)

Although Bede has already noted that Aidan was sent to the court of Oswald,[54] the inclusion of the failed conversion distances Oswald's decision to convert his people from his ability to bring it about. When the first monk returns to Ireland, he blames his failure on the character of the people he was sent to convert: they are "intractable, obstinate, and uncivilized." It is Aidan who recognizes the real problem: the first monk did not offer the Northumbrians "lac doctrinae mollioris" (III.5.228) [the milk of simpler teaching (229)]. His insight results in the reassignment of the mission to him.[55] In Bede's version of the story, if Aidan cannot speak the local language, no note is made of it. Temporal distance—created by the failed teaching of the first monk—replaces linguistic distance, and this difference accentuates the gap in time between Edwin's conversion and Oswald's.

Ælfric's inclusion of translation activities closes the narrative historical distance between non-Christian and Christian Northumbria. No sooner does Oswald inquire about the will of God than he calls for a bishop to be sent to him from the Irish monastery. No sooner does he send for a bishop to teach his people than Aidan is chosen for the mission. The narrative space between Oswald's decision to convert the English and his ability (through Aidan) to bring about that conversion is closed just as the narrative distance between non-Christian and Christian Northumbria is closed. For Ælfric, Oswald's desire to convert his people to belief in Christ leads directly to the act of conversion. The translation effect that highlights linguistic conversion functions similarly to facilitate community in the narrative: a potential delay is avoided, just as other delays present in Bede's account are avoided in Ælfric's. The result in the *Life of Oswald* is a continuity of Christian community that is conspicuously absent from the *Historia Ecclesiastica*. This continuity strengthens the association of Northumbria with the Christianity brought to it through its holy kings.

The omission of narrative distance lessens the amount of time within the *Life* that Northumbria remains non-Christian. This attention to community

---

54. See *HE* III.3.218–19.
55. See *HE* III.5.228–29.

extends to other Ælfrician alterations that erase traces of inter-kingdom conflict in the narrative, which allows the Northumbrian community to more easily stand in for an English Christian community. The English Christian community expands in time in a way that historically it could not possibly have done—and that it only can do here through the figure of a saintly king. In these moments, Ælfric does not draw attention to the process of translation *per se,* and so translation effects as such do not operate. Yet a comparison with Bede's version of events makes his innovation clear.

Analyzing the two major battles in the *Life of Oswald,* Heavenfield and Maserfeld, reveals the extent of Ælfric's interventions in this vein. Chase argues that Bede, through a rather circular treatment of Oswald's death, "effectively masks the possibility that Maserfelth was the continuation of an old blood feud,"[56] in part because it obscures connections between Oswald, Penda, and Edwin. Penda was a Mercian king allied with Cadwalla at the time of Edwin's death. Bede emphasizes that Oswald dies "ab eadem pagana gente paganoque rege Merciorum, a quo et prodecessor eius Eduini" (III.9.240–42) [by the same heathen people and the same heathen Mercian king as his predecessor Edwin (243)]. Bede's rendition of the story of Oswald's death focuses on the Mercian king and his pagan people rather than Cadwalla.

Ælfric's version of Oswald's death, by contrast, highlights the relationship between Cadwalla and Penda:

> Hit gewearð swa be þam þæt him wann on penda
> myrcena cyning . þe æt his mæges slege ær
> eadwines cyninges ceadwallan fylste .
> and se penda ne cuðe be criste nan þincg .
> and eall myrcena folc wæs ungefullod þa git .
> (26.150–54)

> It happened then to him [Oswald was killed] because Penda, King of the Mercians, fought against him, who before had helped Cadwalla slay his kinsman, Edwin. And this Penda did not believe in Christ at all, and all of the Mercian people were not yet baptized.

The difference between Bede and Ælfric on this point is instructive: the association of Penda with Cadwalla associates non-Northumbrian, non-Christian peoples with the non-Christian Britons who were responsible for the death of

---

56. Chase, "Saints' Lives, Royal Lives," in Chase, *Dating of Beowulf,* 165. See also Cramp, "Making of Oswald's Northumbria," in Cambridge and Stancliffe, *Oswald,* 21–22, who notes this episode's possible blood feud component.

another holy king. Bede apologizes for Penda's actions and downplays their significance. Ælfric correlates the two and makes it extremely clear that Northumbrian Christianity is meant to be the ascendant force of Christianity in England. For Ælfric, the later conversion of the Mercian people matters more than their historical mistakes. Christianity offers an opportunity: it can sanctify kingship and create a holy land that transcends inter-kingdom conflicts in early medieval England.

For Bede, even the interment of the saint's holy remains is subject to political rivalries. Initially, monks at Bardney refuse to receive the saint's corpse. Bede explains the relationship between the Queen of Mercia and the kingly martyr[57] but pauses to remark on the monks' hesitation to accept the relics: "Etsi sanctum eum nouerant, tamen quia de alia prouincia ortus fuerat et super eos regnum acceperat, ueteranis eum odiis etiam mortuum insequebantur" (III.11.246) [They knew that Oswald was a saint but, nevertheless, because he belonged to another kingdom and had once conquered them, they pursued him even when dead with their former hatred (247)]. Bede's story directly addresses the problematic relationship between Oswald's kingdom and the kingdom of the Mercians, marking the difficulty created for rival groups when a warrior king becomes a saint. In Bede's narrative, secular allegiance is not always trumped by Christian brotherhood. However, Ælfric alters the reason for the monks' refusal of the saint's remains: they initially reject them "for menniscum gedwylde" (26.179) [because of human error]. Again, Ælfric elides discussion of a potential political conflict in order to place the blame solely on sinful men, who cannot see what it is they turn away from.

Superficially, this change seems somewhat odd. After all, Ælfric has already observed that neither Penda nor the Mercians he leads were Christian at the time of Edwin's death. This moment in Ælfric's text draws attention to a single phrase in the earlier segment that describes the relationship between Penda, Oswald, and Edwin: þa git (26.152) [yet]. The Mercians are described by their future: "and eall myrcena folc wæs ungefullod þa git" (26.152) [and all of the Mercian people had not yet been baptized]. The inclusion of the phrase þa git in this description suggests a continuity granted by Christianity. Although the Mercians had not yet been baptized, they were still possible subjects of Christianity's healing grace. With the hindsight of history, their eventual conversion is inevitable.[58] Thus, when Ælfric reduces the monks' refusal of the bones

---

57. He notes that the movement of Oswald's bones to Bardney was on the order of Queen Osthryth of Mercia, Oswald's niece. See HE III.11.246–47.

58. Waterhouse argues that the þa git is part of the interaction between encoder and decoder, and "foreshadows the conclusion to the life" ("Discourse and Hypersignification," in Szarmach, *Holy Men and Holy Women*, 338).

to simple "human error," he changes the character of their response. Where Bede figures a Mercian response to a former adversary, Ælfric glosses over the monks' secular allegiance to a kingdom in order to emphasize the more important allegiance all men owe to God and, by extension, to his chosen saints.[59] The Mercians had not *yet* been baptized when Penda killed Oswald and when the monks refused the holy relics. Ælfric's smoothing over of their Mercian sentiments fulfills the promise of what was "yet" to come. Just as they would eventually believe in Christ after Penda kills Oswald, the monks would also redeem their rejection of the bones by later accepting them. Ælfric's omission of their secular allegiance emphasizes the power of the Christian faith to unite peoples, in contrast to the secular ties that divide them.

The scenes that follow the monks' refusal to house the holy bones also mark a textual divergence between Ælfric and Bede, one that further highlights Ælfric's commitment to a vision of English Christianity. In the *Historia Ecclesiastica*, God's revelation to the Mercian monks follows the manifestation of a miracle meant to garner the relics' acceptance: "Sed miraculi caelestis ostensio, quam reuerenter eae suscipiendae a cunctis fidelibus essent, patefecit. Nam tota ea nocte columna lucis a carro illo ad caelum usque porrecta omnibus pene eiusdem Lindissae prouinciae locis conspicua stabat" (III.11.246) [But a sign from heaven revealed to them how reverently the relics should have been received by all the faithful. All through the night, a column of light stretched from the carriage right up to heaven and was visible in almost every part of the kingdom of Lindsey (247)]. The monks see the error of their ways writ in the light and recant their position, taking the bones to be housed in their monastery. The monks and people of Lindsey are not the only ones who see the light, however. Several chapters after its first appearance, the light returns: "Nec solum inclyti fama uiri Brittaniae fine lustrauit uniuersos, sed etiam trans Oceanum longe radios salutiferae lucis spargens Germaniae simul et Hiberniae partes attigit" (III.13.252) [Not only did the fame of this renowned king spread through all parts of Britain but the beams of his healing light also spread across the ocean and reached the realms of Germany and Ireland (253)]. In itself, this mention of the light is probably metaphorical: "the beams of his healing light" need not be the same beams that were present at the Lindsey monastery when the monks see the error of their ways. Even as a metaphor, however, their presence is significant.

What matters to Bede is English Christianity in its wider context of European Christianity. The spread of Oswald's cult to the continent is historical

---

59. Despite Ælfric's implication that the Mercians would have not welcomed a conquering king's bones, no matter how sacred, he eschews consideration of that smaller allegiance in favor of his dominant theme of a Christian, English kingdom.

fact.[60] In Ælfric's account, by contrast, the miracles from his "healing light" are confined to England:

> Heofonlic leoht ofer þæt geteld astreht
> stod up to heofonum swilce healic sunnbeam
> ofer ealle þa niht . and þa leoda beheoldon
> geond ealle þa scire swiðe wundrigende.
> (26.183–86)

> A heavenly light stretched over the tent and stood straight up to the heavens like a high sun beam throughout all the night, and the people all around that shire beheld it with great wondering.

The specificity of Ælfric's description of the light leaves little to no room for misinterpretation. The beams are a *heofonlic leoht* [heavenly light] sent by God in order to make Oswald's sanctity clear. The light is confined to the province or shire in which Bardney is located. When the spread of Oswald's cult becomes a focus some seventy lines later, the light is conspicuously absent: "Þa asprang his hlisa geond þa land wide . / and eac swilce to irland and eac suþ to franclande" (26.239–40) [Then his fame spread throughout the lands widely, and also even to Ireland and also south to Frankland]. People from Ireland and Frankland are healed through his holy relics, but the text confines the heavenly light by which Oswald is known to England. The glorious light from heaven suggests a specifically English holiness and emphasizes the Christian community in England as having priority over the Christian community on the continent.

Even the miracles and death of Oswald betray the differing foci of Bede's and Ælfric's versions of the story: Ælfric lessens the narrative distance between Oswald and his miracles, clarifying the nature of his holiness far earlier than does Bede. Bede describes Oswald's death succinctly in Book III.9, but three chapters intervene before its next mention of his death. Intriguingly, Bede does not refer to Oswald's "last words" until the latter instance, placing narrative distance between Oswald's death in the battle of Maserfeld and the words he speaks as he dies there:

> Vulgatum est autem, et in consuetudinum prouerbii uersum, quod etiam inter uerba orationis uitam finierit; namque cum armis et hostibus circumseptus iamiamque uideret se esse perimendum, orauit pro animabus exer-

---

60. See Clemoes, "Cult of Saint Oswald," in Lapidge, *Bede and His World*.

citus sui. Vnde dicunt in prouerbio: "Deus miserere animabus, dixit Osuald cadens in terram." (III.12.250)

It is also a tradition which has become proverbial, that he died with a prayer on his lips. When he was beset by the weapons of his enemies and saw that he was about to perish he prayed for the souls of his army. So the proverb runs, "May God have mercy on their souls, as Oswald said when he fell to the earth." (251)

The chapters between Oswald's death and the purported institutionalization of his last words as proverbial knowledge are filled with miracles. These miracles take place through both Oswald's presence (in relic form) and the places with which he is associated. His final words become proverbial in part because of the holy works he performs after death. Bede's interpretation of these events—that it makes sense that Oswald cares for his people in death because he did so in life[61]—is made clear through the final words of the saintly king. By placing his miracles between Oswald's death and his dying words, Bede's narrative reflects a tradition of holiness that clarifies Oswald's death as martyrdom and emphasizes his role in the community as the provider of saintly wisdom.

In contrast, Ælfric's narrative places these two moments—Oswald's death and his proverbial final words—much closer together, relating them in the same passage. This narrative proximity allows Ælfric to claim sainthood for Oswald and then prove it, whereas Bede uses the miracle stories to create the aura of sanctity first and only then claims Oswald's power to care for his kingdom even after death. These differences are in part due to Ælfric's particular project of hagiography. Rather than the somewhat messy narrative of putatively historical events, Ælfric attempts to mold divine truth out of a holy life, simplifying the events of that life as necessary.[62] Ælfric relates that when Oswald perceives that he will die at Maserfeld at the hands of the Mercians, he "gebæd for his folc þe þær feallende sweolt . / and betæhte heora sawla and hine sylfne gode . / and þus clypode on his fylle . God gemiltsa urum sawlum . (26.159–61) [prayed for his people that were falling dead there and committed their souls and his own to God and thus cried out as he fell, "God have mercy on our souls!"] Ælfric's narrative generally follows the linear trajectory of Oswald's life. The victory at Heavenfield is followed by the miracles that occur with Heavenfield as facilitator. The same is true for the miracles that take place through Maserfeld, which follow the relation of Oswald's death and his final words.

---

61. See *HE* III.12.250.
62. See Chase, "Saints' Lives, Royal Lives," in Chase, *Dating of Beowulf*.

The juxtaposition of Bede's and Ælfric's respective versions of the *Life of Oswald* demonstrates the ramifications of their differences. Bede's conception of England was as a kingdom united by shared faith: "a kingdom not just of bodies but of souls."[63] Ælfric's alterations to his source text, by contrast, demarcate the uses to which a holy king and his legacy might be put. Ælfric makes King Oswald a pan-English saint by ignoring or forgetting the factionalism that marked Bede's rendition of the story. As I shall argue, the result of this "forgetting" is the production of a saint whose holiness extends to the very soil of the English kingdom he represents.

HOLY SAINT, HOLY SOIL

Perhaps the most intriguing part of Ælfric's *Life of Oswald* is its emphasis on the sanctification of the soil on which the king fights and, eventually, dies. This holy soil participates in a complex process that symbolically converts the landscape itself, claiming it for Christianity and the larger vision of England that Ælfric emphasizes in his *Lives of the Saints*. The soil functions as what Clare Lees and Gillian Overing call an "emplaced relic," a term that encapsulates both the relic's specificity and its centrality to communities of belief. Such relics can reveal much about the "identity and the *locus*" of a community of belief, and also illuminate "literal as well as sacred topography."[64] Such sacred topographies could, as John Howe argues, both literally and symbolically Christianize previously non-Christian sites. The geographical references in texts about saints can provide "a series of snapshots witnessing cultic developments over time"[65] because places, once Christianized, could be put to use for traditional gatherings or to indicate that a territory belongs to a Christian people. Crosses in particular "[proclaim] Christian territory"[66] while simultaneously demonstrating the identity of the peoples or rulers associated with such spaces. They claim the community for Christianity as well as the land.

In the *Life of Oswald,* both the Heavenfield cross and Oswald's physical body create relics that have a life beyond that body. One such relic is the soil itself. The land is literally converted from mere dirt to holy dust. The

---

63. Wormald, "Engla Londe," 15.
64. Lees and Overing draw on the work of John Howe to explore the possibility of places *being* Christian, rather than simply being the locale of Christian belief ("Anglo-Saxon Horizons," in Lees and Overing, *A Place to Believe In*, 21). See also Howe, "Conversion of the Physical World," in Muldoon, *Varieties of Religious Conversion*.
65. Howe, "Conversion of the Physical World," 68.
66. Howe, 71.

particularity of this emplaced relic raises several questions: How can community form around literally holy land? To what uses is such holy soil put, and how does its transmission stand in for and amplify the narratives about the martyr that circulate beyond his immediate community? As I will demonstrate, both the soil and the narratives it stands in for function as translation effects, calling together a transtemporal and transgeographical Christian community by emphasizing the inheritance of narrative.

The victory at Heavenfield and its related miracles bring to light a pattern of sanctification that occurs in the soil and is associated with Oswald and his death as a martyr. The distribution of that sanctifying power becomes a key component of Oswald's cult as Ælfric describes it. This pattern is also perceptible in the battle of Maserfeld, in which Oswald's death solidifies his position as a martyr for the Christian faith in England. Even after his death, however, his ongoing concern for and involvement with his kingdom persist in the dust that originates from his body and that behaves as both object and subject of action. That is, the miracles that take place through Maserfeld originate in the soil but are not completely contained there. Rather, like the relics of the saint and the story of his life, Oswald's holy power is transferable from believer to believer because the dust that carries his power is portable—just as the story Ælfric tells of that dust is portable. Its movement from the battlefield to various locations around Northumbria and England emphasizes the dust's role as a mediator between the supernatural power of the saint, his physical (though physically lifeless) body, and the other humans that this soil can act upon. In this way, it highlights the function of relics as agents of healing change, agents that provoke alterations in human behavior. That is, humans behave differently around this sanctified soil, regardless of whether they recognize its power. For Ælfric, the power of the Christian faith, defended by a holy king, becomes a property of the soil which that king died to protect from both invaders and non-believers.

Oswald's death at Maserfeld literally sanctifies the soil of England, but Oswald has already claimed the soil at Heavenfield for Christ. Before his victory in battle over Cadwalla, Oswald raises a cross in order to honor God, and he and his companions pray for victory there (26.17–24). After their victory, the cross becomes a site of healing: "And wurdon fela gehælde / untrumra manna and eac swilce nytena / þurh ða ylcan rode swa swa us rehte beda" (26.31–33) [And many were healed, un-well men and also animals through that same cross, as Bede has told us]. Notably, Ælfric invokes Bede's authority here because Bede does relate this same story.[67] The invocation of Bede is a

---

67. See *HE* III.2.214–19.

translation effect: it highlights narrative transmission, and locates Bede as the authoritative source, despite Ælfric's many alterations to the *Life*. It also prepares the reader of the *Life of Oswald* for what is still to come: the distribution of holiness that the cross creates.

Even though Oswald has not yet died for his faith, his saintly potential is already central to the action at Heavenfield. From the point of view of the narrative, a collapsing of time takes place through this elision. Oswald has not yet become a martyr-king, but his ability to create a holy and meaningful place through his intercession and prayer is clearly manifest. His incipient sainthood permeates the story as much as his holiness alters the properties of the soil. Moreover, the cross marks the first suggestion that Oswald's holiness has the potential to disperse its sanctifying power far away from its place of origin. The cross works miracles at a distance because its holiness spreads to the vegetation that grows upon it:

> Sum man feoll on ise þæt his earm tobærst .
> and læg þa on bedde gebrocod forðearle
> oð þæt man him fette of ðære foresæden rode
> sumne dæl þæs messes þe heo mid beweaxen wæs .
> and se adliga sona on slæpe wearð gehæled
> on ðære ylcan nihte þurh oswoldes geearnungum .
> (26.34–39)

> A certain man fell on ice so that his arm was broken, and he lay then in bed very much injured until a man fetched for him from that aforementioned cross a part of the moss that was growing on it, and the sick man soon became healed in his sleep on that very night through Oswald's worthiness.

The narrative emphasizes the traversal of a physical space, a pervasive theme in the *Life of Oswald* (and most hagiography). In this case, however, such movement takes place not through contact with relics but through a secondary site created by the saint himself. The place of Heavenfield, or rather its holiness, is made present in the material of the moss. The moss can be "fetched" and transported to anywhere it is needed.

Moved from its initial location to wherever it could work healing power, the moss extends the holiness of Heavenfield and the efficacy of its healing cross to locales far from its initial environment. The interaction between the king, the cross, and the land creates a contact relic, but this relic is hardly static. The portability of the moss is implicit in the verb used to describe its movement: *fetian*.⁶⁸ This verb calls attention to one way in which the moss functions within the narrative because its literal meaning contains valences of being sought out, fetched, brought, or moved—all of which prioritize the uses to which the moss is put.⁶⁹ *Fetian*, however, also falls into a semantic range that includes the possible meaning of "to marry."⁷⁰ This less common use of *fetian* functions as an apt metaphor for the way the moss helps create the communities of holiness that Oswald draws together, communities that exceed the strictly human to include elements of the natural environment, the supernatural (God), and the holy king. The moss performs a linking of humans with both the natural and supernatural worlds. As a result, the moss gains a sense of agency—non-human, but still present. Whether it is supernatural or not is ultimately not the fundamental issue. The moss has power. The holiness of the king leads to the holiness of the land. The portability of the moss means that Oswald's holiness can be effective far from his physical presence. The result is a spatially extensive community of English Christians associated with and by the material that Oswald sanctifies.

Even Heavenfield's naming demonstrates Oswald's exceptionality and its extension to his people. In the *Historia Ecclesiastica,* the identity of Heavenfield is associated with the place through its original name, which was given long before Oswald's miraculous battle:

> Vocatur locus ille lingua Anglorum Hefenfeld, quod dici potest latine Caelestis Campus, quod certo utique praesagio futurorum antiquitus nomen accepit; significans nimirum quod ibidem caeleste erigendum tropeum, caelestis inchoanda uictoria, caelestia usque hodie forent miracula celebranda. Est autem locus iuxta murum illum ad aquilonem, quo Romani quondam ob arcendos barbarorum impetus totam a mari ad mare praecinxere Brittaniam, ut supra docuimus. (III.2.216)

> This place is called in English Heavenfield, and in Latin *Caelestis campus,* a name which it certainly received in days of old as an omen of future happenings; it signified that a heavenly sign was to be erected there, a heavenly victory won, and that heavenly miracles were to take place there continuing to this day. The place, on its north side, is close to the wall with which the Romans once girded the whole of Britain from sea to sea, to keep off the attacks of the barbarians as already described. (217)

---

68. DOE, s.v. *fetian*.
69. DOE, s.v. *fetian*[1, 3, 4, 5]
70. DOE, s.v. *fetian*[6]

Bede's narrative positions Heavenfield's name as an inheritance rather than an innovation. He avers that the name itself—*Caelestis campus*—is a sign of the holiness of the place, bestowed (we can assume) in the time of the Romans. They too sought to keep an enemy people from attacking their lands; one need only substitute "non-Christian" for "barbarian" in the passage above to make the similarity clear. Just as the wall kept out a force that threatened to undermine the Roman Empire, the cross at Heavenfield offers testament to the power of that sign to unite and bolster Christians against the forces that threaten them.[71] Moreover, it points to the eventual coming of Christianity and the remaking of Heavenfield through its Christianization—a narrative, Bede suggests, destined to be fulfilled. Ælfric's version of Heavenfield's name, by contrast, is much abridged:

> Seo stow is gehaten heofon-feld on englisc .
> wið þone langan weall þe þa romaniscan worhtan
> þær þær oswold oferwann þon wælhreowan cynincg .
> (26.40–42)

> The place is called Heavenfield in English, against the long wall which the Romans wrought, there where Oswald overcame the cruel king.

Ælfric's interest in the material holiness of the cross at Heavenfield is mirrored by his interest in the means by which the site becomes holy. The process by which Heavenfield gains its name is further evidence of Oswald's ability to create a holy space. Although Ælfric does not posit the naming of Heavenfield as a result of Oswald's actions, the occurrence of the naming after the miracles suggests that the place's holiness becomes known because of his victory through Christ. Oswald, that is, puts Heavenfield on the map.

While Heavenfield proves to be a particularly holy locale, Ælfric goes on to pursue an argument about the holiness of English land more broadly in narrative moments in which he chooses not to give precise information about holy locations. His lack of precision seems to indicate an impulse to make Oswald a more generally English saint, rather than confining the community his sanctity affects to a specific locale. In the relation of the miracle stories that take place at Heavenfield and Maserfeld, Ælfric shows a characteristic avoidance of details that identify either the recipients of the healing or the precise knowl-

---

71. For the absence or presence of Christianity and Christian paraphernalia in and around Oswald's time, see Cramp, "Making of Oswald's Northumbria," in Cambridge and Stancliffe, *Oswald*. For further background on the context of the cross at Heavenfield, see Maclean, "King Oswald's Wooden Cross," in Karkov et al., *Insular Tradition*.

edge of the location's significance on their part. In the case of Heavenfield, the exclusion is quite simple: where Bede avers that the man who experiences healing from his broken arm is a monk at Hexham, Ælfric makes no claim whatsoever for his identity.[72] The man is simply referred to as "a certain man": "Sum man feoll on ise þæt his earm tobærst" (26.34) [A certain man fell on ice so that his arm was broken]. Were this the only such omission, the simplification could be explained as a function of genre and the lack of a need for more specific and local references in the *Life*. Ælfric is, however, almost systematic in his exclusion of details that Bede includes. The bulk of these exclusions make Oswald's holiness a general one, capable of spreading throughout his kingdom and to believers in his sanctity beyond Northumbrian soil. In Ælfric's retelling, Oswald's holiness unites an English Christian community.

In the case of Maserfeld, the different degrees of specificity in locating the holy place indicate the final way in which Ælfric's alteration of Bede suggests a different kind of interest in community, one that seeks to position Oswald as a pan-English saint.[73] The introduction of Maserfeld in the *Historia Ecclesiastica* reveals a higher degree of specificity in Bede's location of the site, as well as in the reproducibility of the miracles that take place through the soil. After noting that many animals and men are healed by the holy soil, Bede makes an implicit claim for the ease of locating the spot. In his time at least, it is marked by a gaping hole: many people removed earth from the place, and in their piety they create a hole "ad mensuram staturae uirilis altam" (III.9.242) [as deep as a man's height (243)]. Perhaps counterintuitively, the very first healing that takes place there is by accident. After his horse is cured of "graui dolore" (III.9.242) [agonizing pain (243)] by touching the spot where Oswald died, a rider "intellexit aliquid mirae sanctitatis huic loco, quo equus est curatus, inesse, et posito ibi signo non multo post ascendit equum atque ad hospitium, quo proposuerat, accessit" (III.9.242) [realized that there must be some special sanctity associated with the place in which the horse was cured. He put up a sign to indicate the site, shortly afterward mounted his horse, and reached the inn where he intended to lodge (243)]. Initially, the rider does not know that this place is holy because of Oswald, but he still marks it with a sign, presumably so that others might return to it. The narrative distance implied by the man's lack of knowledge—the reader knows that he is in a holy place from the beginning but the man does not—serves to make the site itself specific. That is, both the horse that is healed and the paralyzed woman who is brought there afterward to be healed must be in a specific place to experience the heal-

---

72. *HE* III.2.216–17.
73. For an important dissenting point, see Gretsch, *Ælfric and the Cult of the Saints*.

ing. The owner of the horse must mark the place by putting up a sign, making sure that he and others could find it again.

Ælfric, by contrast, omits the rider's sense of place, noting that his horse is cured when "becom hit embe lang þær se cynincg oswold / on þam gefeohte feoll swa swa we ær foresædan" (26.208–9) [it came before long to the place where the king Oswald fell in the fight, as we said before].[74] The narrative does not imply that the rider knows that the place is holy or that Oswald died there. Moreover, the rider does not erect any sign at the place when he leaves; rather, he simply "þa ferde forð on his weg" (26.212) [went forth afterward on his way]. Although the reader is consistently reminded that the ground is holy (and that it is holy because of Oswald's death) the narrative itself only foregrounds the agency of the dirt on which Oswald dies to heal the horse. The rider (if not the reader) is drawn into relationship with the holy soil completely unawares, and leaves no trace of his miraculous encounter. Oswald's holy work can apparently be continued even if those healed by him are not aware either of his power or the need to distribute it. In a certain sense, then, for Ælfric the rider does not need to mark the place—the person for whom this holiness is made manifest is the reader of the saint's story.

Even the natural world conspires to make Oswald's holiness known in Bede's *Historia Ecclesiastica*. The ground where Oswald dies at Maserfeld is qualitatively different from other ground in the same field. It is, the text observes, "greener and more beautiful":

> Eodem tempore uenit alius quidam de natione Brettonum, ut ferunt, inter faciens iuxta ipsum locum, in / quo praefata erat pugna conpleta; et uidit unius loci spatium cetero campo uiridius ac uenustius, coepitque sagaci animo conicere, quod nulla esset alia causa insolitae illo in loco uiriditatis, nisi quia ibidem sanctior cetero exercitu uir aliquis fuisset interfectus (III.10.244)

> The story is told that about this time another man, a Briton, was travelling near that place where the battle had been fought, when he noticed that a certain patch of ground was greener and more beautiful than the rest of the field. He very wisely conjectured that the only cause for the unusual greenness of that part must be that some man holier than the rest of the army had perished there. (245)

---

74. Arthur notes that "Oswald's sainthood is verified by the beast's renewed posture"—i.e., the horse stands up, having been previously rolling indiscriminately on the ground ("Postural Representations," 317).

Oswald's death alters the growth of the grass in this place of holiness: it grows more beautifully, with "unusual greenness." In some sense, it is more full of life—literally and metaphorically—through its association with the sainted king. The Briton man correctly interprets this altered growth pattern to mean that a holy man had died at Maserfeld. Neither is it unimportant that the man who recognizes this altered growth pattern is "de natione Brettonum"—the power of the soil extends across geographical space, and its importance for humans as a marker of identity. Even a Briton, that is, can experience Oswald's holy power by being in the proper place to receive it.

The power of the soil in this miracle protects not just human or animal life but even the buildings that humans construct. The Briton binds some of the dirt from that site in a cloth and takes it to a feast at a house in an unnamed village. During this feast, "contigit uolantibus in altum scintillis culmen domus, quod erat uirgis contextum ac foeno tectum, subitaneis flammis impleri" (III.10.244) [it happened that the sparks flew up to the roof which was made of wattles and thatched with hay, so that it suddenly burst into flames (245)]. No human power could save the house, but the dust from Oswald's site of death retains a protective function: "Consumta ergo domu flammis, posta solummodo, in qua puluis ille inclusus pendebat, tuta ab ignibus et intacta remansit" (III.10.244–45) [So the whole house was burnt down with the single exception that the post on which the soil hung, enclosed in its bag, remained whole and untouched by the fire]. Understandably curious, the witnesses seek more information, and the source of the miracle is revealed: "Inuenerunt, quia de illo loco adsumptus erat puluis, ubi regis Osualdi sanguis fuerat effusus" (III.10.244–45) [They discovered that the soil had been taken from that very place where Oswald's blood had been spilt].

Because Ælfric omits any specific way in which Oswald's place of death is marked out as special, his story of the house fire creates a very different set of narrative circumstances that allow for the saint's miraculous intervention. Ælfric creates one more translation effect by making the *story* of Oswald part of the saint's ability to create a transtemporal community:

Eft siððan ferde eac sum ærendefæst ridda
be þære ylcan stowe . and geband on anum claþe
of þam halgan duste þære deorwurðan stowe.
(26.221–23)

And again, a horseman [was] bound on an errand by that same place, and [he] bound up some of the holy dust from that precious place in a cloth.

The implication in this description—with the absence of any physical marker to show the holy difference of the place in question—is that the errand-bound man *already knows* that this place is special. The dust, hung on a post, saves that post from a fire in this account of the miracle as well, but human minds are not prompted to seek the truth of the holy soil in this instance. Rather, "se post ana ætstod ansund mid þam duste . / and hi swyðe wundrodon þæs halgan weres gearnunga / þæt þæt fyr ne mihte þa moldan forbærnan" (26.234–36) [the post alone stood whole, with the dust, and they greatly wondered at the merit of the holy man that the fire could not burn the earth]. The implication in this scene is that the narrative of Oswald's holiness—perhaps even the hagiography itself—has already disseminated widely enough for these people to know without asking that the martyr-king's holiness is what makes these miracles possible. A last component of the community this saint brings together is thus illuminated. Joining the house, the fire, the dust, Oswald's blood, and the human minds who perceive it all, we have Oswald's story: the accumulation of miraculous evidence that occurs both during and after his holy life. This scene, finally, points to the inheritance of narrative itself, a translation effect that is as portable as the holy dust and that collects believers into a larger community that implicates them in worlds natural, human, and divine.

CONCLUSION

Ælfric's interest in translation in the *Lives of the Saints* emphasizes how narrative transmission creates community across both time and geographical space. By creating a tradition in which English saints can participate alongside earlier saints, Ælfric makes a significant claim: that England itself is worthy of inclusion—and indeed, special merit—in the transgeographical and transtemporal community of Christendom. By emphasizing narrative inheritance and the translation such inheritance occasions, he creates the very community for which he wishes to argue. This process is brought to fruition in his *Life of Oswald*—a story that intertwines the holiness of a king with that of his geographical kingdom. The alterations that Ælfric makes to the version of Oswald's story in Bede's *Historia Ecclesiastica* change the kind of community imagined by the text. Where Bede's narrative emphasizes a Christian community that can be splintered by the divisions that separate the northern English kingdoms and the British Isles more generally, Ælfric's choices in translation remedy this problematic relationship between faith and kingdom. By omitting key details that have to do with places of origin and simplifying the narrative of Oswald's transition from Christian king to Christian martyr, Ælfric creates a Christian community that exceeds and avoids questions of historical conflict and rivalry. In so doing, he creates a saint whose interaction with specifically English land become the basis of his ability, pre- and postmortem, to unite a Christian community by creating holy places—places that are only legible through acts of translation.

CHAPTER 3

Communities of the Page in the Ælfrician Homiletic Corpus

TO THIS POINT, my argument has concerned a series of translations that are localizable on the level of both semantic and narrative equivalence: translations that are recognizably versions of earlier narratives, retold in a different language. Put another way, the texts I have thus far treated are translations in the traditional sense, and the translation effects I highlight within them function in that context—they are effects of narrative and narrative temporality, of the transfer of material from a source text to a target language. Moreover, the communities these translations imagine are artifacts of the authors and translators: each translation imagines an audience that will form its eventual textual community.

In contrast, this chapter focuses on how readers and scribes respond to translated texts, and by doing so inscribe themselves into the textual community of the manuscript. My archive is the Ælfrician corpus of homilies, a set of manuscripts whose production ranges from near Ælfric's lifetime in the tenth century through to the twelfth century and whose subsequent use continues into the seventeenth century. I argue that by paying attention to the glosses—interlinear and marginal—as well as emendations and additions that accrued to the manuscripts of Ælfric's homilies, we begin to see how translation effects can indicate a different kind of community from the ones that we have thus far considered. This textual community extends in time, but its habitation is not a thought-world of texts and stories; rather, it is a community that exists only in and on the manuscript page.[1]

This "community of the page," as it were, is not always a historical textual community, limited to one locale or time. Rather, this textual community consists of readers (and writers) who may well be separated by centuries. In some cases, it can be comprised only of a lone annotator responding to their own annotations. However, through their various interactions with the manuscripts they annotate, these glossators, amenders, and copyists demonstrate awareness of and concern for translation—and for how different audiences might respond to and read multilinguality. In this way, the impressions that such readers leave in manuscripts raise similar questions of time, language, and community as do the translation effects of my preceding chapters.

To understand how, I will first engage with glossing in early medieval England, as well as this tradition's extension into the post-Conquest period, by examining the work of the Tremulous Hand of Worcester. I then turn to a consideration of *De Octo Vitiis* ("The Eight Vices"), a homily that appears in a diverse range of manuscripts and forms that span the medieval period in both production and subsequent use. I argue that selective use of the punctus, red ink decoration on *litterae notabiliores,* and intralinear discourse markers (in addition to the selective glossing that appears within the manuscripts of these homilies) constitute a visual, manuscript-based translation effect. Together, these strategies highlight how the awareness of translation is made legible on the manuscript page by the scribes who copied the homilies. These scribal interventions indicate an extended temporality for the textual communities such manuscripts create. Finally, I will turn to a more localized consideration of several longer additions that appear in Cambridge, University Library

---

1. Here I draw on the work of Christine Schott, who argues that "in contrast to the coterie groups discussed by scholars like Brian Stock, Ralph Hanna, and A. I. Doyle, which cohered around a text or set of texts but which frequently pre-existed the text or had other primary causes for unity, the 'communities' I explore here frequently exist only on the page" ("Intimate Reading," 28). Her discussion of the Peterborough manuscript in particular illuminates the "sheer scale of time" involved in such conversations, which has the effect of "stretch[ing] the boundaries of that community into something more properly termed metaphorical, or at least metaphysical" (28). Although the marginalia and annotations I examine are engaged primarily with multilingualism and translation, I owe much to Schott's idea of the "intimacy of texts," which compellingly describes the kinds of communities of the page with which I am concerned in this chapter. Fisher's monograph on scribal invention in manuscripts posits a similar sense of agency in its exploration of derivative textuality, while Wakelin's exploration of scribal correction in late medieval manuscripts also suggests that the kinds of interventions I examine in this chapter approach an interaction akin to literary criticism (although his corpus is several centuries later than my own). See Fisher, *Scribal Authorship;* Wakelin, *Scribal Correction and Literary Craft.* See also Bryan, *Collaborative Meaning.*

Ii.1.33, one of the major manuscript witnesses of Ælfric's *Lives of the Saints*. Although these marginalia do not necessarily register as clear translations, I argue that they do count as translation *effects*, moments in which the manuscript draws attention to the fact of translation through its multilinguality. The manuscript thus both participates in and creates a transtemporal community.

GLOSSING THE LETTER

As I have argued in the preceding chapters, translation is first and foremost an interpretive process that leaves traces of itself in the narratives and texts it transforms. Although it is a process that moves between languages, it is more importantly "a problem of moving between individual minds, varieties of textual authority [. . .] cultural worlds, and systems of thought and belief."[2] Robert Stanton's emphasis on process here creates a useful distinction between translation as an activity that takes place in and over time (i.e., a process) and translation as a product that results from that activity.[3] Put another way: in order to have the product of translation, someone must have once undertaken a process of translating, with all of the attendant decisions that entails.[4] Glosses to early medieval English manuscripts are one arena in which this thesis—that the process of translation can be evident in its product—is readily apparent. Using the glossing activities of the Tremulous Hand of Worcester as an example, this section of my chapter will suggest some methods by which glossing highlights translation effects in a manuscript context.

Stanton's work shows that glossed manuscripts in early medieval England "[make] visible the symbiotic relationship between the text, as an object of understanding, and the gloss, as a guide to the specific, historically situated interpretive act."[5] Glosses also indicate *translatio studii, translatio imperii*—they usurp the interpretive process in favor of a momentary intervention into

---

2. Stanton, *Culture of Translation*, 172.

3. Warren's work on translation in Middle English is central to my thought process here. See Warren, "Translation," in Strohm, *Middle English*.

4. In this sense, translation might be considered as similar to manuscript production. As Johnston and Van Dussen argue, "The manuscript is a process as much as it is a product, resulting in absolute numerical uniqueness" (*Medieval Manuscript Book*, 4). Although they refer specifically to a late medieval context (1–16), this observation certainly applies to both early medieval manuscript culture (albeit in a more restrained way) and to the ways in which translation reimagines and recreates the texts it translates.

5. Stanton, *Culture of Translation*, 10.

a text.⁶ The translation effects that glossing produces are also broadly related to the way that *ordinatio* (the intellectual structures that determined manuscript layout) affected the composition of medieval texts, as M. B. Parkes has examined.⁷ He connects *ordinatio* and glossing to the growing prominence of the *compilator*, who unlike both commentator and scribe, could "[impose] a new *ordinatio* on the materials he extracted from others."⁸ The work of the *compilator* grew out of less comprehensive methods of arranging and organizing written materials, including systems of glossing, rubrication, and the use of *litterae notabiliores*.⁹ Although Parkes's focus is on a later period than my own, the centrality of *ordinatio* to manuscript production is apparent in the large number of earlier manuscripts that use elements of *mise-en-page* like rubrics and decoration to help readers navigate the materials in question. In particular, I argue that these manuscripts employ such indicators in order to help users navigate a multilingual text. This apparatus becomes a formal feature of the way in which texts that include both Latin and Old English are presented on the manuscript page, as Katherine O'Brien O'Keefe influentially observed.¹⁰ O'Brien O'Keeffe notes that "the less predictable a work [is] to its reader [...] the more necessary become graphic cues to assist its reading and decoding."¹¹ Her early identification of writing and layout as "technolog[ies]" of multilinguality allows us to better assess how glossing and manuscript layout intersect.¹²

Due to disagreement over both his aims and his tremble, the Tremulous Hand of Worcester makes a useful case study for understanding the temporal

---

6. See Curtius, *European Literature and the Latin Middle Ages*, 28–29. This sense of *translatio* is, moreover, a moment of usurpation of the meaning of a text: as Stanton observes, the gloss "derives its explanatory power from the exclusion of competing interpretations, and hence positions itself as definitive" (*Culture of Translation*, 25). For the relationship between translation and glossing in the Old English *Boethius*, see Hobson, "Translation as Gloss." For the relationship between glossing and the Anglo-Latin "hermeneutic style," see Lapidge, "Hermeneutic Style," and Stephenson, *Politics of Language*.

7. In his examination of the relationship between *ordinatio* and glossing, Parkes examines the development in the twelfth through fourteenth centuries of increasingly complex apparatuses for helping readers to navigate texts. See Parkes, "*Ordinatio* and *Compilatio*," in *Scribes, Scripts, and Readers*, 35–70.

8. Parkes, 59.

9. Parkes, 35–70.

10. Here I build on O'Brien O'Keeffe's work on visual cues in Old English, especially her analysis of the relationship between the writing of a text and the technologies by which such writing takes place, including that "the physical arrangement of a text on a page [...] becomes a crucial constituent of its meaning" (*Visible Song*, 5).

11. O'Brien O'Keeffe, 5.

12. O'Brien O'Keeffe, 13. O'Brien O'Keeffe's argument primarily concerns verse works; my interest here is in prose texts. See both O'Brien O'Keeffe, *Visible Song* and "Graphic Cues."

function of glosses, as well as their community-building capacity. For one, the multilinguality of glossing activities on the part of the Tremulous Hand demonstrates the importance of glossing's temporal structure: it preserves an interaction between the early and late stages of the scribe's activities.[13] A number of scholars have remarked on the Tremulous Hand's interest in Old English works by Ælfric, which he glosses extensively over a period of years,[14] with some identifying him as "the first formal student of Old English."[15] Although Seth Lerer sees in the scribe's activity a nostalgic impulse, both Elaine Treharne and Christine Franzen disagree with that assessment. Franzen's analysis suggests that the interventions themselves do not seem antiquarian, and Treharne argues that the Tremulous Hand is one of "myriad other readerly witnesses occupied in making their presence felt in manuscripts containing Ælfric's many compositions."[16] That is, the work of the Tremulous Hand is part of a wider movement in the Middle English period wherein readers seek to reshape the earlier texts that they read.

Distinct from the preceding scholars, my interest in the Tremulous Hand and his glosses is a specifically temporal one. Given that he is not an isolated figure and that the Tremulous Hand often returns to the same manuscripts at various points in his glossing career, what do his glossing activities in the Ælfrician homiletic corpus tell us about how a specific reader imagined his relationship to a manuscript (or a group of them) over time? As Stanton observes, glosses could derive from a number of sources, ranging from the idiosyncrasy of opinion to a corpus of prior glosses.[17] For example, the Tremulous Hand "built and used an English-Latin word list, the earliest known glossary in first-letter alphabetical sequence by English word."[18] Moreover, his "fragmentary glossaries are some of the earliest known in the English lan-

---

13. For a thorough recent consideration of the Tremulous Hand and his glossing activities, see Butler, *Language and Community*, 129–57.

14. See Treharne, "Making Their Presence Felt," in Magennis and Swan, *Companion to Ælfric*; Lerer, "Old English and Its Afterlife," in Wallace, *Cambridge History of Medieval English Literature*.

15. Hahn, "Early Middle English," in Wallace, *Cambridge History of Medieval English Literature*, 73. Franzen takes a slightly more restrained approach, noting that her "study of the scribe indicates that he went through a clear and methodical learning process in the course of his glossing of these manuscripts," even if the intention behind those activities is unclear (*Tremulous Hand*, 2).

16. Lerer, "Old English and Its Afterlife," in Wallace, *Cambridge History of Medieval English Literature*, 10; Treharne, "Making Their Presence Felt," in Magennis and Swan, *Companion to Ælfric*, 404; Franzen, *Tremulous Hand*.

17. Stanton, *Culture of Translation*, 9.

18. Franzen, *Tremulous Hand*, 3–4. See also Schipper, "Worksheet of the Worcester 'Tremulous' Glossator."

guage in this form."[19] In certain instances, he quite clearly consults with and then employs Latin texts in order to create glosses in Old English ones.[20] On the whole, the care with which the Tremulous Hand undertook his work suggests that he engaged in a conversation with the texts he glossed. This textual conversation led him not only to gloss but to further modify the texts he worked with to make them more easily accessible.[21]

The lack of certainty regarding either the Tremulous Hand's identity or his motivation makes it hard to situate his glossing activities as part of a clear consciousness of community. His activity therefore lends itself to considering what Christine Schott calls the "intimacy of texts"[22]—"an interaction on the page" that does not presuppose a single time in which readers add their annotations. The intimacy of texts in medieval manuscripts creates a community that is not necessarily localizable to a single time and place. It therefore requires a different approach than pursuing ideas of a "coterie" of readers or of historical textual communities. Schott argues that this community of voices only exists "in the marks left on the page"; however, their work exhibits clear intentionality, and Schott argues that "those who came early on very much intended to communicate with future readers, and those who came later interacted with and responded to the notes of their predecessors as though the separation of time meant nothing."[23]

Schott's concept of the intimacy of texts is a crucial part of what I earlier termed the "community of the page." Moreover, it highlights two of the key attributes of the annotations, emendations, and marginalia I consider later in this chapter. First, the community of the page is not always localizable to a single time: these are readers who are separated, in some instances, by centuries. Yet in their interactions with manuscripts, they leave traces of the reading process that we can understand as central to their experience of translation in a manuscript culture. Second, these additions to the manuscript are fundamentally extended in time: they are oriented toward both the past of the manuscript's text and the future of its reception. In this way, interventions on

---

19. Collier, "Tremulous Worcester Hand," in Swan and Treharne, *Rewriting Old English*, 197.

20. Collier.

21. Butler suggests that the Tremulous Hand's phonological modifications to manuscripts imply "that he had a real interest in the linguistic gap itself, in the simultaneous familiarity and unfamiliarity of the language of these texts" (*Language and Community*, 141).

22. Schott, "Intimate Reading," 18. Schott focuses on the Peterborough chronicle, but her insights regarding the interaction of gloss and text are still relevant to a reading of earlier texts.

23. Schott, 29. Schott argues that "if they were not part of what we would strictly consider a quantifiable readerly community, they seemed not to know that." ("Intimate Reading," 29). See also Wakelin, *Scribal Correction and Literary Craft*.

the page of the manuscript partake of the logic of translation effects and the questions that they raise about community, identity, and time. The glossing activity of the Tremulous Hand, I argue, creates a community across time—by glossing the text, the Tremulous Hand demonstrates awareness of a possible future audience that might benefit from his labor. His later additions and corrections to his work solidify that vision: the scribe himself becomes the community toward which his original interventions are oriented.[24]

The work of the Tremulous Hand is particularly suited to temporal analysis for two reasons.[25] The first is his distinctive trembly letter forms, a characteristic which makes him remarkably easy to identify as a scribe. Second, the deteriorative properties of his likely disease allow scholars to date his work self-referentially, allowing for a clear picture of the temporal disposition of his glosses and additions. Indeed, Franzen uses the progression of the scribe's tremble as the primary way to order the glosses that he composed.[26] For example, in Oxford, Bodleian Library Hatton 116,[27] she identifies several of the usual layers of Tremulous Hand glosses. The hands she refers to as P (pencil), B (bold), C (crayon), M (mature), and L (large) all appear in this manuscript.[28] The annotations in Hatton 116 gloss texts that are "found in more than one manuscript, and there is evidence that glosses to multiple copies of the same text were sometimes copied from one manuscript to another" by the Tremulous Hand.[29] His work was multidirectional in terms of its timing: certain glosses from Hatton 116 appear to be reproduced from Oxford, Bodleian Library, Hatton 114,[30] but glosses from Hatton 116 are also used in a later state of the scribe's hand in Oxford, Bodleian Library, MS Hatton 115.[31]

In addition to being multitemporal, the work of the Tremulous Hand is also multilingual: it appears in both Latin and Middle English. In Hatton 116,[32] in addition to Latin and Middle English glosses throughout, the otherwise blank final pages of the manuscript include several additions, including "two

---

24. This assertion resonates with Bakhtin's analysis of what he called "the living word" (*Diaglogic Imagination*, 276–77). See Chapter 1, n. 53. See also n. 58 below.

25. See Franzen, *Tremulous Hand*.

26. Franzen further argues that the chronology "for the layers can be established by studying how they built upon each other and from this chronology we can see how he went about glossing the Old English texts, what he knew, and what he had to learn" (*Tremulous Hand*, 3).

27. Franzen's MS F; Ker no. 333.

28. Franzen, *Tremulous Hand*, 44–48.

29. Franzen, 47.

30. Franzen's MS D; Ker no. 331; Gneuss-Lapidge no. 638. See Franzen, 48.

31. Franzen's MS E; Ker no. 332; Gneuss-Lapidge no. 639. In this case, the relational dating is possible because early B state glosses in Hatton 116 appear in the later M state in Hatton 115. See Franzen, 48.

32. See Treharne, "Hatton 116," in Da Rold et al., *Production and Use of English Manuscripts*.

lines of music written in his hand" and also "a few Latin-[Middle English] word pairs which are drawn from glosses in the manuscript. Some are in pencil and are too faint to read."[33] Others are in the earliest D (dark) state of the tremulous scribe's hand.[34] Like his other glosses, these remain somewhat obscure—it is difficult to tell whether or not they either had or succeeded in a specific aim.[35]

Although these word lists were likely more readable closer to the time they were produced, they still highlight the function that the Tremulous Hand's other glosses were meant to perform. By situating his work in a multilingual context that includes Latin as well as both Old and Middle English, the word list and other ephemera that the Tremulous Hand copies in the final pages of Hatton 116 suggests his ongoing commitment to legibility between Latin and English. That is, these word pairs highlight the function of his glosses as translation effects: moments in which an interlinear gloss calls attention to linguistic difference.

The multitemporal dimension of the Tremulous Hand's work becomes legible only through comparison, however: in other parts of Hatton 116, the scribe has added newer glosses, gone back over his work, and altered his initial emendations. He works with the Old English language as well, altering phonological elements of Old English to make it more legible to Middle English speakers; moreover, he draws dotted lines between words that run together and adds a plethora of *puncti* as a guide to reading this earlier form of the language.[36] Hatton 116, then, illustrates the kinds of revisiting that one scribe might perform in his lifetime. Moreover, it highlights two aspects of the Tremulous Hand's activities. First, it demonstrates the extension of his work in linear time, to the point of creating a collaboration *with his own former work* in glossing the manuscript. Second, it shows that his investment in each of the three languages with which he worked—Old English, Latin, and Early Middle English—was present from the very beginning of that work.

---

33. Franzen, *Tremulous Hand*, 47. To this end, Franzen cites the edition of the *Life of Saint Chad* by Rudolf Vleeskruyer, who observes these specific inclusions in the manuscript. See Vleeskruyer, *Life of Saint Chad*. Treharne argues that the inclusion of the poetic line "ic am nout for þisse þinges wo" can "[remind] us of the sorrow of the Tremulous Hand so famously inscribed in his lament for a lost England that might have provided the inspiration for his detailed work recuperating earlier English texts for those in his care" (*Living through Conquest*, 145–46).

34. Franzen, *Tremulous Hand*, 27.

35. Franzen, 193–94.

36. See Butler, *Language and Community*, 141. Collier, moreover, notes that "in most of the glossed texts the Tremulous Hand attempts to make the Old English text more readable by inserting dotted lines to divide words which were run together by the original scribe" ("Tremulous Worcester Hand," in Swan and Treharne, *Rewriting Old English*, 197).

My purpose in this brief discussion of the Tremulous Hand is first to point out that a single user might have a multitemporal relationship to a manuscript book: a glossator can return to the same texts at different historical moments. The Tremulous Hand annotates manuscripts across a distinct period: "whatever prompted his work, something sustained it for a considerable period of time—the amount of glossing and the number of manuscripts involved would suggest several years of work."[37] Yet despite his singularity, he is still very much an example of the kinds of communities of translators and readers that I have explored elsewhere in this book. Here we have a scribe who interacts with the Old English past—in the guise of Ælfrician homilies—glossing in Latin and Middle English in order to facilitate reuse or learning by himself *or* by others.[38] He returns to his work at different moments in his career, often reglossing the same manuscripts at a later time. His work is both backward- and forward-looking: he interacts with the manuscript in full expectation of the other readers or potential annotators who may need his work. That these alterations and additions are glosses is also central to his activity and its import: these glosses are themselves a type of translation effect, drawing attention to the processes of language transformation and remediation that can only take place across time.

HIERARCHIES OF LANGUAGE

Although the Tremulous Hand's glossing epitomizes the kinds of work that translation effects perform in manuscripts, it does not exhaust them. Indeed, translation effects in manuscripts often exceed glossing's word-for-word approach to translation. That is, translation effects can also be visual or lexical—they can be made clear by elements of page layout, using specific kinds of punctuation and marking, or by the insertion of phrases and other marginalia into the manuscript itself.

In this section, I address the Old English *De Octo Vitiis* tradition.[39] A sermon attributed to Ælfric of Eynsham, *De Octo Vitiis* appears in multiple

---

37. Franzen, *Tremulous Hand*, 193.

38. Butler points out that "the Tremulous glosses and annotations demonstrate their own communal engagement with earlier texts, and more obviously communal, these annotations provided important support for later work on Old English texts" (*Language and Community*, 129). See also Collier, "Tremulous Worcester Hand," in Swan and Treharne, *Rewriting Old English*; Franzen, *Tremulous Hand*; Treharne, "Making Their Presence Felt," in Magennis and Swan, *Companion to Ælfric*.

39. Clayton, *Two Ælfric Texts*. I owe a debt of gratitude to Professor Clayton, whose helpful comments and bibliographic suggestions on an early draft of this work presented at the

homiliaries of the period in several variant forms, including as part of the *De Memoria Sanctorum* homily in the *Lives of the Saints* collection. A brief list of the manuscripts that form the core of the *De Octo Vitiis* tradition will help situate my discussion. The main text of the homily—*De Octo Vitiis*—is found in seven manuscripts.[40] Cambridge, Corpus Christi College 178; Oxford, Bodleian Library, Hatton 116; and London, Lambeth Palace 487 all contain what Mary Clayton calls the "composite text" of *De Octo Vitiis*.[41] Three other manuscripts include the text as part of a homily called *De Memoria Sanctorum*, also known as *Lives of the Saints* XVI.[42] These include London, British Library, Cotton Julius E.vii; Cambridge, University Library Ii.1.33; and Cambridge, Corpus Christi College 303.[43] Another version, somewhat different from the preceding ones in content and form, is found in London, British Library, Cotton Vespasian D.xiv, where, as Clayton notes, extracts from *LS* XVI appear under the titles "De . VIII. principalibus uiciis" and "De . VIII. principalibus virtutibus."[44] As a whole, the tradition indicated by these numerous variants demonstrates the diverse strategies of decoration and punctuation that are used to demarcate linguistic difference in manuscripts, thus drawing attention to the process of translation even when it takes the form of a word-for-word Old English gloss of Latin materials.[45]

The translation effects that attend such manuscript presentation techniques are inherently visual: rather than emphasizing content, they draw attention to the act of translation as a relationship between readers and the

---

2015 ISAS Glasgow conference were crucial to the emergence of my argument in its current form.

40. For a full account of each manuscript, see Clayton, *Two Ælfric Texts*, 1–18. This group is in addition to the manuscripts that include a related text, *De duodecim abusiuis*: Oxford, Bodleian Library Hatton 115; London, British Library Cotton Vespasian D.xiv; and Cambridge, Corpus Christi College 303.

41. For CCCC 178, see Ker no. 41; Gneuss-Lapidge no. 54; and Treharne, "Cambridge, Corpus Christi College, 178," in Da Rold et al., *Production and Use of English Manuscripts*. For London, Lambeth Palace 487, see Ker no. 282; Swan, "London, Lambeth Palace, 487," in Da Rold et al., *Production and Use of English Manuscripts*.

42. See Skeat, *Ælfric's Lives of the Saints*.

43. For London, British Library, Cotton Julius E.vii, see Ker no. 162; Gneuss-Lapidge no. 339. For Cambridge, University Library Ii.1.33, see Ker no. 18; and Da Rold, "Cambridge, University Library, Ii.1.33," in Da Rold et al., *Production and Use of English Manuscripts*. For CCCC 303, see Ker no. 57; Treharne, "Cambridge, Corpus Christi College, 303," in Da Rold et al., *Production and Use of English Manuscripts*.

44. See Clayton, *Two Ælfric Texts*, 8. For British Library, Cotton Vespasian D xiv, see Ker no. 209; Gneuss-Lapidge no. 392; Treharne, "London, British Library, Cotton Vespasian D.xiv," in Da Rold, et al., *Production and Use of English Manuscripts*.

45. For the utility of homilies as a corpus for linguistic analysis of multilingualism, see Cain, "Performing Multilingualism," in Machan, *Imagining Medieval English*. Cain surveys the discourse markers that attend these kinds of performative inclusions of the Latin.

books they read, creating a community that can only inhere on the page.[46] What O'Brien O'Keeffe calls "non-lexical graphic cues"[47]—in this case, *litterae notabiliores,* hierarchies of script, and various kinds of puncti—are, in the *De Octo Vitiis* corpus, used to demonstrate differences between languages *visually* as well as lexically. These extra-textual signifiers function as translation effects because they highlight translation activity that prepares the manuscript for a future community of readers.[48]

Red ink, *litterae notabiliores,* and punctuation all demonstrate the scribal investment in making translation highly visible in the manuscripts in which *De Octo Vitiis* appears. I begin, however, with a brief case study: London, British Library Cotton Vespasian D.xiv and how it uses red ink to indicate translation effects in the manuscript. Although the use of red ink is by no means ubiquitous in early medieval English manuscripts, several of the manuscript attestations of *De Octo Vitiis* do use it, often in concert with punctuation, to highlight moments of translation. Taken collectively, these translation effects demonstrate an extension of scribal thinking in time, toward a future audience who will use the manuscript and who may need more assistance with the Latin text than with the Old English.[49] I begin with Cotton Vespasian D.xiv because it offers the most visually striking form that translation effects take in these manuscripts: the use of red-ink-decorated *litterae notabiliores* to demarcate linguistic difference.[50] Distinct from rubrication, which is reserved for titles and subtitles, the red ink decoration of *litterae notabiliores* often marks only a single letter or word, rather than an entire subsection of the manuscript page.[51]

Cotton Vespasian D.xiv is a twelfth-century compilation of "homiletic, hagiographic and educative material, much of it drawn from the first and

---

46. See Schott, "Intimate Readers." For further reflection on the ethical stakes of glossing and the *ordinatio* of the medieval manuscript, see Dagenais, *Ethics of Reading in Manuscript Culture*; Treharne, *Living through Conquest.*

47. O'Brien O'Keeffe, *Visible Song,* 5. See also O'Brien O'Keeffe, "Graphic Cues."

48. In the texts that I examine, I do not consider variations in script itself. Following Julia Crick, we know that in this period all Latin and Old English texts were easily distinguished by the differences between Caroline Minuscule and Vernacular Minuscule scripts. See Crick, "English Vernacular Script," in Gameson, *History of the Book,* 174–86.

49. For a thorough discussion of "scribal thinking," see Wakelin, *Scribal Correction,* 54.

50. *The Production and Use of English Manuscripts 1060–1220* defines *litterae notabiliores* as "any capitals that are offset in some way: by size, by decorative features, or by design, to make them visually more obvious than other graphs on the folio." See Da Rold et al., "Principles of Description," in Da Rold et al., *Production and Use of English Manuscripts.*

51. See Brown, *Understanding Illuminated Manuscripts,* 111.

second series of Ælfric's *Catholic Homilies.*"[52] The text opens on f. 15r with a rubric that labels the text "De xii abusiuis secund[e]m disputacione[m] S[an] c[t]i Cipriani martyris." The rubric is, obviously, in Latin, though the text itself is in Old English.[53] But from the very beginning, a translation effect appears: the opening of the text remarks that "Nu synd twelf abusiva . þ[æt] synd twelf unðeawes þe we eow secgeð on leden . 7 syððen on ænglisc" (3–4) [now there are twelve *abusiua,* that is twelve abuses, that we will tell you in Latin and then in English].[54] From the very outset of the homily, there is an assertion of linguistic difference, to be mitigated by the duplication of text in two languages. In order to distinguish between the languages on a visual level, the scribe utilizes subtle red ink decoration on the initial letter of each abuse.

The transcription below demonstrates the difference between Latin and Old English in the manuscript based on the use of *litterae notabiliores* decorated with red ink. The inclusion of red ink decoration only begins with the inclusion of the Latin text. In fact, the first word of each clause or semantic unit in the Latin is thus highlighted, as this example from *Duodecim Abusivis* demonstrates (with red ink decoration represented by bold characters):

Duodecim abusiua sunt s[e]c[u]li. **H**oc est. **S**apiens sine operib[us] bonis. **S**enex sine religione. **A**dolescens sine obedientia. **D**iues sine elemosina. **F**emina sine pudicitia. **D**[omi]n[u]s sine virtute. **C**[hrist]ianus contentiosus. **P**aup[er] sup[er]bus. **R**ex iniquus. **E**p[iscopu]s negligens. **P**lebs sine disciplina. **P**op[u]l[u]s sine lege. **E**t sic suffocat[ur] iusticia dei. (4–8)

(There) are twelve abuses in the world. They are: a wise man without good works; an old man without religion; an adolescent without obedience; a wealthy man without acts of mercy; a woman without modesty; a lord without virtue; a quarrelsome Christian; an overbearing poor person; an unjust king; a negligent bishop; general citizens without discipline; a citizenry without law; and thus (these) choke the justice of God.

This visual clarity of the scribe's interest in Latin would be less compelling, however, if it did not precede the Old English translation of the list. The Old

---

52. Treharne, "London, British Library, Cotton Vespasian D.xiv," in Da Rold et al., *Production and Use of English Manuscripts.*

53. MS Cotton Vespasian D. xiv has been fully digitized by the British Library: see http://www.bl.uk/manuscripts/Viewer.aspx?ref=cotton_ms_vespasian_d_xiv_f004r.

54. Line numbers for *Duodecim Abusivis* and *De Octo Vitiis* are drawn from Clayton, *Two Ælfric Texts*; however, Old English transcriptions from the manuscripts for both are my own, unless otherwise indicated. Translations are my own, following Clayton.

English uses red ink somewhat differently, as the following transcription suggests:

> Twelf unðeawes synden on þyssen wurulde to hearme eallen mannen gyf heo moten rixigen . 7 heo aclecgeð rihtwisnysse . 7 þone geleafe amerreð . 7 mancynn gebringeð gyf heo moten to helle . þ[æt] is . Gyf se wyte beo bute gode weorcan . 7 gyf se ealde beo butan eawfæstnysse . Se junge buten gehyrsumnysse 7 se welige buton ælmesdæden . wif buten sydefullnysse . 7 hlaford bute mihte . 7 gyf se cristene byð sacfull . 7 gyf þearfe bið modig . Gyf se cyng byð unrihtwis . 7 se bisceop gemeleas . þ[æt] folc buten steore oððe folc buten æ. (9–16)

> There are twelve abuses in this world that harm all of mankind if they are allowed to rule, and they diminish righteousness and exterminate belief, and [they] bring mankind to hell if they are allowed. They are: if the wise man is without good works; and if the old man is without firmness in religion; if the young man is without obedience and if the wealthy man is without almsgiving; the woman without modesty and the lord without might/virtue and if the Christian is contentious and if the needy man is proud. If the king is unrighteous, and the bishop is negligent; the people without regulation or the people without law.

The comparatively sporadic red ink decoration in the Old English list of abuses demonstrates the scribal attention to the difference between Latin and Old English, potentially even in the sense of how his audience might receive it.[55] Where the Latin uses *litterae notabiliores* to mark syntactic units at the level of the clause—and thus to indicate each abuse in turn—the Old English only marks the beginning of full sentences, and not in a particularly consistent manner. The net effect of such usage is the suggestion that the Latin needs more clarifying apparatus than the Old English. It thus illustrates a specific attitude both toward the content of the material and toward the multilinguality of the text.

The *litterae notabiliores* decorated with red ink to serve as visual markers of Latin and Old English in Cotton Vespasian D.xiv establish a useful heuristic for understanding how the rest of the manuscripts of *De Octo Vitiis* deploy similar distinctions. They function as translation effects because they

---

55. As O'Brien O'Keeffe observes, this is also characteristic of verse layouts in the period, as well: "Latin manuscripts written in England regularly distinguished verse from prose through the use of a set of conventional visual cues," which distinguishes them from Old English manuscripts of the same period (*Visible Song*, 3).

call attention to the fact of translation: one cannot ignore the distinctions made between the Latin text and its Old English counterpart because the red ink decoration makes it explicit.[56] This kind of marking, moreover, implies a community of readers who are dispersed in time. The most obvious members of this community are the original writer and the copyist scribe who comes some centuries after the text was first written down. Just as important, however, is the implied audience of users of the manuscripts who are temporally later than the scribe. The red ink decoration that draws attention to the multilinguality of the text assumes that this later audience will need such demarcations made visually clear, perhaps implying that they will need more assistance to navigate a text in Latin rather than Old English.[57] Put another way: even as the scribe copies the manuscript, the visual translation effects in Cotton Vespasian D.xiv demonstrate that the scribe's vision of the readers who will one day use the text shapes his present copying process. The text's possible future reception—anticipated by the copyist scribe—shapes its production.[58] This dynamic of manuscript production is, of course, a central concern of *ordinatio*.[59] The addition of translation as a key component in the *De Octo Vitiis* complicates the relationship, however, making these communities of the page and the translation effects that anticipate them not only multitemporal but multilingual as well.

MARKING VICES AND VIRTUES

Litterae notabiliores are only one method among many by which translation effects can be highlighted using visual cues in Old English homiletic manuscripts. Because the discourse on the vices and virtues has a relatively stable format over the breadth of the manuscripts in which it appears, it offers a useful archive for exploring some of the other ways in which linguistic difference is indicated via visual cues in the Ælfrician homiletic corpus. *De Octo Vitiis*

---

56. See O'Brien O'Keefe, *Visible Song*; Parkes, *Pause and Effect*.

57. See Fisher, who argues that "writing is always intended. Whether that writing is composition or copying, medieval manuscripts did not come into being by accident. In manuscripts, insular history writing is itself historical, copied and authored, by hand, by scribes" (*Scribal Authorship*, 13). Fisher's point here is expanded upon in Wakelin, *Scribal Correction*, 16.

58. Here we might usefully invoke Bakhtin's concept of the heteroglossia of the "living word," from his *Dialogic Imagination* (276–77). This temporal structure illuminates the work of a scribe as much as a writer: a manuscript is always already determined in form by the *use* to which it will be put. In this way, its future inscribes itself on its creation. See also Chapter 1, n. 53.

59. Parkes, "Ordinatio and Compilatio," in *Scribes, Scripts, and Readers*. See also Fisher, *Scribal Authorship*.

uses the insertion of a Latin word or phrase in the body of the text, followed immediately by its Old English translation. A discourse marker such as "þ[æt] is [. . .] on englisc" may or may not be included. For clarity's sake, I will provide an overview of strategies for indicating linguistic difference in the corpus, while focusing the bulk of my attention on a single case of scribal practice in marking translation—Lambeth Palace 487. The manuscripts under consideration—Cotton Vespasian D.xiv; Hatton 116; Lambeth Palace 487; CCCC 178; CCCC 303; Cotton Julius E.vii; and CUL Ii.1.33—represent a broad range of medieval interactions with the Ælfrician *De Octo Vitiis* material and were written, compiled, and annotated over a period from the late tenth to early eleventh century (Cotton Julius E.vii) to the late twelfth to early thirteenth century (Lambeth Palace 487).[60]

The kinds of visual cues and verbal markers surveyed in these seven manuscripts of *De Octo Vitiis* fall into several categories. Three of the seven manuscripts utilize red ink decoration in some way, as previously discussed. All seven use the punctus as a method of indicating the Latin names of the vices and virtues and, less frequently, to mark the English translations of those names. The punctus and red ink decoration are visual analogues to the use of discourse markers like "þ[æt] is" and "þ[æt] is [. . .] on englisc" and its variants. They draw attention to the fact of linguistic difference and the manuscripts' engagement in the act of direct translation, thus serving as visual translation effects.

The punctus is by far the most common method of highlighting the Latin names of the vices and virtues. In the 291 instances of visual or verbal cues that signal translation in the seven manuscripts containing *De Octo Vitiis*, a punctus—in black or red ink, to the right or left of the Latin—occurs 110 times, as opposed to 47 times marking the English translations of the Latin names. Moreover, the Latin names are far more likely to include a *littera notabilior* marked with red ink: in the three manuscripts where red ink decoration is used, there are 30 instances of such decoration on Latin words, as opposed to one instance of decoration on English names of the vices or virtues, and only 7 *litterae notabiliores* in the discourse marker "þ[æt] is" (in any form). This distinction in the use of red ink decoration is made more significant by the number of times that "þ[æt] is" or "þ[æt] is [. . .] on englisc" (or variants) appear in the manuscripts. These discourse markers appear 91 separate times, meaning that less than eight percent receive any distinguishing decoration.[61]

---

60. For the development of scripts in this period, see Crick, "English Vernacular Script."

61. Even if we ignore the manuscripts that do not include red ink decoration at all, this number is still low: 7 out of 39 instances, or less than eighteen percent of the total number of discourse markers for translation.

The two earliest manuscripts—Cotton Julius E.vii and CCCC 178—feature the fewest markers, 30 and 28, respectively, whereas the later manuscripts of the group (all copied post-Conquest) feature between 42 and 56.

London, Lambeth Palace Library 487, however, stands out in this group as a bit of an anomaly. A somewhat smaller collection of homilies, this manuscript features 56 separate markers of translation in its version of *De Octo Vitiis*. It is also the version that pays the most attention to the difference between Latin and Old English. Dated to either the late twelfth or early thirteenth century,[62] Lambeth Palace 487 speaks to the ongoing interest in Old English homiliaries in the period—indeed, it undertakes a translation of the *De Octo Vitiis* text into a form of Early Middle English.[63] Like many of the manuscripts I treat in this chapter, it exists at a remove from the period in which its texts were initially written.[64] Lambeth Palace 487 is one of three manuscripts that utilize red ink to demarcate linguistic difference in *De Octo Vitiis*; however, rather than the *litterae notabiliores* used in Cotton Vespasian D.xiv and CUL Ii.1.33, it uses red ink not only for Latin names of virtues and vices but also for much of the other Latin that appears in both the *De Octo Vitiis* homily and the manuscript as a whole. These differences make it a good case study of how visual translation effects can work in concert with discourse markers to demonstrate the extension of implied readerly communities across time.

Lambeth Palace 487 uses red ink for a variety of Latin materials in the text, from a single word to full lines and whole paragraphs. The text of *De Octo Vitiis & de duodecim abusivis huius seculi* begins on f. 37v, with a Latin rubric setting off the opening of the text from the one that precedes it. The rubric is written in seemingly the same ink as the first line of the homily, which is also in Latin. The line was clearly meant to have a decorated initial; instead, a small penciled "O" stands in for it. The Latin incipit is, like the rubric, in red: "Omnia nimia nocent et temp[er]a[n]tia mater virtutum dicitur" (2) [All excessive things (cause) harm and temperance is said to be the mother of virtues]. Using the locution "þet is on englisc," the text proceeds to translate the Latin quotation into Old English, saying, "Alle oferdone þing deriað 7 imet-

---

62. Swan, "Ælfric's *Catholic Homilies*," in Swan and Treharne, *Rewriting Old English*, 71.

63. See Swan, "Ælfric's *Catholic Homilies*"; Pelle, "Source Studies in the Lambeth Homilies." For other studies of the materials in Lambeth Palace 487, see Sisam, "Scribal Tradition"; Millett, "Pastoral Context," in Scase, *Essays in Manuscript Geography*; Swan, "Preaching Past the Conquest," in Kleist, *Old English Homily*; Hanna, "Lambeth Palace Library, MS 487," in Innes-Parker and Gunn, *Texts and Traditions*.

64. According to Swan, Lambeth Palace 487 contains "recontextualizations of *Catholic Homilies*" material ("Ælfric's *Catholic Homilies*," 71). Hanna argues that "codicological evidence" in such manuscripts "might well imply a much less centralized and organized group of texts" on which producers could draw ("Lambeth Palace Library, MS 487," 87–88).

ness is alre mihta moder" (3) [All things done to excess harm and temperance is of all virtues the mother].

The scribe immediately sets up a hierarchy of scripts between Latin and English. The red ink decorated incipit of the homily is in Latin; however, the scribe also uses red ink for the other Latin words that appear in the homily. The collocation of the red ink for the Latin text with the missing but clearly intended decorative initial serves two primary functions. The first is to prioritize the title and opening line, offering an easy way to locate where this particular homily begins. The second, however, only becomes clear when understood in the context of the way that the remainder of the manuscript uses color: it demarcates Latin and Old English through the use of red ink, creating a visual translation effect. Put another way, it draws attention to the *fact* of translation in excess of its content.[65] Similarly to Cotton Vespasian D.xiv, red ink decoration in Lambeth Palace 487 can also mark places in the homily at which a new segment of text begins. This usage of red ink is related to the primary function of the rubric above. It allows a reader quickly scanning through the text to find relevant passages for their interests, without needing to read every segment.[66] It thus implies a readership for whom this work will need to be carefully laid out.

Although the use of red ink to indicate new sections in the manuscript is not a translation effect, its deployment in this context highlights its use in a second one: red ink is used to mark the Latin name of the vices and virtues in the manuscript. Take, for example, the Latin vice *Gula*, which appears five lines from the bottom of f. 37v. *Gula* itself is written in red, set off by one black punctus and one red; moreover, the text includes the "þ[æt] is [. . .] on englisc" construction to mark translation: " · **Gula** · þ[æt] is giferness on englisc" (13) [*Gula,* that is gluttony in English]. The punctus distribution here is particularly interesting: we can tell that the punctus is meant to end what precedes it. A red punctus follows the red *Gula*, while the Old English words preceding *Gula* are followed by a black punctus. This separation of the Latin from the Old English suggests, as it does in the rest of Lambeth Palace 487, that the quality of *this word* is fundamentally different from the quality of other words in the manuscript. Like its use of red ink to write its Latin pas-

---

65. In Lambeth 487, "rubrics and Latin quotations [are] mostly added in red by the main scribe. Space was left at the start of each item, apparently for a decorated enlarged initial, but these were not written in. A few small and now illegible guiding letters are visible in the left- or right-hand margin, in red or black. Red is used for some Latin snippets and some capital letters of words in sentences in English" (Swan, "London, Lambeth Palace, 487," in Da Rold et al., *Production and Use of English Manuscripts*).

66. See de Hamel, *Manuscript Illumination,* 16–17.

sages, this distinction is oriented toward readers. Because of the use of the "þ[æt] is [. . .] on englisc" construction, it is also inextricably bound to questions of translation. Thus, although it most certainly partakes of what Parkes describes as the increasing attention to *ordinatio* in later manuscripts, it also goes beyond the compilation-driven concerns of *ordinatio* to engage with the complexities of translation. As a translation effect, it indicates awareness of a future multilingual readership for this manuscript, for whom translation is not only a central concern but also a central component of any approach to the manuscript itself.[67]

Across the entire *De Octo Vitiis* tradition, fourteen vices and virtues regularly receive both a Latin name and its Old English translation. In Lambeth Palace 487, eleven of these Latin names appear alongside their translations.[68] Intriguingly, space is left where the other three Latin names should be inserted. Lambeth Palace 487 is one of only two versions of the vices and virtues that alter the pattern of discourse markers found in the other five manuscripts.[69] This pattern is otherwise perfectly followed. *Avaritia, tristicia, pacientia, spirtualis leticia,* and *instancia boni operis* indicate translation with the discourse marker "þ[æt] is." For example: "Se þridda is *auaritia*, þæt is seo yfele gitsung, and seo is wyrtruma ælcere wohnysse" (21–22) [The third (vice) is *avaritia,* that is evil yearning, and it is the root of every iniquity].[70] *Gula, ira, accidia, iactantia, superbia, temperantia, castitas,* and *largitas* all use the discourse marker "þ[æt] is [. . .] on englisc." Again, the entry for *Gula* is instructive: "An is gecwæden *gula,* þæt is gyfernyss on Englisc, seo deð þæt man ytt ær timan and drincð, oððe he eft to mycel nimð on æte oððe on wæte" (12–14) [The first is called *gula,* that is gluttony in English, that makes it so a person eats and drinks before the time, or that one often takes too much in food or in drink].[71] In the entry for *pacientia,* however, where the other six manuscripts utilize "þ[æt is]," Lambeth Palace 487 f. 39r uses the longer "þ[æt] is [. . .] on englisc": "· **pacientia** · þ[æt] is on englisc iþuld ·" [*patiencia,* that is in English, patience]. It seems likely that the alteration in

---

67. See Parkes, "*Ordinatio* and *Compilatio,*" in *Scribes, Scripts, and Readers*; Fisher, *Scribal Authority*; Crick, "English Vernacular Script," in Gameson, *History of the Book*.

68. Swan notes that this use of Latin "is the highest level of visual marking the scribe engages in," and "it highlights the assertion of Latin as an authority, underpinning the Old English which translates it" ("Reading for the Ear," 223).

69. The only other change in the pattern occurs in CCCC 303, for the vice *fornicatio*. In this instance, however, the Latin name of the vice precedes the English name, whereas in the other manuscripts the English precedes the Latin. The text includes the discourse marker "se is" preceding the Old English translation of the Latin name.

70. Old English text is drawn from Clayton, *Two Ælfric Texts*.

71. Old English text is drawn from Clayton, *Two Ælfric Texts*.

this insertion is partially a function of the later date of Lambeth Palace 487; in fact, the only other alteration to the pattern of markers in the manuscripts is in CCCC 303, which is a similarly late manuscript. The alteration to the pattern of discourse markers suggests that the later manuscripts may treat the multilinguality of the text differently than their earlier counterparts—or, indeed, that the use of red ink for the Latin obviates the need in certain cases to specify the language of translation as English. Put another way, these copyists participate in a longer tradition of translation than their predecessors. They can expect their audiences to be familiar with the layout conventions of these texts and can therefore rely upon that knowledge as they create their own manuscript layouts.

What particularly stands out about Lambeth Palace 487 and its use of red ink is not necessarily what *is* there, but rather what is not. As mentioned previously, three of the virtues in the manuscript do not include Latin names at all, but leave a space where the Latin name would be added in red ink after the black ink of the main text was written. Two additional virtues have similar unfilled spaces for their Latin names. On f. 39v, both "soð luve to gode 7 to monnen" [true love toward God and men] and "soð e[a]dmodnesse to gode 7 to mon[n]en" [true humility toward God and men] are preceded by a space for their Latin name to be inserted in red ink.[72] This is the only indication— in any of the seven manuscripts that include the vices and virtues—of Latin names for these two virtues, which are otherwise consistently named only in Old English.

These omissions might well be accidental. Yet alone among the manuscripts of *De Octo Vitiis*, Lambeth Palace 487 leaves space for these untranslated words. Even when ultimately not added in, the Latin names are important enough to require space: that they are absent reminds us that they, too, would have been in red ink. The pattern of the text allows a reader or rubricator to fill in the gaps, so to speak: to imagine a Latin word that would translate the English virtue. Through its use of red ink and, more intriguingly, the moments in which a scribe has left out the Latin words that should be marked in it, Lambeth Palace 487 demonstrates one function of translation effects in a manuscript context. Translation effects point to a manuscript copyist's awareness of translation, its audience, and the different methods that can be employed to help a future readership parse the words of the past.[73]

---

72. It is of course worth noting that there is little space to actually insert the Latin name of the virtue.

73. There is a lingering question here concerning whether the blank space was geared toward an eventual reader or a rubricator who was separate from the main copyist. Here, I follow Mary Swan, who sees Item 10 as characteristic of the Lambeth 487 scribe, who "is re-

Þ[ÆT] IS [. . .] ON ENGLISC: COTTON JULIUS E.VII AND CUL II.1.33

Of the manuscripts that include *De Octo Vitiis,* the two that most clearly demonstrate the consequences of translation effects in manuscript production and use are London, British Library Cotton Julius E.vii and Cambridge, University Library Ii.1.33. These two manuscripts are from opposite ends of the tradition examined in this chapter—Cotton Julius E.vii was copied in the eleventh century, while CUL Ii.1.33 was likely copied in the late twelfth century.[74] The divergent approaches they employ for indicating translation make a particularly compelling comparison, not least of all because of their difference in time: a late-twelfth-century audience of the Ælfrician sermons collected in CUL Ii.1.33 would very likely need a different set of ancillary materials to aid in comprehending the texts than would the early-eleventh-century audience of Cotton Julius E.vii. As a result, the range of translation effects deployed in the manuscript are quite different. In the Cotton Julius E.vii version of the sermon, discourse markers are used to indicate translation. In CUL Ii.1.33, a wider range of translation effects are present, including a reduced use of discourse markers alongside red ink decoration on the names of the vices and virtues.

The opening folio of the "Sermo de Memoria Sanctorum" in British Library, Cotton Julius E.vii, f. 77r demonstrates the investment of the manuscript in the form of translation.[75] It begins with a Latin text, swiftly translated into English: "Ego sum alfa et [omega]- initium et finis dicit d[omi]n[u]s d[eu]s . qui est & qui erat & qui venturus est om[n]ip[oten]s . Ðæt is on englisc . Ic eom angin . 7 ende . cwæþ drihten god se ðe is . 7 se ðe wæs . 7 se ðe towerd is ælmihtig . <god>" (LS 16.i–iv) [I am the alpha and omega, the beginning and the end said the Lord God almighty, who is, who was, and who will be. That is, in English, I am the beginning and end, said the Lord God, he who is and he who was, and he who is in the future almighty (god)]. The "e" of *Ego* is a decorated initial in red. The text is predominantly in black ink,

---

reading source-texts in anticipation of a future reception—a future reading—of them" ("Reading for the Ear," 223). However, in either case, the temporality of the absence remains at issue: the blank space is meant to spur a future user of the manuscript (reader or rubricator) to interact with it in a certain way, to supply the Latin name for the English.

74. For Cotton Julius E.vii, its origin, and its dating, see Ker, *Catalogue of Manuscripts,* 206–10; see further Bussières, "MS British Library Cotton Julius E.vii." For CUL Ii.1.33, see Traxel, *Language Change.*

75. See British Library, "Cotton MS Julius E.vii," available at http://www.bl.uk/manuscripts/Viewer.aspx?ref=cotton_ms_julius_e_vii_fs001ar.

and so the manuscript distinguishes between Latin and Old English through the use of an intralinear phrase: "Ðæt is on englisc" [That is, in English]. The initial *eth* of this phrase has light red decoration, darkened and discolored by time, yet the implied relationship between the Latin and the Old English is quite clear. The Old English is important, but only because it makes the Latin incipit accessible.[76]

CUL Ii.1.33, on the other hand, has a different set of operating principles that are related but not reducible to its later date of origin.[77] Most importantly, perhaps, this collection of materials—and its subsequent additions and emendations—illustrates a specific attitude toward homiliaries in the twelfth century, in addition to their importance both as a cultural touchstone and as a central series of texts. That there is an Old English homily tradition being copied at all in the twelfth century speaks to the ongoing relevance of the materials to religious thinking in the period.[78] Some of the differences between CUL Ii.1.33 and Cotton Julius E.vii are clear from the opening folio of the homily. Where Julius E.vii utilizes some red ink to indicate translation with the phrase "Ðæt is on englisc," CUL Ii.1.33 (f. 114r) includes far more: both the decorated initial "e" in "Ego" and the following "g" receive red ink. Moreover, the use of *litterae notabiliores* is extended beyond the incipit in CUL Ii.1.33: red decoration appears on initial letters in both the Latin (**Eg**o) and the Old English translation (**Ic**), but also on the thorn in the discourse marker "**þ**æt is on Englisc," which appears in excess of the usual emphasis on syntactic marking in the manuscript (i.e., a red ink *littera notabilior* at the start of each sentence). Although these differences may seem small, when catalogued across the entirety of the homily in both manuscripts, they indicate the multitude of ways that these translation effects function both within and across time.

---

76. As Cain argues, "The linguistic framing of Latin and English in comparison worked to help establish the hierarchical relationship between the two, in which Latin is naturally the higher-prestige authentic voice" ("Performing Multilingualism," in Machan, *Imagining Medieval English*, 96). British Library, Cotton Julius E.vii has been most thoroughly described and studied by Bussières. She notes that the texts of the collection are "principalement hagiographiques" [principally hagiographic] and derive mainly from feasts "celebrées dans l'église Anglo-Saxonne" [celebrated in the Anglo-Saxon church], excepting those already included in the *Catholic Homilies* collection ("MS British Library, Cotton Julius E.vii," 134). Translations from Bussière's French are my own. See also Magennis, "Adaptation, Appropriation, and the Disappearing Book," in Kelly and Thompson, *Imagining the Book*.

77. Irvine assigns its creation to "a twelfth-century compiler" based on the "physical composition of the manuscripts, textual transmission, and inclusion of post-Conquest compositions" ("Compilation and Use," in Swan and Treharne, *Rewriting Old English*, 45).

78. See Treharne and Swan, *Rewriting Old English*, 1–10; Treharne, *Living through Conquest*, 127–36.

An example of text from Cotton Julius E.vii and CUL Ii.1.33 demonstrates some of the differences between the two manuscripts. CUL Ii.1.33, f. 116r employs a simple method of indicating translation: " · **P**enit[en]tiam nam agite ad p[ro]pinquabit eni[m] regnu[m] celor[um] · **W**yrcað dæd bote eowra mis dæda for ðan þe heofonarice efne genealæcð" (LS 16.131–33) [*Penitentiam nam agite ad propinquabit enim regnum celorum* · Work deeds of remedy for your sins because the kingdom of heaven approaches even now]. As the bolded letters indicate, the first initial of the Latin is given red decoration and separated from both the preceding Old English passage and the Old English translation by a black punctus. The Old English translation of the passage is also marked by a red-ink-decorated *littera notabilior*. What is notably missing, however, is the discourse marker that so often appears in the manuscript: neither "þ[æt] is" nor "þ[æt] is [. . .] on englisc" appear here. By contrast, although these discourse markers also do not appear in the primary text on Cotton Julius E.vii, f. 79r, an enterprising correcting hand has taken the opportunity to add "þ[æt] is on englisc" above the line where the translation appears: " · Penitentiam agite ad propinquabit enim regnum cælorum <þ[æt] is onenglisc;> Wyrcað dæd bote eowra mis dæda for ðan þe heofonan rice efne genealæchð" (LS 16.131–33). The insertion demonstrates that this later correcting hand both noted the presence of translation in Cotton Julius E.vii and acted on that presence, adding back in the habitual Ælfrician discourse marker where one was not originally included.

In fact, Cotton Julius E.vii exhibits a number of corrections and additions, many of which fall into the category of translation effects. According to Michelle Bussières, these alterations can be attributed to two different sources: the A copyist, which is the main hand present in the manuscript, and a separate, later copyist, which she calls "D."[79] The D hand is active through the middle of the manuscript. Based on the kind and number of interventions it makes into the manuscript, Bussières argues that the correcting hand D is removed in time from the original copyists and did not work from an exemplar.[80] Moreover, his choice of texts to annotate breaks down along unsurprising lines—they usually appear on materials that were most likely to be read: "Of the fifteen texts that [the D hand] annotates, five are lives of the English Saints (all of the ones that are contained in the collection) and five are sermons and biblical stories."[81] That a full third of the fifteen texts annotated by the D hand are English saints makes a certain amount of sense: the D copyist

---

79. Bussières, "MS British Library Cotton Julius E.vii," 172.
80. See Bussières, 177–78.
81. "C'est que sur les 15 textes qu'il annote, 5 sont des Vies de Saints anglais (tous ceux contenus dans le recueil) et 5 sont des sermons et des récits bibliques" (Bussières, 178). Bussières

seems to be annotating those sermons that would hold the most interest for his projected audience. With regard to translation, the annotator's primary intervention is the addition of the phrase "þ[æt] is [. . .] on englisc" (and variants).[82] This addition makes the difference between Latin and Old English legible in a different way—not in terms of the visual distinctions of the two languages at the time of Cotton Julius E.vii's production, but in the insertion of a distinction where one otherwise would not exist.

A straightforward example of the correcting hand's activities serves to underscore their importance. On Cotton Julius E.vii, f. 77v, the homily translates a fairly restricted use of Latin: "god him gesette þa oðerne naman Israhel, þ[æt] is uir uidens d[eu]m ; <ðæt is ongliscre spræce ;> se wer þe God gesihð" (LS 16.32–33). This line includes an instance of translation that spans three different languages: "God gave him the second name *Israhel*, that is *vir videns deum* ; <that is in English speech ;> the man that sees God"—that is, Jacob. Although the copyist has clearly made an error—*on englisc* becomes *ongliscre*—the meaning of the phrase is still clear. Moreover, it demonstrates the investment of the correcting hand in making such moments of translation legible to his audience, although his reasons for doing so must necessarily remain opaque. As a translation effect, this insertion demonstrates how such interventions invoke both the past and the future. The correcting scribe, having read the collection he copies, knows that "þ[æt] is [. . .] on englisc" is a common phrase in the Ælfrician corpus.[83] As a result, he adds this phrase into the manuscript even though it does not appear in the original. He does not do so for himself, obviously: he must already know the difference between Latin and Old English if he is able to distinguish between them interlinearly. Therefore, we can infer that he does so for a future audience—one that does not exist yet—that will need the discourse marker, or at least find it useful.[84] In adding this marker, he interpellates that same audience: he creates it, or the conditions for its existence, through his own intervention. The imagined

---

also notes that the remaining annotated sermons are *Eugenia*, *The Forty Soldiers*, *Apollinarius*, *The Seven Sleepers*, and *Eustace*.

82. Bussières observes that "'þæt is on englisc' est rajouté en interligne chaque fois qu'une citation latine est suivie de sa traduction en vieil anglais" (Bussières, 176) ["'þæt is on englisc' is added interlinearly each time a Latin citation is followed by its translation in Old English"].

83. See *inter alia*, Bussières. See also Weaver, "Formal Orders." Moreover, as Cain argues, "the expansion of Latin quotation and use of *þæt is* [. . .] constructions in later homiletic compositions (especially as found in Ælfric's works) express a shift in the rhetorical strategies of performing multilingualism in preaching" ("Performing Multilingualism," in Machan, *Imagining Medieval English*, 96–97).

84. See here, *inter alia*, Swan, who argues that "altered copies of texts are made by readers who write. They are always the result of reading, and they constitute rereadings themselves" ("Reading for the Ear," 216).

community of the page extends from the past into the future through the scribe's hand.

CUL Ii.1.33 distinguishes between Latin and Old English somewhat differently. Although the manuscript deploys red ink decoration in this homily, the decoration is syntax-based rather than keyed to translation; it appears at the start of each new sentence in this part of the manuscript. The quotidian work of translation is not distinguished by red ink—Old English simply follows Latin, with the reader clearly meant to simply see and understand that translation has taken place, as in this example from f. 116r:

> Discite a me quia mitis sum et humilis corde . et inuenietis requiem animab[us] u[est]ris. Leorniað æt me þ[æt] ic manþwære eom 7 eadmod on heortan 7 ge gemetað reste eowru[m] sawlu[m] . þis sæd drihten. (LS 16.123–26)

> *Discite a me quia mitis sum et humilis corde, et invenietis requiem animabus vestris ;* Learn from me, for I am gentle and humble in heart and you may find rest for your souls, thus said the Lord.

In this instance, the text does not even include "þ[æt] is" to distinguish syntactically between the Latin and Old English locutions.

The same passage in Cotton Julius E.vii, at f. 78v, uses interlinear insertion to make the distinction between Old English and Latin text:

> Discite a me quia mitis sum et humilis corde . et inuenietis requiem animabus u[est]ris. <þ[æt] is on englisc; > Leorniað æt me þ[æt] ic manþwære eom 7 eadmod on heortan 7 ge gemetað reste eowrum sawlum . Þis sæd drihten. (LS 16.123–26)

As in the preceding example from Cotton Julius E.vii, the correcting hand D has added the phrase "þ[æt] is on englisc" between the Latin and Old English text. A correction marker is notably absent in the line of main text the copyist alters, but the usual *punctus versus* marks the end of the alteration itself (if not the location the alteration is meant to refer to in the manuscript). The result of this insertion is, as before, a visual translation effect. The point of this insertion has nothing to do with *what* the translation is or means. Rather, the point is to show that the text *is* a translation.

Returning to the vices and virtues passage of the *De Memoria Sanctorum*, Cotton Julius E.vii and CUL Ii.1.33 offer further evidence of the importance and function of translation effects on the manuscript page. Both manuscripts indicate the Latin names of the vices and virtues in *De Octo Vitiis*, but they do so in divergent ways that become indicative of the kinds of communities these translation effects enable. In Cotton Julius E.vii, a black punctus indicates the names of the vices and virtues, usually only to the right of the Latin and the Old English. An intralinear "þ[æt] is on englisc" designates the translations. Again, the vice *gula* at f. 80v offers a good example: "· An is gecwæden gula · þ[æt] is gyfernyss on englisc" (LS 16.268) [The first is called *gula*, that is, gluttony in English]. *Gula* is marked off by a punctus following the Latin, then is followed by the "þ[æt] is [. . .] on englisc" construction. No decoration indicates the phrase; rather, it simply appears as any other part of the text does. The intralinear appearance of the phrase "þ[æt] is [. . .] on englisc" is made remarkable only by the work of the correcting hand elsewhere in the manuscript. Earlier in the same homily, where the demarcation of Latin and Old English is less clear, the correcting hand intervenes.

CUL Ii.1.33 f. 118v demonstrates a use of red ink that is familiar from the above consideration of Lambeth Palace 487: to demarcate linguistic difference in a manner that allows a reader to perceive it visually, without necessarily reading the words. Taking the entry for *gula* again as an example—"· Gula · þ[æt] is gifernyss on englisc" (LS 16.268) [*Gula*, that is gluttony in English]—there are two translation effects present. First, the "þ[æt] is [. . .] on englisc" construction appears intralinearly, written by the primary copyist as in the Cotton Julius E.vii example above. Second, the example uses red ink decoration on the initial letter of *gula*. Red ink demarcates the beginning of new syntactic units—each sentence also begins with a larger capital than its surrounding letters.[85] However, throughout the segment on vices and virtues it also marks the initial letter of each Latin name with *litterae notabiliores*. By including the red ink decoration on the Latin text as well, the manuscript implicitly draws attention to the difference between Latin and Old English in the manuscript, creating another visual translation effect.

The community of the page that becomes evident in Cotton Julius E.vii and CUL Ii.1.33 serves to codify the translation effects I have examined thus far. Some Old English manuscripts—like CUL Ii.1.33—utilize synchronous indications of translation effects in their materials. That is, the indication of translation, if there is any, is intralinear and part of the sense of the text rather than the manuscript. Other Old English manuscripts, like Cotton Julius E.vii, exhibit asynchronous use of translation effects. They are added to the manuscript by readers who wish to indicate moments of translation in a very literal sense. These translation effects are part of a manuscript use history that

---

85. See above discussion of Cotton Vespasian D.xiv.

stretches away from the composition of the manuscript and into a perceived future, where these kinds of indicators are part of the ongoing reception history of the manuscript. Moreover, they initiate the reader into a multilingual, multitemporal community: they demonstrate how translation might condition its readers to respond to a multilingual text, even to the point of inscribing marginal additions that do not bear any relationship—as translation or otherwise—to the "primary" text on the page.

MARGINAL STORIES

Much of this chapter has focused on specific manuscript attestations of the *De Octo Vitiis* tradition in order to demonstrate how translation effects draw attention to the potentially multilingual communities of the manuscript page. I now turn to several larger marginal insertions that appear in CUL Ii.1.33.[86] This kind of marginalia functions as a very different sort of translation effect, comprising the multilingual inclusion of materials that extend, revise, or otherwise reconsider the story recorded in the main text. Such additions create a temporal expansion of community through the circulation of stories that are ancillary, but related, to the main text of the manuscript in which they appear. Although these texts may well be translations, it is their function as translation *effects* that interests me here. These interventions in the manuscript draw attention to narrative transmission and thus invoke a future community of readers who will need the information they contain. This future community is multilingual and multitemporal—and attention to these scribal interventions allows modern critics to better understand how medieval scribes and copyists thought about their work.[87]

On CUL Ii.1.33 f. 70v, in the midst of a version of the *Life of Saint Andrew*, a scribe has inserted two marginal additions: one in Middle English and one in French. The Middle English is a prose addition in the left margin of the page, while the French is in verse at the bottom.[88] Oliver M. Traxel argues that the hand of the main text of the hagiography is different than the one responsible for the marginal additions. He identifies this hand as scribe 4; however,

---

86. In addition to Traxel, see Frankis, "Varieties of Language Contact," in Cambridge and Hawkes, *Crossing Boundaries*; and Frankis, "Languages and Cultures in Contact."
87. Here I follow Treharne, who argues that, for twelfth-century copies of Old English texts, "there is no single textual community [. . .], no monolithic audience of illiterate lay people" (*Living through Conquest*, 127).
88. See Traxel, *Language Change*, 68–77.

other scholars have suggested that the additions are by Traxel's scribe 1, the folio's main hand.[89]

Regardless of the differentiation between the two hands, the additions offer an important perspective in how readers—synchronous or not—encountered the materials of the texts that they copied and read.[90] The Middle English addition, for example, concerns a woman named "Maximilla," who is part of the Andrew tradition:

> Maximilla was an læfdie inne þære burh ofer þa oðre hlæfdie. heo weorðede saint Andreu. 7 com mid heore cnihte. 7 nam þone halige licame mid mycele wyrðmunte. 7 hine smerede mid aromate. Aromat is gemacad of godes cynnes weorte ðe wille swote stince. hu hæfde gecore ænne swiðne fairne stede on to licgende. þær hu leide saintes Andreas lichame mid weorðmunte.[91]

> Maximilla was a lady in the castle above the other ladies. She venerated Saint Andrew and came with her servant and took the holy body with great dignity and anointed it with an aromatic substance. The aromatic substance is made of an herb of good quality which will smell sweet. She had chosen a very beautiful place lying nearby. There she put St. Andrew's body with dignity.[92]

Maximilla was a noble woman who venerates Saint Andrew and removes his body so that he can be properly buried. Traxel observes that the passage bears some linguistic indications that it is early Middle English and thus removed in time from the original composition of the homily, if not from its appearance in CUL Ii.1.33.[93] This ancillary text bears a close relationship both to other stories of Andrew and to the fragment of the narrative of his passion that appears on f. 70v. The portion of the homily that appears in the main text of the page focuses on the moments directly adjacent to and following Andrew's death.

---

89. Most notably Ker, *Catalogue of Manuscripts*, 23–27; and Da Rold, "Cambridge, University Library, Ii.1.33," in Da Rold et al., *Production and Use of English Manuscripts*.

90. This example is somewhat analogous to what Wakelin identifies as a moment in which correcting a manuscript "nurtures intelligent responses to literary works and, in a knot that cannot be untied, is also nurtured by these responses. Thereby the craft of correcting becomes a little like literary criticism" (*Scribal Correction*, 8). See also Frankis, "Language and Cultures in Contact."

91. Transcription of the addition is from Traxel, *Language Change*, 68.

92. Translation of the addition is from Traxel, 68n49.

93. Traxel, 73–76.

Most notably, it speaks of the fate of Andrew's tormentor Ægeas and also of Ægeas's brother, who takes the saint's body to an honorable place for burial and "heold þæs halgan andreas lic mid micelre arwyrðnysse" (344–45) [held the body of the holy Andreas with great honor].[94] The hagiography, unsurprisingly, emphasizes the miracles that attend Andrew's death: "Swa micel oga asprang ofer eallum þam mennisce . þ[æt] ðær nan ne be laf þe ne gelyfde on god" (345–47) [So great a fear sprang up over all the people that there were none left who did not believe in God]. The dual focus of the homilist on Andrew's death and what was done with his body connects the text quite closely to the marginal addition.

Indeed, some critics have argued for the clear interrelation of the marginal text and sermon. Traxel suggests that the Middle English addition bears a close relationship to a Latin life of Andrew, BHL 429, although he cannot determine with certainty whether the scribe had access to the Latin text.[95] The scribe may well have recalled details of the addition from memory.[96] However, I would suggest that a number of the alterations signal intellectual engagement in excess of rote reproduction and translation.[97] In the Latin, for example, Maximilla "cum reuerentia colligens corpusculum conditum aromatibus optimo in loco sepeliuit" [took up the little body, which had been anointed with spices, with reverence and buried it in a good place].[98] *Colligens* appears in the third-person singular, suggesting she moves the body by herself.[99] In the Middle English, *colligens* is translated by the word *nam*, from the Old English verb *niman* meaning "to take" or "seize."[100] *Niman* also appears in the third-

---

94. For the excerpts from Ælfric's *Life of Andrew*, I have transcribed the material directly from f. 77v. Line numbers refer to Clemoes, *Ælfric's Catholic Homilies*.

95. See Traxel, *Language Change*, 67n41 and 69.

96. Traxel argues that the scribe "altered and elaborated [the addition to the homily] for his English translation" (Traxel, 69). Traxel compares both the content and form of the Middle English addition to expose the syntactic similarities that imply the scribe's familiarity with the Latin text (see his comparative Table 6 at 70). It is worth noting that Da Rold and Swan argue that the "scribes and compilers, and presumably their intended readers, are not preoccupied by—and perhaps not aware of—a boundary between what we might label late Old English and early Middle English" ("Linguistic Contiguities" in Tyler, *Conceptualizing Multilingualism*, 265).

97. See Traxel, *Language Change*, 69–73. Again, Wakelin's argument concerning later manuscripts provides a useful analogue to what occurs here. As he argues, "Correcting requires scribes to attend closely to what they copy, as though every word matters, and to think about style, form, and structure. They do not explain their close reading or general thinking in works of their own; we can, though, infer their attitudes from their corrections" (*Scribal Correction*, 8).

98. Text and translation from Traxel, *Language Change*, 69 and 69n52.

99. Traxel, 71.

100. BT, s.v. *niman*.

person singular: "com mid heore cnihte. 7 nam þone halige licame" [came with her knight and took the holy body]. The addition of the servant indicates a moment of interpretation on the part of the copyist, "since the audience might not have believed that a single woman was capable of carrying a human body over a great distance."[101] Moreover, adding the servant reinforces the aristocratic position of Maximilla.

The addition of the knight to the story—as either a helper for a presumably weaker woman or as a sign of her aristocratic status—holds significant theoretical import for my argument. It indicates the annotator's consideration of an audience who would need or want such a clarification. Although the grammatical and social implications of the additions are clear, I would add a third consideration: time.[102] By altering the materials in order to explain how a single woman could move a presumably heavy body, the scribe who writes the addition on f. 70v implies an imagined community of readers, one that can only be called together on this particular manuscript page. A reasoning mind—either of the original scribe or a later annotator—creates a translation effect by not only translating a Latin text into Middle English but also altering it with his own future audience in mind as he adds it to the margin of the manuscript. Even if this clarification comes from an unknown Latin version of the life, its addition here—in a story that does not include this portion of the legend of Andrew—suggests that the future audience of the text changes the kind of information that the scribe decides to transmit in his annotation.

The temporal complexity of this community of readers is enlarged by multilingualism. In the bottom margin of f. 70v, the manuscript includes two lines of French verse that indicate the location in which the action takes place:

Icest auint en Achaia.
dunt plusur unt oi parler
dedenz la cite de patras
que uus auez oi numer.

This happened in Achaea, of which many have heard speak, within the city of Patras, which you have heard named.[103]

As with the Middle English addition, the French supplies information related to the passion that would have been familiar from other versions of the story. The hand appears to belong to the same scribe as the previous example. Nota-

---

101. Traxel, *Language Change*, 71.
102. Traxel.
103. Traxel, 77. Translation by Judy Weiss.

bly, however, the darker ink suggests that it was added to the manuscript at a different time than the Middle English.[104]

Indeed, the initial line of the Old French addition gives information that is already contained in the manuscript, thus fulfilling the second line's promise that this is something "dunt plusur unt oi parler" [of which many have heard speak]. The opening line of the homily as it appears in CUL Ii.1.33, f. 65v gives the location of the action as Achaia: "Se apostol Andreas æfter Christes ðrowunge ferde to ðam lande þe is gehaten Achaia . 7 ðær bodade Drihtnes geleafan . 7 middangeardes alysednyss . ðurh his ðrowunge" (170–72) [The apostle Andrew, after Christ's suffering, traveled to the land that is called Achaia and there preached the faith of God and the world's salvation through his suffering]. Although Achaia is mentioned, the specific city of Patras is not, and so the second half of the French addition adds information which, though it might have been known elsewhere, is not part of the circulation of this particular copy of the text.

The French insertion in the manuscript causes several interpretive difficulties. Traxel does not identify any specific source for the verse in question: it differs from other Old French versions of the Life of Saint Andrew, not least of all in its use of the *abab* rhyme pattern, where both extant Old French poetic texts use an *aabb* scheme.[105] Traxel argues that the passage was likely composed by the scribe who wrote it down. In this case, the scribe would have inserted information into the manuscript that he knew from somewhere, mixing up the rhyme scheme in the process of writing it down from memory.[106] Moreover, the joint alliteration and end rhyme in the passage suggests a kind of *mélange* of French and English poetic effects, which Traxel suggests is part of the scribe's familiarity with multiple languages and poetic traditions. He ultimately concludes that the "intended audience cannot have been exclusively French-speaking," else why include French in an English-language manuscript? As a result, we must assume that the implied audience of the text had knowledge of both English and French.[107]

---

104. Traxel, 77. See also Frankis, who argues that "the Anglo-Norman note seems to evoke a response in English from another annotator, almost as if two late twelfth-century readers of Ælfric's homilies were engaged in a bilingual conversation" ("Varieties of Language Contact," in Cambridge and Hawkes, *Crossing Boundaries*, 261).

105. Traxel, *Language Change*, 78. Frankis notes that the rhyme scheme is "rather crude, [. . .] with an easy rhyme supplied by repeating identical syntax [which] suggests that it may be an *ad hoc* composition by the scribe" ("Languages and Cultures in Contact," 106).

106. Traxel, *Language Change*, 78.

107. Traxel, 79. Again, it is worth noting that the linguistic difference in question might not have been particularly remarkable to its readers. See Crick, "English Vernacular Script," in Gameson, *History of the Book*.

The multilinguality of these additions raises questions about the nature of the translation effects that they indicate. On the one hand, they obviously assume that the future audience of the manuscript is, at least in part, multilingual. On the other hand, this addition is not, strictly speaking, a translation. Indeed, even if there were an extant, identifiable source for each of the additions, those sources are illegible to the user of the manuscript. Yet the very presence of these multilingual interpolations into the manuscript still invoke a *figure* of translation: they are fundamentally different from the materials on the rest of the manuscript page, but they are also clearly related to the narrative that the page transmits. They create a multitemporal community through their invocation of other texts, other genres, and other languages in the margins of the life of Andrew.

Although the additions on f. 70v are the most dramatic of the Middle English and French marginalia in the manuscript because of their collocation on a single manuscript page, they are not the only occurrence of multilingualism in CUL Ii.1.33. A brief consideration of two other additions—one in French on f. 120r and one in Middle English on ff. 224v–225r—will help to contextualize the kinds of additions that the scribes made in the manuscript. These additions ultimately exhibit a fundamental difference from the two on f. 70v. The first, on f. 120r, consists of several proverbs of the *vilun* or peasant; the second, on ff. 224v–225r, contains two putative sayings of Solomon concerning the evils of wives.

The proverbs of the *vilun* appear alongside the manuscript's version of the *Memory of the Saints*. It reads as follows:

> Li uilain dit en repruuier
> de iueune seint uiel auersier
> pur ceo dit li uilain uerite.
> Tels l'unt ki ne ten seuent gre.
> Qu'entre l'aueir e le bricun.
> Ne sunt pas longes cumpaignun
> li uilains dit la u il ueolt.
> Que oil ne ueit a cuer ne duelt.

The peasant says in a proverb: "From young saint, old devil." In this the peasant says the truth—some have it who are not grateful to you—that between the wealth and the fool is no association for long. The peasant says when he wishes it: "What the eye does not see will not grieve the heart."[108]

---

108. Text and translation from Traxel, *Language Change*, 105 and 105n301. Translation by Judy Weiss and Peter Rickard.

Written in the same hand as the Old French passage on f. 70v,[109] these proverbs likely originate in *La Vie de Sainte Gilles*, which John Frankis calls "the work of an exceptionally gifted poet."[110] Regardless of the now-irretrievable intention of the amender of the manuscript, the addition of these proverbs is somewhat more curious than the addition of the Old French material on f. 70v. Where the lines concerning Achaia and Patras have a direct correspondence to the manuscript page on which they are inserted, the connection here is slightly more oblique, requiring careful thought on the part of the student of the manuscript. Put another way: the reader is asked to parse the connections between these verses and the materials they accompany, mimicking a kind of devotional process.[111]

The second set of insertions, in Middle English, is somewhat more opaque. Two "proverbs of Solomon" appear in an English dialect in the top and bottom margins of the manuscript. Attributed by Traxel to either scribe 1 or 4, the additions come from the first series of Ælfric's *Catholic Homilies* and read as follows:

Se þisa salomon cp[æð]. þ[æt] selre pære to punienne mid leon ; <7 mid draca;> þonne mid yfelu[m] pife. and oferspræcu[m]. (f. 224v)

Se þisa eft cp[æð]. þ[æt] nan pild deor ne on feoper fotu[m]. ne on creopendu[m] nis to pið metenne yfelu[m] pife. (f. 225r)

The wise Solomon said: that it is better to dwell with lions and with dragons than with an evil and excessively talkative woman.

The wise one also said: No wild animal, either crawling or on four feet can compare to an evil woman.

Both of these "proverbs" appear—although in a different order, in the homily on the beheading of John the Baptist:[112]

---

109. Traxel, 106.
110. Frankis, "Language and Cultures in Contact," 124. Traxel argues that the addition of these materials to the homily's margins is likely a result of the copyist finding similarities in the interests of the two texts. Traxel, *Language Change*, 110.
111. Here I owe thanks to Gina Marie Hurley, who pointed out the possible devotional aspect of these annotations.
112. Text of marginal proverbs transcribed directly from CUL Ii.1.33, translations my own. The Old English text of the *Decollation of Saint John the Baptist* is drawn from Clemoes, *Ælfric's Catholic Homilies*, 451–58.

> Nu cweð se trahtnere þæt nan wildedeor. ne on fiþerfotum ne on creopendum nis to wiðmetenne yfelum wife. [. . .] Ac se wisa salomon cwæð þæt selre wære to wunienne. mid leon. 7 dracan. þonne mid yfelum wife & ofersprecum. (172–73; 175–76)

> Now said the commentator that no wild beast, neither on four feet or crawling can compete with an evil woman. [. . .] But the wise Solomon said that it is better to dwell amid lions and dragons than with an evil and excessively talkative woman.

Interestingly, although both seem related to the same homily, the attributions are changed somewhat. Solomon remains the progenitor of the second piece of wisdom; yet *trahtnere,* which means "an expositor, commentator"[113] becomes simply *se wisa,* the wise one. Mary Swan argues that "the main text's verses offer no trigger for a discussion of women, unless this is provided by the reference in the verses at the end of fol. 224v to the misery of earthly desires."[114] This point raises a provocative question that can extend to many marginal additions to manuscripts: are they related to the thematic preoccupations of the written words or are they unique to the annotator?[115] This movement of text across both context and time suggests a very different attitude toward text and composition than our modern preoccupations.[116]

The comparison of both the proverbs of the *vilun* and those of Solomon highlights the differences between each of them and the additions on f. 70v. While these additions are themselves quite different in terms of both their content and their form, the important point is that the attitude toward emendation implied by each addition is also different. The additions of the proverbs of the *vilun* on f. 120r and the proverbs of Solomon on ff. 224v–225r suggest an implicit connection with the materials that make up the "main" text of the page. The additions to the *Life of Andrew* make that implicit connection explicit: these are shorter texts drawn from the very tradition into which they are being reinscribed. They enact a kind of *translatio* in themselves—speaking across earlier and later forms of English even as they engage with French verse, and implicitly, with a Latin exemplar that is reshaped in twelfth-century

---

113. BT, s.v. *trahtnere.*

114. Swan, "Ælfric's *Catholic Homilies,*" in Swan and Treharne, *Rewriting Old English,* 79.

115. Swan argues that such additions may serve "as an amplifying and familiar comment to increase the range of reference of the main text, and perhaps also as a betrayal of a particular reader's preoccupations" (80).

116. Moreover, Swan notes that such insertions suggest that Ælfric's homilies were "profoundly integrated" into twelfth-century homiletic traditions (82).

prose. The attitude toward the circulation of knowledge in CUL Ii.1.33 demonstrates a keen sense of multilingual identity. It also suggests that translation (always implicit in multilingual milieux) would have been at the forefront of the copyists' and correctors' minds. The community imagined on these pages demonstrates connections across time, space, and linguistic difference to create a group identity brought together only through their knowledge of these particular homilies and their corrections.

But how does the work done in the emendations and additions on f. 70v constitute a translation effect? The answer goes to the very heart of the distinction between translation proper and the translation effects I examine in this monograph. While a translation transforms one language into another, the translation effect need not be so direct in its work. The work of translation in its most fundamental sense is clearly indicated by the longer English addition in the margin of the text, in the story of Maximilla and how she treated the body of Andrew after his death, which comes from a Latin text.[117] But the *translation effect* is present in both the English addition and the French one, because they both present themselves as linguistically different additions to the manuscript. They have some of the effects that a "true" translation might have: they call attention to multilingualism and they demonstrate the accretive function of knowledge through manuscript emendations. More importantly, they call together a community of people who can read multiple languages, of people who know different stories, and of people who exist in different relationships to the knowledge presented on the page. The result is an imagined audience distributed in time across the writing, amending, and reading of the manuscript—the formation of a textual community of the page.

CONCLUSION

Throughout this chapter, I have catalogued and interpreted many ways that manuscript compilers, copyists, and correctors highlight translation as a process-oriented practice rather than a single product. As a result, they create translation effects that imply audiences who might want to differentiate between languages by means that are not easily reduced to a reading practice. The various compilations of the homilies of Ælfric suggest careful attention to linguistic difference—moving from the use of simple pointing techniques, to a more elaborate deployment of red ink to distinguish between Latin and English in various settings, to the insertion of "typical" Ælfrician phrases to

---

117. See Traxel, *Language Change*, 73–76.

further highlight the interplay of languages in the homilies. These techniques each betray a concern with the future reading audience of these manuscripts and how those readers will see differences of language played out on the page.

Although they do not always engage with translation directly, the longer insertions in CUL Ii.1.33 represent another context for this multilingual mindset. Demonstrating the breadth of Ælfric's use-history, each addition creates a link across time, stories, and—in the cases we can reconstruct even partial stemma for—the codices. Yet the effect of linguistic difference laid out on the page creates a community of both readers and of stories, enlarging the "range of reference of the main text," but also its temporal boundaries.[118]

To close, I return to the glossing practice of the Tremulous Hand. This glossator's activities—the only literal translation I have examined in this chapter—demonstrates a multitemporal engagement with linguistic difference on the part of a single mind working across several years. Although we cannot know whether the Tremulous Hand was working solely for himself or for future readers, the result of his activity is the interplay of languages on the page and a collocation of earlier and later versions of his translating mind at work, in both Latin and Middle English. His corpus demonstrates the flexibility of both the translation effect and the community of the page: a mind at work over multiple readings can, through the accretion and transfer of additions and emendations, even exist in a metaphorical textual community with itself. In any case, it is always—and only—through the medium of the page that such a community is made possible.

---

118. Swan, "Ælfric's *Catholic Homilies*," in Swan and Treharne, *Rewriting Old English*, 80.

CHAPTER 4

Becoming England
The Northumbrian Conversion in Trevet, Gower, and Chaucer

IN THE OPENING of the Northumbrian section of Chaucer's *Man of Law's Tale,* the waters that border the province are given a prominent position: Custance arrives "into oure occian" (II.505) and "oure wilde see" (II.506).[1] Eventually, her specific location is revealed: she arrives at "Northhumberlond" (II.508).[2] Chaucer's choice of geographical designation has two main effects. First, the use of the first-person plural "oure" creates an identification between the speaker and his audience—the pilgrims to whom the Man of Law speaks, certainly, but also the English-speaking audience to whom Chaucer addresses the *Canterbury Tales.* However, the generality of the geographical features—an "occian" and a "wilde see"—contrasts sharply with the specificity of the term "oure" that modifies the body of water in question.[3] Despite the identification invited by the pronoun "oure," the realm these waters surround is temporally distant from the present of the Man of Law and the other pilgrims. The designation might, as Kathleen Davis suggests, produce "the sense of political

---

1. Throughout this chapter, I refer to the characters in each of the versions of the Constance-story by their name as it appears in that version. So, for example, segments discussing the *Man of Law's Tale* will refer to Custance, Olda, and Alla, those discussing Trevet's "Of the Noble Lady Constance" will refer to Constance, Elda, and Ælle, etc.

2. All Middle English text is drawn from Benson, *Riverside Chaucer.*

3. Taylor argues that this moment "[implies] that smooth oceanic space can promote communal collectivity outside any fixed location" ("Toward Premodern Globalism," 258). See also Hsy, "'Oure Occian,'" in Gifford and Hauswedell, *Europe and Its Others,* 219.

borders," but such borders are also firmly situated in the past: in Chaucer's time, Northumbria is no longer its own political territory under sovereign rule.[4]

The story that follows traces the path of Northumbria from a heathen kingdom to one that becomes more familiar as it becomes Christian. Only at the close of this conversion story does the term "Engelond" (II.1130) name the location in which the narrative takes place. Critically, then, the Northumbrian King Alla returns at the end of the story to a place that is only proleptically England in Chaucer's narrative. Existing out of its proper time, the vision of a community-in-progress that develops over the course of the *Man of Law's Tale* derives from the multiple temporalities with which Chaucer engages in the narrative: the pre-Conquest Northumbrian past and the post-Conquest Christian England of his own time. Such preoccupations form part of an emerging engagement—beyond Chaucer himself—with the pre-Conquest past during the fourteenth century. By situating the *Man of Law's Tale* alongside Gower's *Confessio Amantis* and Nicholas Trevet's "Of the Noble Lady Constance" from his Anglo-Norman *Chronicle*, this discourse comes into finer resolution, revealing the concerns of language, time, and community-building that attend Chaucer's attempt to write the history of "Engelond."[5]

Chaucer wrote the *Man of Law's Tale* over two hundred years after the latest copy of Ælfric's homilies that were discussed in Chapter Three and over four hundred years after the works at the center of Chapters One and Two. I take this temporal leap across the Norman Conquest for two reasons. First, Chaucer is the inheritor of the kinds of thinking that the preceding chapters' translation effects illustrate. As a result, his negotiation of linguistic difference and translation demonstrates not only a commitment to narrative transmission but also to the modification of these translations for specific ends. Second, Chaucer's position as a writer fully immersed in a multilingual post-Conquest literary tradition offers an intriguing interlocutor for the foregoing analyses. As a translator, Chaucer had little compunction about altering his

---

4. Davis, "Time behind the Veil," in Cohen, *Postcolonial Middle Ages*, 117.

5. Understanding the possibilities of national or protonational identity in the *Man of Law's Tale* is beyond the scope of this chapter; however, for the purposes of my work here, I understand the kingdoms described in the *Tale* following Susan Reynolds, who argues that the status of "a people" exists without a discernible relationship between that people in the Middle Ages and the existence of a modern nation-state (*Kingdoms and Communities*, 253). Heng makes a compelling argument that the Constance narratives use "the nexus of family figures" as a foundation for "proto-nationalist discourse, or the imagined community of the nation" (*Empire of Magic*, 208). See also Hodges, "Malory's Launcelot"; Davis, "Time behind the Veil," in Cohen, *Postcolonial Middle Ages*; Nakley, "Sovereignty Matters" and *Living in the Future*.

source texts.⁶ By examining the translation effects that appear in the *Man of Law's Tale,* we can begin to see how imagined textual communities are affected by post-Conquest translation. How does a new English vernacular change the composition of such textual communities?

In the proliferation of postcolonial, feminist, queer, and historical criticism about the *Man of Law's Tale,* much of the scholarly focus rightly lingers on its portrayal of "the East" and the role that Syria plays in the opening of the story.⁷ These readings have included considerations of orientalism, gender, race, and temporality, among other themes. The scholarship about Syria also addresses the importance of an anachronistic fantasy of Syrian sovereignty to the tale's creation of an idea of the nation.⁸ Another common approach prioritizes the centrality of Rome to the *Man of Law's Tale.*⁹ This emphasis, however, draws attention away from the relationship that emerges *between* Rome and pre-Conquest England—a relationship founded on conversion and religious power.¹⁰ To complement and extend the critical focus on Rome and Syria, this chapter centers on the portrayal of Northumbria in Chaucer's *Man of Law's Tale,* Trevet's "Of the Noble Lady Constance," and Gower's *Confessio Amantis.* I argue that the varying emphases among these three texts underscore the

---

6. To be more precise, Chaucer's compunctions about altering his sources are balanced by his reliance on the humility topos that insists, often, on his marked lack of originality. As Tim Machan observes, "Rather than the anxiety of influence, it was apparently the anxiety of *originality* that informed Chaucer's procedures"—that is, Chaucer utilizes the figure or rhetoric of translation in order to obscure his own invention ("Chaucer as Translator," 60). See also Taylor, *Chaucer Translator.*

7. For criticism on the *Man of Law's Tale,* see Dinshaw, "New Approaches to Chaucer," in Boitano and Mann, *Cambridge Companion to Chaucer;* Dinshaw, "Pale Faces"; Schibanoff, "Orientalism, Antifeminism, and Heresy"; Delany, "Womanliness"; Robertson, "'Elvyssh' Power of Constance"; Kruger, "Conversion and Medieval Sexual, Religious, and Racial Categories," in Lochrie et al., *Constructing Medieval Sexuality;* Davis, "Time behind the Veil," in Cohen, *Postcolonial Middle Ages;* Nakley, *Living in the Future;* Whitaker, "Race and Racism in the *Man of Law's Tale.*"

8. See Davis, "Time behind the Veil," in Cohen, *Postcolonial Middle Ages;* Heng, *Empire of Magic,* 181–237; Nakley, "Sovereignty Matters" and *Living in the Future.* Heng stresses the centrality of "crusade, cultural-style, feminine-style" to the narrative tradition of the Constance-story (*Empire of Magic,* 189).

9. See Frantzen, *Before the Closet;* Stanbury, "*Man of Law's Tale* and Rome."

10. Cawsey focuses on religious and cultural difference rather than sexual difference, arguing that "both Gower and Chaucer's versions of the story of Constance continue the literary tradition of paralleling Northern pagans with Muslim Saracens" ("Disorienting Orientalism," 387). Frankis also argues that the *Man of Law's Tale*'s interest lies in no small part with its focus on sixth-century England, as does Smith. See Frankis, "King Ælle and the Conversion of the English," in Scragg and Weinburg, *Literary Appropriations;* Smith "Writing, Rewriting, and Disrupting," in Gates and O'Camb, *Remembering the Medieval Present.* See also Lavezzo, *Angels on the Edge of the World.*

representations of linguistic identity, translation, and power that permeate these post-Conquest visions of early medieval England.[11]

Although my examination of the *Man of Law's Tale* is very much indebted to scholars who have explored the text in regard to its relationship to both Gower and Trevet,[12] I propose a slightly different approach to the comparison, focusing on qualitative differences of translation rather than quantitative ones.[13] Despite the varying emphases of Trevet, Chaucer, and Gower in their versions of the Constance-legend, I will demonstrate that these three texts are united by their temporally heterogeneous portrayals of an emerging sense of "Engelond." The problematic temporalities latent in these texts become evident through their shared, if dissimilar, focus on key events that lead to the conversion of the Saxons.[14] In these moments of conversion, translation effects are prominent: they become sites where the power of linguistic difference to form community becomes a central concern of the text. By examining the translation effects that occur in each of these narratives, I demonstrate Chaucer's keen interest in a contemporary discourse about the pre-Conquest English past. The *Man of Law's Tale* gives us what might be our only sustained insight into how Chaucer viewed his predecessors in what he considered to be England.[15]

My consideration of this narrative unfolds in two parts. First, I examine the acts of translation—linguistic, religious, and cultural—that occur in each narrative, as well as the translation effects they occasion. The nature of

---

11. I follow A. C. Spearing, who argues that identifying this text solely with its fictional narrator misses much of the text's complexity. See Spearing, "Narrative Voice." For a recent dissenting view, see Smith, "Writing, Rewriting, and Disrupting," in Gates and O'Camb, *Remembering the Medieval Present*; Nelson, "Premodern Media."

12. Edward Block's 1953 quantitative comparison between Trevet and Chaucer underlies many understandings of the relationship between Chaucer and his source texts. See Block, "Originality, Controlling Purpose, and Craftsmanship"; Pratt, "Chaucer and *Les Cronicles*," in Atwood and Hill, *Studies in Language, Literature, and Culture*.

13. Here I follow in a long tradition of such studies, including Legassie, "Among Other Possible Things," in Ganim and Legassie, *Cosmopolitanism and the Middle Ages*; Heng, *Empire of Magic*; and Hsy, *Trading Tongues*.

14. This chapter marks a partial exception to my general avoidance of the term "Anglo-Saxon": Chaucer uses the term "Saxon" in the *Man of Law's Tale*, and moreover specifically links the people designated with this term to his own time. I retain his usage to demonstrate its utility for authors whose works use it to promote a hegemonic, mono-cultural vision of England across time. Moreover, my retention of the term "Saxon" highlights a crucial difference between Chaucer and Trevet's respective terminology and our own. See Reynolds, "'Anglo-Saxon' and 'Anglo-Saxons.'"

15. Whereas Trevet's *Chronicle* creates a status for the Saxons that could potentially trouble the Norman hierarchy whose ancestors conquered them, the *Man of Law's Tale* "removes the disruptive potentiality that the Anglo-Saxon past represented to late medieval, Anglo-Norman historiographers" (Dugas, "Legitimization of Royal Power," 38).

language and its representation in these three texts offer a range of linguistic identities for the characters within them. Moreover, the centrality of translation to a post-Conquest consideration of historical continuity and change demonstrates its ubiquitous availability as a spyglass through which writers like Chaucer could view and reinterpret the past.[16] Second, I explore the specific representation of the Britons in each narrative in order to better understand the ramifications of these portrayals of cultural translation. I conclude with a brief examination of several key moments in Nicholas Trevet's Anglo-Norman *Chronicle,* which serves to contextualize the version of the Constance narrative offered in his text and brings the two later versions of the story into sharper relief.

THREE STORIES OF ENGLISH CONVERSION

Chaucer's, Gower's, and Trevet's versions of the Constance legend all share basic narrative elements: Constance, the daughter of the Emperor of Rome, is promised in marriage to the Muslim sultan of Syria, who in turn promises to convert to Christianity.[17] Upon Constance's arrival, the sultan's mother plots to kill her son and Constance's escorts because of her anger at the proposed conversion. She sends Constance to sea in a rudderless boat. Guided by God, Constance arrives in Saxon Northumbria. A knight whose sexual advances she rebuffs frames Constance for murder, and God's miraculous testimony at her subsequent trial converts the Saxon king and his people. Constance marries the king, but her mother-in-law hates the Roman for taking her son from their non-Christian faith. When the king is away fighting a war, the mother-in-law replaces a letter announcing the birth of his son with one announcing the birth of a monster. The king's response shows compassion, so the mother-in-law steals that letter as well, forging a letter that exiles Constance instead. Constance eventually returns to Rome and, years later, the king is reunited with his wife and their son while on pilgrimage there. While Chaucer's story shares these basic elements with the other two, the modifications in his text highlight his concern with creating a specifically English past in his narrative.

---

16. For further considerations of Chaucer's investment in multilingualism, see Hsy "'Oure Occian,'" in Gifford and Hauswedell, *Europe and Its Others* and *Trading Tongues;* Phillips, "Chaucer's Language Lessons"; Burrow, "A Maner Latyn Corrupt."

17. For a list of examples of what Schlauch and others have called the "accused queen" narratives, including *The King of Tars, Emaré,* and the story of Chrosoes, see Correale and Hamel, *Sources and Analogues,* 2:277–93. Heng argues that crusader logic is at work in the text (*Empire of Magic,* 181–237). See also Stavsky, "Translating the Near East."

Although Chaucer's *Man of Law's Tale* focuses two-thirds of its narrative energies on the interaction between Northumberland and Rome, the opening of the story does little to anticipate its eventual focus on English history. It begins far from its Northumbrian subject matter: "In Surrye whilom dwelte a compaignye / Of chapmen riche" (II.134–35). Moreover, the *Man of Law's Tale* goes on to a second distant geographical setting for the narrative immediately after its mention of Syria, when these merchants travel to Rome: "Now fil it that the maistres of that sort / Han shapen hem to Rome for to wende" (II.141–42). The emphasis on travel—the merchants "wende" to Rome, after all[18]—foregrounds early the potential complications of *cultural* difference that will become a central theme.[19] Potential problems of *language* and *linguistic* difference, however, are conspicuously absent from this account.

Christine Cooper notes that, in the *Man of Law's Tale*, "moments of actual, difficult, or miraculous translation in the tale draw our attention to those places where translation is not mentioned at all, or to those places in which translation is purposefully ambiguous."[20] Following her cogent observation, I argue that translation effects in Chaucer's narrative can take paradoxical forms, not least including moments where Chaucer's omission of translation—translation that is sometimes (though not always) explicitly present in his source texts—draws attention to linguistic difference in the narrative. In these instances, the absence of allusions to translation in places where it must logically occur comprises the translation effect and highlights the temporal and linguistic distance of communities drawn together in medieval texts.

The merchants at the outset of the tale occasion one such translation effect. As we might expect, they seem to have no difficulty either in gathering intelligence from the Romans concerning Custance nor in conveying the import of that information to their sultan. The narrative presents the description of Custance as "the commune voys of every man" (II.155), followed by what Gania Barlow terms the "virtue-blazon" that defines Custance as a pseudo-romance heroine and gives equivalent status to courtly and religious ideas of

---

18. McSparran et al., *Middle English Dictionary Online*, s.v. wenden[2a]. Hereafter, this resource is cited as *MED Online*.

19. As Davis observes, the "tale retrospectively defines the terms of success and failure for attaining an identity within the European system from the perspective of fourteenth-century England" ("Time behind the Veil," in Cohen, *Postcolonial Middle Ages*, 115). That is, these merchants must "fit in" to English cultural norms—something Chaucer writes them to do, deftly evading questions of difference by the a priori assimilation of the merchants to England. See Legassie, "Among Other Possible Things," in Ganim and Legassie, *Cosmopolitanism and the Middle Ages*.

20. Cooper, "Translating Custance," 36–37.

virtue.²¹ "Voys," usually glossed as "opinion," also evokes a sense of the speaking voices that would have shaped this image of Custance with words.²² These voices are definitively Roman: the tale "makes no mention of the cultural and religious differences [. . .] between Syrians and Romans. Instead, [it] works to establish the closeness, both geographically and culturally, between the two" in the tale's opening scenes.²³ The Syrian merchants hear, understand, and presumably translate the words that describe Custance for their sultan. Yet they do so with no mention of linguistic difference.²⁴ This absence is itself a kind of invisible translation effect: we know translation must be taking place (or at the very least that multilingualism is in play), but the text does not focus on language, only the story it conveys. The lack of explicit translation, that is, highlights translation as an issue in the text as a whole. The shared story of Custance's virtue—told and retold by this "commune voys"—creates a community of observers who praise Custance.

Moreover, the "commune voys" of the Roman citizens sing Custance's praises in Middle English. This silent act of translation into the vernacular also creates a telescoping of times: presumably Latinate voices are made to speak in a Middle English dialect that would not have existed in their time. Rome, Syria, and the England of Chaucer's day are represented by a single language despite their temporal, geographical, and linguistic differences. This substantial flattening of multiple forms of alterity creates a temporal problem: the *Man of Law's Tale* maps fourteenth-century Middle English onto the text, increasing the discordance of the initial geographical treatment of the English landmass on the one hand as surrounded by the proximate "oure occian" and on the other hand as being temporally remote and alien by virtue of its lack of Christianity.

The lack of emphasis Chaucer places on linguistic difference is particularly evident when considered in comparison to Trevet's version of the Constance story. In "Of the Noble Lady Constance," the protagonist's use of knowledge—both linguistic and religious—converts the merchants who later sing her praises. Constance's father, "pur ceo qe nul autre enfaunt avoit" (297.12–13) [because he had no other child],²⁵ goes to great lengths to make sure his daughter is well educated:

---

21. Barlow, "Thrifty Tale," 405.
22. *MED Online*, s.v. *voys*.
23. Schibanoff, "Orientalism, Anti-Feminism, and Heresy," 78.
24. Phillips notes that "what is surprising about these tidings is not their content or prevalence, but rather the fact that the merchants understand them without any difficulty" ("Chaucer's Language Lessons," 53).
25. All Anglo-Norman text and English translation for Trevet's "Of the Noble Lady Constance" and Middle English text for Gower are from Correale and Hamel, *Sources and*

A grant diligence la fist enseigner la foi Cristiene, et endoctriner par mestres sachauntz en les sept sciences, qe sount [logiciene], naturele, morale, astronomie, geometrie, musiqe, [perspective], qe sont philosophies seculers apelez, et la fist endoctriner en diverses langages. (297.13–17)

With great diligence he had her taught the Christian faith and instructed by learned masters in the seven sciences, which are logic, physics, morals, astronomy, geometry, music, and optics, called the secular sciences, and had her taught various languages. (296)

That Constance is instructed in *diverses langages* marks another kind of translation effect. Foreshadowing its function in Northumbria, here we see the first instance where Constance's ability with language smooths a narrative problem.[26] Trevet's insistence on observing her ability raises questions about how she deploys her knowledge, of both faith and language: "Et quant ele [entendi] q'il estoient paens, lour precha la foi Cristiene. Et puis q'il avoient assentu a la foi Cristiene les fist baptizer et enseigner parfitement en la foi Jhesu Crist" (297.21–24) [And when she understood that they were heathens, she preached the Christian faith to them. And when they had assented to the Christian faith, she had them baptized and instructed perfectly in the faith of Jesus Christ (296)]. Constance, already revealed to be skilled in language, converses with these foreigners without difficulty. Although it is not mentioned whether she speaks with them in their language or her own, she is able to find some linguistic common ground, which she uses first to learn about them and then to convert and teach them.[27] In other words, she uses her knowledge of languages to effect conversion—it is an artifact of both her "clerical education and missionary functions."[28] The contrast between Chaucer and Trevet on this point highlights the *Man of Law's Tale*'s tendency to flatten linguistic and cultural difference in favor of the overarching monoculturalism (and perhaps even monolingualism) of Christianity that allows a fourteenth-century

---

Analogues, Vol. 2. Anglo-Norman from elsewhere in Trevet's *Chronicle* is drawn from Rutherford, "Anglo-Norman Chronicle." Translations of these segments are my own.

26. Legassie argues that "for Trevet, the cosmopolitanism of the court is the intersection of international commerce, courtly refinement, familial sentiment, and higher learning, all of which combine to advance the universal expansion of orthodox Christian belief" ("Among Other Possible Things," in Ganim and Legassie, *Cosmopolitanism and the Middle Ages*, 186–87).

27. Hsy argues that this difference in Constance's ability with languages indicates the aims of the text as a whole: where Trevet is fundamentally "clerical or hagiographical," Chaucer is mercantile in his intents (*Trading Tongues*, 70).

28. Hsy, 71. See also Heng, *Empire of Magic*, 191.

"Engelond" to overlie a sixth-century Northumberland. It also highlights a translation effect: language has to be of import, as does linguistic difference.

Where Christianity and Custance are concerned, linguistic difference—whether between Rome and Syria or between Rome and England—is largely ignored in favor of comprehension that proceeds either easily or by readily attained stopgaps. These moments of easy understanding, however, are thrown into high relief by an example in which translation is not so easily achieved: there is no one in the narrative who can read the stars, either literally or metaphorically. In a description of the heavens as a book to be read and comprehended, both the sultan's decision to convert and the Roman emperor's decision to allow Custance to marry a foreigner are portrayed in terms of reading. A narratorial aside, notably absent from both Gower's and Trevet's versions of the story, laments the sultan's fate and speculates on the possibility of it being presaged in astrological signs:

> Paraventure in thilke large book
> Which that men clepe the hevene ywriten was
> With sterres, whan that he his birthe took,
> That he for love sholde han his deeth, allas!
> For in the sterres, clerer than is glas,
> Is writen, God woot, whoso koude it rede,
> The deeth of every man, withouten drede.
> (II.190–96)

Although the "large book" of the heavens contains the lives—and deaths—of all humans within it, the apprehension of that knowledge relies at least partially on the ability of any given man or woman to read it. That is, although the heavens are the proverbial open book, they reveal their secrets only to "whoso koude it rede." Such knowledge, the narrator observes, is rare: even though the meaning of the stars should be clear, "mennes wittes ben so dulle / That no wight kan wel rede it atte fulle" (II.202–3). The book of the heavens is not easily read or interpreted, and its translation from starry script to human language, knowledge, and action is difficult due to human linguistic failings.[29]

---

29. Later, the narrator asks whether or not there was a better time for Custance to travel or a "philosophre" (II.310) who could have helped the Emperor of Rome make this choice. "Allas," he laments, "we been to lewed or to slowe" (II.315) to understand the importance of such decisions. Legassie argues that this moment in the text is meant to highlight "a lack of international courtly culture in the Emperor's household," which sets it apart from the more cosmopolitan culture at the court of the Sultan ("Among Other Possible Things," in Ganim and Legassie, *Cosmopolitanism and the Middle Ages*, 185).

By drawing attention to a moment in which people fail to translate adequately, Chaucer highlights another instance of what might be understood as either linguistic deficiency or linguistic innovation, depending upon its interpretation. When she arrives in Northumberland, Custance communicates with the constable in a language that he understands, but only barely: "A maner Latyn corrupt was hir speche, / But algates therby was she understonde" (II.519–20).[30] Custance's difficulty in finding a common language with the constable has two implications. First, it highlights the centrality of language to England's conversion because it obliquely refers to the difficulty inherent in traversing both cultural and linguistic space. Custance arrives in England and through God's power converts the non-Christian Saxons—but to do so, she first must find a common language. Second, these linguistic measures function as a translation effect: they call attention to translation through contrast with the merchants' easy comprehension of the "commune voys" that praises Custance's virtues and intelligence. The merchants required no moment of translation to communicate.[31]

Chaucer's alternating interest in and disregard for linguistic difference differs from the treatment of language in either Trevet or Gower.[32] Trevet's description of Constance's linguistic abilities suggests the incorporation of a long lineage of English historical narrative; moreover, it suggests that linguistic identities are mutable. Trevet's Constance was tutored in *diverses langages* (297.17) [various languages]—as Heng notes, "including, conveniently, Saxon English"[33]—in addition to other indispensable skills for a Christian, Roman princess to learn. Trevet does not explicitly state which languages Constance learns at the outset of the story, but this omission symbolically elevates Saxon to the same linguistic plane as other more learned languages. Where Chaucer's

---

30. Cooper sees this as a miracle of *xenoglossia* ("Translating Custance"); Hsy sees it as "a mixed Latinate speech" attributed "not to clerics but merchants" (Hsy, *Trading Tongues*, 71). Burrow defines this speech as "a *lingua franca* current in mercantile and maritime districts [. . .] owing its origin [. . .] to the necessities of trade" ("A Maner Latyn Corrupt," 36). Legassie argues that this linguistic gap "recalls the medieval tendency to explain linguistic kinship and difference in terms of the rise and fall of empires and the schema of salvation history" ("Among Other Possible Things," 191). Shyama Rajendran terms this form of a Latin "a contact language," drawing on Hsy's deployment of "contact zones" ("Undoing 'the Vernacular,'" 8).

31. Of course, the merchants may well have known enough Latin to communicate with their customers. See Hsy, *Trading Tongues*, 68–69; Phillips, "Chaucer's Language Lessons," 53–54; Burrow, "A Maner Latyn Corrupt." For the mercantile transformation of the story from Trevet to Chaucer, see Wallace, *Chaucerian Polity*, 205–6.

32. Some writers see this particular difference as a greater attention to detail. For example, see Block, "Originality, Controlling Purpose, and Craftsmanship." Legassie, by contrast, sees this as part of the "art of making do" that is central to cosmopolitanisms ("Among Other Possible Things," in Ganim and Legassie, *Cosmopolitanism and the Middle Ages*, 188).

33. Heng, *Empire of Magic*, 191.

Custance speaks a corrupted form of Latin to enable a piecemeal communication with the constable and his wife, Hermengyld, Trevet's Constance meets the Saxons on their own linguistic territory.[34]

The narrative results of this linguistic ability suggest a very specific alignment between Trevet's depiction of language and the identities that those languages make possible.[35] The constable, Olda, exhibits surprise at her command of the Saxon language, which in turn influences his interpretation of the riches found with her on the rudderless boat. Combining linguistic and material markers of identity, Olda creates an origin story that casts Constance as a Saxon princess:

> Et puis qe Olda l'avoit oy si renablement parler sa lange, et trova ove lui si grant tresour, esperoit qe ele estoit fille de ascun roi des Sessouns outre mere, come d'Alemayne, oue de Sessoine, ou de Suece, oue de Denemarche. (303–5.137–40)
>
> And when Olda had heard her speak his language so competently and found such great treasure with her, he supposed she was the daughter of some king of the Saxons beyond the sea, as of Germany, or Saxony, or Sweden, or Denmark (302–4)

Language—and the absence of the need for translation—provides an impetus toward interpretation for Olda. He assigns Constance an identity based almost solely on her linguistic ability: she clearly must be some kind of Saxon in order to speak their language. Yet the material objects he finds with her indicate that she is a special *kind* of Saxon: royalty. This royalty, for Olda, is located *outre mere* [beyond the sea]. Furthermore, Olda broadly associates this Saxon identity with a larger geographic one, citing both western (Germany and Saxony) as well as northern (Sweden and Denmark) "Germanic" locations as possible homelands for the presumed princess.[36] This association suggests that Olda's

---

34. Additionally, it gracefully sidesteps any concerns that might have been raised by Constance's conversations with and conversions of the Syrian merchants earlier in the tale—diverse languages could also include *their* language. Another reading of these rhetorical situations might suggest that Constance engages in an act of code-switching. For a survey of recent work on premodern code-switching (predominantly in nonliterary texts), see Schendl and Wright, *Code-Switching in Early English*, 1–14. For an analysis of code-switching in Chaucer in particular, see Putter, "Code-Switching in Langland, Chaucer, and the Gawain-poet," in Schendel and Wright, *Code-Switching in Early English*, 281–302. See also Hsy, *Trading Tongues*, 59–60.

35. Schiff has questioned ideas of linguistic identity as it intersects with national or ethnic identity (*Revivalist Fantasy*).

36. These linguistic terms—"Northern" and "Western" Germanic—come from a modern viewpoint of historical linguistics, but they allow us to see the import of the claim that Olda

own language proceeds from, or is otherwise closely related to, other Saxon languages. Unaware of her training in various languages, Olda interprets Constance's skill in speaking Saxon in a way that is limited by his knowledge of his people's cultural and linguistic heritage. In fact, Olda's assumptions about his visitor's origins bear some similarity to broader themes in early medieval English literature, although they are taken from the perspective of an Anglo-Norman hierarchy that displaced it.

Although it refers to her personal history rather than to cultural memory, Olda's understanding of Constance as part of a Saxon hierarchy *outre mere* suggests that, from his point of view, the language and the community that speaks it are coterminous.[37] Olda assumes that their shared language comes from another kingdom related to his own through linguistic inheritance. He thus imagines a linguistic community that is larger than his local community of Northumbrian Saxon speakers. His reaction also participates in a larger cultural mode of interpretation in pre-Conquest England that Nicholas Howe terms the "Migration Myth." Defined somewhat broadly, this term refers to the belief in and representation of the migration of the Angles, Saxons, and Jutes to England from continental homelands.[38] Howe argues that "despite frequent political rivalries, religious disputes, and some degree of dialect variation, [the early medieval English] could gather a sense of unity from their continental origins as these were memorialized in the central works of the culture."[39] Thus the migration from "Germania" became an important topos of pre-Conquest England's origin myths.[40] Olda himself seems to participate in a similar (if further fictionalized) cultural awareness and identification. He does so not only through the movement of people across space but also through the movement of the languages such people speak.

Olda's assumptions about Constance's background constitute a translation effect: they call attention to linguistic difference (via its absence) while posit-

---

makes over Constance's origin. He is, essentially, positing a language that is coterminous with specific geographical areas of origin.

37. For an analysis of the reasoning behind this change in Chaucer—essentially, the danger that a foreign woman would face in the "threatening postcolonial situation of Northumberlond"—see Hamaguchi, "Custance as a Foreign Woman," 421.

38. Germania referred both to the locale from which these tribes migrated and to the Germanic tribes who were still located in continental Europe and Scandinavia. In modernity, the myth of Germania is closely associated with white supremacist ideologies.

39. Howe, *Migration and Mythmaking*, 6.

40. It is important to note that the idea of a nation having its roots in a collective identity is very much under debate. Reynolds, for example, argues persuasively that such identities emerged out of sovereign rule, in contrast to the possibility that these collective identities led to the need for sovereign rule in the Middle Ages. See Reynolds, *Kingdoms and Community*; also Hodges, "Malory's Launcelot."

ing a community drawn together by language, shared stories of migration, and identity. As such, this translation effect has significant narrative consequences. Fabienne Michelet reminds us that "narrative [. . .] constitutes a powerful weapon in the struggle for control and appropriation of space."[41] The work of translation effects is similar: Olda's comprehension of Constance sparks the creation of another narrative, meant to bring together her origins with his. The explanation Olda constructs in Trevet's *Chronicle* appropriates a relationship to a foreign space through narrative: it creates a story that connects disparate speakers of similar languages. However, the more significant appropriative gesture Olda makes is over Constance. By imaginatively assigning a role to Constance that positions her as part of a shared but imagined "Germanic" past, Olda claims her for a Saxon—and therefore Northumbrian—tradition. Most importantly, her linguistic ability negates any need for translation at all.

Gower's version of the narrative sheds further light on both Chaucer and Trevet by completely omitting the question of language in all but the most oblique way when Constance arrives on Northumberland's shores. Gower's Constance is profoundly silent in this section of the text, as she is elsewhere. Although Elda (here, "the kinges chamberlein," [332.726]) and Hermyngheld "axen what sche was" (333.739), Constance "hire wold noght confesse" (333.738). Elda and his wife find joy as they welcome Constance into "felaschipe" (333.742), but Constance's reaction is one of pure sorrow for the lack of Christianity that she finds among this people. Gower's description of her time with them prior to Hermyngheld's conversion is thus particularly poignant: "Bot elles sche hath al hire wille, / And thus with hem sche duelleth stille" (733.747–48). Constance's silence—signified by her dwelling "stille" among the Northumberland pagans—marks her as an outsider.[42] Her voice is not metaphorically heard in Northumberland until Constance begins to convert her hosts, suggesting that this role gives the otherwise silent woman the voice she previously lacked. As Constance and Hermyngheld grow closer—and thus as Hermyngheld grows closer to her eventual conversion—they "spekende alday betwen hem two" (333.752). Even as we metaphorically see Constance speak in the *Confessio Amantis*, however, we are distanced from the actual words she says, and moreover, from the language in which she says them.

In fact, throughout his version of the narrative, Gower features very little direct address by his heroine. This contrast between her initial silence and her loquacious (if distanced) power to convert Hermyngheld is mirrored by

---

41. Michelet, *Creation, Migration, and Conquest*, 11.

42. Constance's silence, figured here as "restraint," also points to the possibility of "sinister things: it inhibits and victimizes the heroine and masks responsibility for her plight" (Allen, "Chaucer Answers Gower," 642).

Gower's version of the opening of the story with its interaction between Constance and the Syrian merchants. In the *Confessio Amantis,* Gower makes no mention either of Constance's education or of her language. Rather, when she encounters the merchants, the text merely states

> Sche hath hem with hire wordes wise
> Of Cristes feith so full enformed
> That thei therto ben all conformed,
> So that baptesme thei receiven
> And alle here false goddes weyven.
> (330.606–9)

Constance's words here, as in her multiple conversionary conversations with Hermyngheld, are silenced in favor of the simple report of their efficacy. They are wise, but they are not heard, and they only seem to matter in so far as they convert.[43] In Gower, language (like translation) is thus a means to an end. Relying neither on imperfect Latin for communication nor on the knowledge of Saxon that associates her with other non-Christian climes, Gower's Constance speaks only when her voice can be useful: that is, she speaks to convert her pagan interlocutors, and though her words are effective, they are, textually at least, remote.

Despite this difference of narration, however, Gower's association of speech and conversion finds a parallel in Trevet's positioning of the Saxon language in Constance's conversions. When Hermegild cures the blind man, for example, the Saxon language merits special mention and even representation: "Et Hermegild, devaunt Olda et sa meine qe lui sui, de bone foi et ferme fist sus les euz de lui enveuglé la seinte croiz et lui dit en sa langage Sessoine, 'Bisne man [in] Jhesu name in [rode] yslawe, have thi siht'" (307.183–86) [And Hermegild, before Olda and his retinue which followed him, in good and firm faith made the holy cross on the eyes of the blind man, and said to him in her Saxon language: "Blind man, in the name of Jesus, slain on the cross, have thy sight" (306)]. Trevet's change of language—a moment that Jonathan Hsy identifies as "code-switching" from Anglo-Norman to English—draws attention to linguistic difference and the necessity of translation to form a community of faith.[44] As a translation effect, it serves as a reminder that Hermegild speaks Saxon at the very moment where she performs the miracle that will convert

---

43. See Allen, "Chaucer Answers Gower"; Cooper, "Translating Custance"; Robertson, "'Elvyssh' Power of Custance."

44. Hsy, *Trading Tongues,* 78. Hsy notes that this switch both "lends veracity to the account" and "thematically links Hermegild's utterance to her imminent conversion" (78).

her husband: moreover, it records her actual words in the Saxon language she purportedly used to say them.[45] The *Chronicle* thus focuses its narrative attention not only on the conversion of Saxon characters but also on the fact that *they are Saxon*. It does so by highlighting the language that they speak. This emphasis accords a further measure of importance to their language as a marker of identity. The translation effect that attends the moment of a miracle also heals a community of Christians dispersed by non-Christian Saxons.

Although the version of the Constance legend that appears in the *Confessio Amantis* is in the aggregate more similar to Chaucer's than Trevet's, Gower's relation of Hermyngheld's words is intriguingly close to Trevet's version in the *Chronicle*: "In trust of Cristes lawe, / Which don was on the crois and slawe, / Thou bysne man, behold and se" (333.769–71). Hermyngheld's words, although they are not clearly in Saxon, are still spoken by Hermyngheld herself in Gower's Constance narrative. Moreover, as Hsy notes, the use of the Old English *bysne* where Gower usually prefers *blind* "effects a form of cross-temporal code-switching."[46] Importantly, Hermyngheld's speech here also acts as a command. The narrative transfers the power of language from the silent Constance to Hermyngheld herself.

In contrast to both the *Chronicle* and *Confessio Amantis* versions of the healing, the *Man of Law's Tale* entirely removes the Saxon language from Custance's conversions in Northumberland, suggesting that language as a cultural marker bears somewhat less importance within the narrative. Moreover, it removes specific quotation from this critical juncture entirely. When the "blinde Britoun" asks Hermengyld to "yif me my sighte agayn," (II.561–62), the narrative only relates her fear that such an act will provoke her husband to kill her: "This lady weex affrayed of the soun / Lest that hir housbonde, shortly for to sayn, / Wolde hire for Jhesu Cristes love han slayn," (II.563–65). We hear neither her words nor the language in which she speaks them; moreover, "the passage never *actually* states" that Hermengyld cures the man at all.[47] The explanation of the miracle thus does not come from Hermengyld, who performs it, but from Custance. After Custance "made [Hermengyld] boold" (II.566) the constable demands an explanation and Custance gives him one:

---

45. In Trevet, Olda is referred to as a Saxon, whereas Hermegild is referred to only as his wife. Still, her linguistic identity is firmly in the Saxon category. See Frankis, "King Ælle and the Conversion of the English," in Scragg and Weinburg, *Literary Appropriations*, 89–90.

46. Hsy notes that this word choice suggests "the alterity of the English past" (*Trading Tongues*, 78). Legassie argues that *bysne* "seems to function as a dialect word and an archaism, a token of the way that languages preserve—amber-like—long-forgotten microhistories of contact and compromise" ("Among Other Possible Things," in Ganim and Legassie, *Cosmopolitanism and the Middle Ages*, 194).

47. Cooper, "Translating Custance," 33.

> "Sire, it is Cristes myght,
> That helpeth folk out of the feendes snare."
> And so ferforth she gan oure lay declare
> That she the constable, er that it was eve
> Converteth, and on Crist made hym bileve.
> (II.570–74)

As Christine Cooper observes of the scene, "It is not important that Custance herself hears and understands; what matters is that she preaches persuasively and her language is ingested."[48] Despite the direct report of Custance's words, it is unclear what language she speaks. She certainly appears to speak Chaucer's Middle English, but we are a mere forty lines from her initial communication with Olda in a "maner Latyn corrupt"—although it is worth noting that Hermengyld is converted after Custance "hath so longe sojourned there" (II.536), indicating a lengthy stay. Yet Chaucer's version of the story again does not make clear the language that makes such conversion possible and so raises the specter of translation only to foreclose the discussion of linguistic difference. Moreover, by reappropriating these words to Custance, the *Man of Law's Tale* transposes the ability to convert Northumbria from the Saxon Hermengyld to her Roman converter.

TIME, POWER, AND RELIGIOUS COMMUNITY

The problematic representation of moments of linguistic difference—or their lack of representation—that occasions translation effects in the *Man of Law's Tale* highlights the relationship between the present and former inhabitants of Saxon Northumbria. Of similar concern—for Gower and Trevet in addition to Chaucer—is the status of religious continuity when considering the pre-Conquest past, especially as it pertains to the relationship between the Britons and their Saxon conquerors. The *Man of Law's Tale,* however, foregrounds the potentially disruptive—and transformative—role that the Britons who remain on the island play in the destiny of Northumbria. But as Trevet's narrative follows a more traditional interpretation of the lack of religious continuity that leads to the Briton's loss of rule, it is instructive to start with his narrative as a basis for comparison to Chaucer's.[49]

---

48. Cooper, 35.

49. See, for example, Bede's version of the Saxon invasion in Colgrave and Mynors, *Bede's Ecclesiastical History,* I.22.68.

In Trevet, Constance's encounter with Olda is prefaced by a brief parenthetical statement wherein Trevet explains that "les Brutons avoient ja perdue la seignurie de l'ysle, come avant est counté en la fin de l'estoire l'emperour Justinian le Grant" (303.125–26) [the Britons had already lost control of the island, as is related above in the end of the story of the Emperor Justinian the Great (302)]. By itself, this comment might easily be passed over as a simple aside regarding historical fact, but a similar comment later in the narrative suggests that the Britons' loss leads directly to the Saxons' gain. When Constance is taken into the house of Olda and his wife Hermegild, Trevet's description of the couple refers obliquely to the exchange of power between Briton and Saxon: "Qar Hermegild et Olda et les autres Sessons q'avoient donc la seignurie de la terre estoient encore paens" (305.159–60) [For Hermegild and Olda and the other Saxons who had control over the land were still pagans (304)]. The same term used in the first aside to describe the earlier loss of British rule—*seignurie*—appears here as something that now applies to the Saxons.

Trevet's understanding of this transfer of *seignurie* comes primarily from his engagement with earlier historical texts. Rutherford notes that Trevet engaged with a variety of precursors, potentially including Bede's *Historia Ecclesiastica*, where Bede clearly establishes his line of thinking on the subject.[50] He argues that the Britons lost lordship over the island of Britain in part because they did not convert the invading Saxons.[51] Trevet does not make such a clear statement about the reasons behind the Britons' loss of power, but the emergence of *seignurie* in his discussion of Constance's story makes an implicit claim for the relationship between the Saxon migration to the island and the Britons' exile from its center. In other words, if the Britons had already lost control or power over Britain in Trevet's narrative, then it is clearly the Saxons who took it from them.

The *Man of Law's Tale*, by contrast, positions the Britons' loss of power not in terms of *seignurie*, but in terms of religious conflict. "No Cristen dorste route" (II.540) in Alla's kingdom because when the "payens, that conquereden al aboute / The plages of the north, by land and see" (II.542–43) landed in England, the Christians were forced to escape to Wales. The religious overtones in this passage reveal a very different vision of English identity.[52] The religious

---

50. See Rutherford, who includes a list of potential sources for Trevet ("Anglo-Norman Chronicle," 20). For a summary of Trevet's possible sources, see Correale and Hamel, *Sources and Analogues*, 2:277–83; Krappe, "Offa-Constance Legend"; Wynn, "Conversion Story"; Frantzen, *Before the Closet*.

51. See Colgrave and Mynors, *Bede's Ecclesiastical History*, I.22.68.

52. Gower's version of Constance's arrival simply states that: "sche no maner joie made, / Bot sorweth sore of that sche fond / No Cristendom in thilke lond" (333.744–46).

population of "olde Britons" flee to the borderlands of the island. Although the "payens" conquer the north, they do not defeat the religion itself—they only dislodge its practitioners. Chaucer's version thus leaves open a space for "Cristyanytee" to one day return from its marginal dwelling place. Moreover, the Christian population of Britons is not exiled in perpetuity. Rather, the text avers that "to Walys fledde the Cristyanytee / Of olde Britons dwellynge in this ile; / Ther was hir refut, for the meene while" (544–46). In this passage, the resurrection of Christian preeminence is inevitable, suggesting a teleology that presupposes Christian return.

The inevitability of such a return is reinforced by the knowledge that not all of the Christians had fled to Wales after this conquest. Several Christians remain in close proximity to the constable's dwelling:

> But yet nere Cristene Britons so exiled
> That ther nere somme that in hir privetee
> Honoured Crist and hethen folk bigiled,
> And ny the castel swiche ther dwelten three. (II.547–50)

It would seem that, despite the "official" exile of the Christians to the Welsh borderlands, not all "Cristene Britons" were thus marginalized. There are still practicing Christians who honor Christ "in hir privetee" and manage to keep the "hethen folk bigiled." Indeed, three such secret Christian Britons live near the castle to which the constable takes Custance. Read in concert with the early comments about Christianity's remote dwelling in Wales, these lines allow the reader to intuit that the three Christians dwelling near the castle were waiting for their renewed historical moment, always alert to the possibility that they would one day be able to propagate their faith again. These Christians have a special role in England's religious history according to Chaucer: their presence allows Hermengyld to perform the miracle of restoring sight to the blind man—a man who, crucially, is not even associated with a specific identity in Gower, although he is identified as "un povre Cristien Bruton enveuglés" (305.176) [a poor blind Christian Briton (304)] in Trevet.[53] This miraculous cure is central to the *Man of Law's Tale* because it sets into motion the events that will eventually convert the king himself.

The presence of the phrase "for the meene while" in the *Man of Law's Tale* highlights an interstitial space, a gap that must be traversed in order for God's will of a Christian England to come to pass. Furthermore, the "meene

---

53. The *Confessio Amantis* simply notes that "a blind man" asks Hermyngheld to heal him (333.759).

while" pertains specifically to the Britons and their role as the source of English Christianity in the text. It recurs some lines later, at II.668, when a book is brought forth for the knight to swear upon in the course of his trial:

> A Britoun book, written with Evaungiles,
> Was fet, and on this book he swoor anoon
> She gilty was, and in the meene whiles
> An hand hym smoot upon the nekke-boon,
> That doun he fil atones as a stoon,
> And bothe his eyen broste out of his face
> In sighte of every body in that place.
> (II.666–72)

The phrase "in the meene whiles"—critically similar to the earlier "for the meene while"—here highlights proximity rather than distance. The knight testifies falsely against Custance, and "in the meene whiles," God destroys him. Once again, this phrase implies the inevitability of what it refers to—in this case, divine retribution.[54] Its second appearance strengthens the intensity of its first. What was an interstitial absence becomes a token of the imminence of Christianity's return and the divine Providence that makes such a return possible.

The Britoun book itself is the clearest manifestation of the interstitial and fleeting status of the "meene while" and functions as a material instance of a translation effect, linking humans to the Christian past and Christian future, as well as to God's divine understanding.[55] It is literally a book in another language: Breeze argues that the "Britoun book, written with Evaungiles" is best understood as a Gospel book "in Latin, written and illuminated in the Celtic manner."[56] The presence of this Latin book can signify not only justice and a means of conversion but also learning that is transmitted by the Britons to their Saxon successors.[57] As a result, the book itself signifies the "meene while"—the time during which Christian Britons were absent from the scene

---

54. Cooney argues that Chaucer's version of the trial contrasts sharply with Trevet's in terms of how divine justice signifies ("Wonder and Immanent Justice," 270). Lavezzo argues that the juridical is central to the story as a whole. See Lavezzo, *Angels on the Edge of the World* and "Beyond Rome."

55. See Dugas, "Legitimization of Royal Power," 35. Dugas writes that the book "functions as a symbol of both past and future."

56. Breeze, "Celtic Gospels," 336. Cooper argues that this marks an instance where problematic translation is foregrounded without comment ("Translating Custance," 28).

57. Dugas identifies the Britoun book as a moment of *translatio imperii* within the *Man of Law's Tale* (Dugas, "Legitimization of Royal Power.")

but destined to return. It calls together a community that exists across time and linguistic difference: Christian Britons and their books are connected to the future Saxons who will, through an interaction with this specific Gospel book, eventually join a transtemporal Christian community. Moreover, the difference between Briton language and Saxon language will ultimately be erased: the Gospel book itself, of course, is most likely in Latin.

The Britoun book is the medium through which God works vengeance on the false knight, but its significance exceeds the divine intervention its use brings about. The book that appears in Chaucer's account derives from Trevet's version of the story, which notes that the knight "en hast prist entre ses mains le livere l'evesque Lucius, avantnomé, q'estoit livre des Evangeils, quel les seint femmes Hermegild et Constaunce, chescune nuyt par devocion avoient en costé eles" (309.241–44) [took in his hands the book of the aforesaid Bishop Lucius, which was a book of the gospels that the holy women Hermegild and Constance had beside them every night for devotion (308)]. Although Bishop Lucius is the priest brought back to Olda and Hermegild to baptize them and is described earlier as a "un evesqe Bruton" (307.195) [British bishop (306)], Trevet distances the book from its British origins and does not designate the book *itself* as British.[58] Moreover, the miraculous testimony from on high referred to in Trevet's version of the story also differs from the account in Chaucer's tale: it reflects different sentiments and occurs in a different language, averring, "Adversus filiam matris ecclesie ponebas scandalum; hoc fecisti et non tacui" (311.251–52) [You were placing a stumbling block against the daughter of mother Church; this you have done and I have not remained silent (308–10)]. The words of God gloss the action of his vengeance explicitly; however, they do so in Latin, highlighting a linguistic difference between the characters in the story and the church that eventually unites them. Similarly, Gower's version of the narrative glosses divine retribution quite directly and furthermore demands that the false knight testify to his own guilt.[59]

Chaucer's representation of the book, however, occasions a very different interpretation of God's intervening words: "Thou has desclaundred, giltelees, / The doghter of hooly chirche in heighe presence; / Thus hastou doon, and yet holde I my pees!" (II.674–76). As in the version by Trevet, the knight's false oath occasions direct glossing and interpretation by God himself, but this time the words come out somewhat strangely. God claims to hold his peace

---

58. Gower's version of the story omits the book's origin, referring to it simply as "a bok" (335.868).

59. See 335.880–83.

but does nothing of the sort.⁶⁰ In fact, he breaks his silence just as he says he does in Trevet, through both words and actions. This use of both the Britoun book and God's glossing of his actions demonstrate another contour of the translation effect marked by the book. In this case, the book connects the all-seeing authority of God with the earthly unfolding of events. Less intertextual or transtemporal than transdimensional, the translation effect of the Britoun book allows a community to come together—through divine intervention—in a soon-to-be shared system of beliefs.⁶¹

Both Chaucer's "Britoun book" and Trevet's "book of the Bishop Lucius" figure in the same punishment of the false knight, but the context and background for the book alters the portrayal of linguistic and cultural difference in the *Man of Law's Tale*. It does so in part because the interpretation of the book is central to Alla's conversion. The false knight's oath occasions a miracle, and this miracle in turn converts the king:

> And for this miracle, in conclusioun,
> And by Custances mediacioun,
> The kyng—and many another in that place—
> Converted was, thanked be Cristes grace!
> (II.683–86)

Alla's conversion takes place because of the miracle, but the miracle—and God's divine judgment—is mediated through the Britoun book. Thus, the book itself marks conversion as a byproduct of the continued presence of Christian Britons who had remained in England "for the meene while." Even Custance's "mediacioun" in the conversion seems to be particularly passive.⁶² In the *Chronicle*, by contrast, Ælle is not converted until somewhat later in the text. This lack of immediacy removes the question of the role that the holy book plays, instead focusing first on Constance and Ælle's love for her, and only then on God's miracles. Chaucer's alterations here suggest that we can understand Custance as mediating not only between God and the Saxons but also between the Britons and the Saxons. Custance provides the necessary provocation for both the blind Briton's cure and the Britoun book's mediation of God's vengeance. The role of the Saxons in this conversion becomes a secondary concern. As a result, the community that emerges in the text does

---

60. See *MED Online*, s.v. *pes⁷*. *Pes* does have several variant meanings including "the peace resulting from the observation of God's will" (s.v. *pes²*).
61. In Gower, God's demand that the knight make known "the sothe er that thou dye" (335.880–83) amplifies the glossing effect of the divine intervention.
62. See Raybin, "Custance and History."

so as a multicultural and multilingual construction. Both Roman and Briton influences are necessary to bring England into being. They fulfill their function through the Christianity that links them with a shared faith, brought together through the material translation effect of the Britoun book.

CONCLUSION: FROM BRUTAGNE TO ENGLETERRE

John Bowers argues that Chaucer's *Man of Law's Tale* is an explicit "rejection of Bede's authoritative Latin account" of the conversion of the English—an assertion that would complicate matters deeply, were it true.[63] Although there is no concrete evidence that Chaucer knew Bede's version of the story of Saint Gregory the Great and the angelic Angles in the Roman slave market, Trevet not only knew but expanded upon the traditional version of the story, whether learned from Bede or elsewhere. In the *Historia Ecclesiastica*, Bede makes a distinct break with the past as he considers the unfolding inheritance of Christianity. The Britons fail in their primary mission as Christians because they do not convert the Angles and Saxons—as a result, Bede identifies the conquering Saxons as the *dignore gens*—worthier people (*HE* I.22.68). Because they are chosen by God to replace the Britons and spread Christianity in a way that Bede claims the Britons did not, they have a similarly prestigious patron: Saint Gregory the Great. Although Bede is careful to note that "alios [. . .] praedicatores mittens" (II.1.134) [he sent other preachers (135)], he avers that Gregory "ipse praedicationem ut fructificaret suis exhortationibus ac precibus adiuuans" (II.1.134) [himself helped their preaching to bear fruit by his encouragement and prayers (135)]. Bede's alignment of the Saxons with both God's will and the will of Pope Saint Gregory the Great suggests a lofty inheritance for English Christianity that comes to pass as a result of the supersession of its British past.[64]

This idea of the Britons having lost their sovereignty over the island as part of their failure as Christians is central to Trevet's version of the story of Gregory, as well as his version of the Constance legend (as discussed above). However, as Robert Correale observes, "whatever other sources Trevet used in fashioning his story of Constance, he was influenced to a larger extent than [previous critics] have realized by people and events recorded elsewhere in

---

63. Bowers, "Colonialism, Latinity, and Resistance," in Fein and Raybin, *Chaucer: Contemporary Approaches*, 128.

64. See Lees, "In Ælfric's Words," in Magennis and Swan, *Companion to Ælfric*; Lavezzo, *Angels on the Edge of the World*.

his own chronicle."[65] Correale comments specifically on Trevet's use and reuse of words and descriptions. The statement applies equally well, however, to the content of the work—the events that Trevet deemed worthy of record and comment. That is, Trevet returns to certain themes elsewhere in his *Chronicle* that are persistently present in "Of the Noble Lady Constance." The most important of these for my argument concerns the history of Northumbria and the role the Saxons play in the eventual conversion of England: a byproduct of the idea that the Britons' failure as Christians related to their failure as rulers. A brief account of these ideas brings the consideration of the past offered by Trevet, Chaucer, and Gower into a wider context of thinking about pre-Conquest England in the fourteenth century.

The *Chronicle* displays a sustained interest in pre-Conquest Christianity in England. It does so by incorporating biblical materials into regnal lists and by relating an account of the conversion quite similar to the one found in Bede's *Historia Ecclesiastica* and elsewhere. Trevet uses regnal lists in the *Chronicle* to create a myth of English origin that blends biblical traditions with Germanic mythology. For example, the genealogical lists in his account of the Kingdom of Wessex participate in a long-established tradition that traces the descent of the royal houses of England back to the Norse god Woden:

Le primer roi apelé Cerdyk, le fitz Elesa, qe fu le fitz Elsa, qe fu le fitz Gemmus, qe fu le fitz Wyg, qe fu le fitz Ffrewyn, qe fu le fitz Ffredegar, qe fu le fitz Broand, qe fu le fitz Beldeg, qe fu le fitz Woden, pere de plusours rois, qe estoit del linage Sem le fitz Noe, si come est escript en l'estoire de Sem q'est en le livre de Genesis. (189.24–190.1)

The first king was called Cerdyk, the son of Elesa, who was the son of Elsa, who was the son of Gemmus, who was the son of Wyg, who was the son of Ffrewyn, who was the son of Ffredegar, who was the son of Broand, who was the son of Beldeg, who was the son of Woden, father of many kings, who was of the lineage of Shem, the son of Noah, as it is written in the story of Shem that is in the Book of Genesis.

As Robin Fleming has suggested, in the case of early medieval English kings, a regnal list can convey "political ideology and invention rather than blood."[66] In

---

65. Correale and Hamel, *Sources and Analogues*, 2:284.
66. Fleming, *Kings and Lords*, 3. Moreover, the genealogies of the royal houses of "Bernician, Kentish, East Anglian, Mercian and Deiran dynasties (cc. 57–61) all trace their descent from the Germanic god, Woden" (Brooks, *Anglo-Saxon Myths*, 85). See also Dumville, "Kingship, Genealogies, and Regnal Lists," in Sawyer and Wood, *Early Medieval Kingship*.

the genealogy reported by Trevet, Woden is related directly to Noah. This regnal list participates in a longer tradition of genealogical listings, in which "all Angles and Saxons [. . .] were thus presented as related through both Adam and Scef (Scyf)—through both Christian and Germanic lines."[67] Although Trevet substitutes the biblical son of Noah named Shem for Scef (who was also considered a son of Noah in some early medieval English regnal genealogies), the way in which his genealogy blends Germanic and Christian traditions implies "the existence of an order of identity which understands a common religious past and a common ethnic past."[68] This order of identity informs Trevet's understanding of the history of Christianity in pre-Conquest England.

Trevet's representation of the conversion process in "Of the Noble Lady Constance" is also partially influenced by his earlier portrayal of the events that surround the conversion of Northumbria. At the behest of Saint Gregory, Augustine of Canterbury was sent to England in the sixth century to convert the people living there. According to legend, Gregory makes this decision because of an encounter he has with some enslaved English people in a market in Rome. Trevet's rendition of the story is for the most part quite similar to the one familiar from Bede, but he adds a significant pun that is not present in the *Historia*:

> Demaunda qi ceux enfauntz estoient, et homme lui respoundi q'il estoient Engleis. Et il demaunda de quele province de la terre, et hom lui dist de Deyra, q'est un pais de Northumbreland, et qe lour roi estoit Alla. Lors dit Seint Gregoire qe droit serroit qe Anglay fuissent associétz as aungels, et qe lour terre estoit ja nomé Engleterre et pur cel encheson estoit la terre de Brutaigne desormé apelé Engleterre, et qe ceux de Deyra fuissent deliveréz de yre, et qe les suggéz le roi Alle fuissent apris chaunter Alleluia, et maintenant surpris de la beaute dez enfauntz q'il appela aungeles. (199.16–30)

> He asked who the children were, and a man replied that they were English. And he asked from which province of the land, and a man said from Deira, which is a country in Northumbria, and that their king was Alla. Then Saint Gregory said that it was right that the English be associated with angels, and that their land be called England; and for that reason from then on the land of Britain would be called England, and that the Deira should be delivered from the wrath [of God], and that the name of Alla suggested it was meant

---

67. Harris, *Race and Ethnicity in Anglo-Saxon Literature*, 87.
68. Harris, 87.

to be "to sing Alleluia," and he was surprised by the beauty of the children that he called angels.

Despite writing in Anglo-Norman rather than Bede's Latin, Trevet carefully retains the linguistic games that make this section of Bede's *Historia Ecclesiastica* so remarkable. These English angels must be saved from the wrath of God, with the Latin *de ire* converting the kingdom of the Deirans. Gregory states that they ought be made to sing "Alleluia" in accordance with the name of their king, Ælle. All of these puns appear in the *Historia* as well, but Trevet includes one additional linguistic transformation.[69] This metaphorical conversion takes place between the term "Brutaigne" and "Engleterre" in its final lines. The change in terminology moves English Christianity away from its British roots. Britain becomes England: the land of the Angles.

Trevet extends Gregory's linguistic conversions from the name of a people and their king to the name of the country from which they hail.[70] In so doing, he also makes a claim for a different kind of inheritance: the association of land, religion, and linguistic identity.[71] The conversion of "Brutaigne" to "Engleterre" marks a characteristic moment of Trevet's understanding of how Christianity in England is established and sustained in "Of the Noble Lady Constance." Although the *Man of Law's Tale* presents a story of the conversion of the English set largely pre-Conquest, the rest of the *Canterbury Tales* does not address the Saxons at all.[72] On the one hand, Trevet's treatment of pre-Conquest history and the development of "Engleterre" from "Brutaigne" emphasizes the rupture in Christian faith that allows Rome to convert the Saxons directly and ultimately transfer religious authority to them. Chaucer, on the other hand, includes the Britons that Trevet's understanding of the story minimizes and so connects the eventual emergence of "Engelonde" in the *Man of Law's Tale* with a Christian past that begins and lingers in the geographical boundaries of the island.

---

69. See Colgrave and Mynors, *Bede's Ecclesiastical History*, II.1.134. Although Bede includes the puns on *Angli*, *Deiri*, and *Ælle*, he does not include any mention of the conversion between "Brutaigne" and "Engleterre."

70. Lees argues that a similar movement in Ælfric's *Life of Gregory* sees that "the nation of the English—as people, land and language—has [. . .] retrospectively co-opted" both Britain and Deira ("In Ælfric's Words," in Magennis and Swan, *Companion to Ælfric*, 285).

71. Hastings argues that these are the hallmarks of a protonation (*Construction of Nationhood*, 35–65). This is also quite similar to Nakley's claim that Chaucer "renders the British past capable of producing an English future" (*Living in the Future*, 152). For Chaucer's nationalist impulses in the narrative, see Heng, *Empire of Magic*, 181–237.

72. Possible exceptions might be made with the brief mention of Edward the Confessor in the *Monk's Tale* or the story of St. Kenelm.

The journey that converts a non-Christian Northumbrian kingdom into a Christian England has different valences in Trevet, Gower, and Chaucer—valences made accessible by the methods each writer utilizes to deploy translation and translation effects, but not reducible to them. By emphasizing the lapse of Christianity in Northumbria as a traversable space—a departure from destiny only "for the meene while"—the *Man of Law's Tale* focuses not on the breaks in the narrative of Northumbria's eventual conversion but on what still remains there. Like the translation it evokes but also distances itself from, the *Man of Law's Tale* invests itself not in the particularity of the past but in the way that past will be deployed to create a new future—and a new Christian community. Custance's role of "mediacioun," the Britons who take refuge in Wales "for the meene while," and the facilitation of the Britoun book all create these connections between the non-Christian past of Northumbria and its English, Christian future. The *Man of Law's Tale*, by its insistence on the intersections between past, present, and future Christianity in the narrative, redeems the lapse of evangelical zeal that Bede argues led to the Britons' loss of power without ever needing to refer to it. Moreover, it demonstrates the stakes of translation and the translation effects that highlight both translation's presence and its problematic absence. Translation is necessary to the narrative—but it is also fundamentally not Chaucer's main point in retelling it. Ultimately, the Christian Britons bring England's destiny to pass, and the story of Custance becomes a story not only of a holy woman, but of a holy England.[73] My consideration of these three texts in terms of their representation of Northumbria reveals the distinct methods by which they each consider the emergence of a community in translation, an emergence that differs in its specifics but that ultimately leads in a single direction: from Alla's "Northumberlond" to Chaucer's "Engelonde."

---

73. Heng, *Empire of Magic*, 237. See also Nakely, *Living in the Future*, 151–79. I modify her linking of a "British past [to an] English future" (152), however, in order to foreground the differing aims of Trevet, Gower, and Chaucer in their renderings of that past.

CHAPTER 5

Beowulf's Collectivities

> Awareness of historical change, of the pastness of a
> past that itself has depth, is not instinctive to man;
> there is nothing natural about a sense of history.
> —ROBERTA FRANK[1]

FROM ITS OUTSET, *Beowulf* serves as a meditation on the enduring power of stories:

Hwæt, we Gar-Dena in geardagum,
þeodcyninga þrym gefrunon,
hu ða æþelingas ellen fremedon.
Oft Scyld Scefing sceaþena þreatum,
monegum mægþum meodosetla ofteah,
egsode eorl[as], syððan ærest wearð
feasceaft funden. He þæs frofre gebad:
weox under wolcnum, weorðmyndum þah,
oð þæt him æghwylc þara ymbsittendra
ofer hronrade hyran scolde,
gomban gyldan. Þæt wæs god cyning.
(1–11)[2]

Hwæt! We have heard of the glory of the Spear-Danes, the kings of the people, in days of yore—how the princes performed deeds of courage! Often

---

1. Frank, "Sense of History," in *Beowulf*, trans. Heaney, ed. Donoghue, 168.
2. The Old English text of *Beowulf* is drawn from Fulk et al., *Klaeber's Beowulf*.

> Scyld Scefing seized mead-benches from enemy troops, from many a clan, he terrified warriors, after he was first found bereft, helpless. For that he experienced comfort, and he grew under skies, prospered in honors until every last one of the bordering nations beyond the whale-road had to obey him, pay him tribute. He was a good king.

We have heard, the poem suggests, of a number of different groups: the Spear-Danes, the kings of the people who performed great deeds, the terrified warriors, and the bordering nations across the "whale-road."[3] These groups exist primarily in relationship to Scyld Scefing. He terrifies earls and forces bordering nations to pay tribute to him. The poem describes these groups not by their separation, but by what brings them into relationship with one another. Scyld, violence and all, creates community.

In addition to the sets of people defined by their relationship to Scyld, the initial lines of *Beowulf* identify two other groups that rely on one another in order to be remembered. Scyld Scefing is a Spear-Dane, and his great feats are known through story, as are others performed by those "kings of the people." Yet the poem waits until its fourth line before identifying this *god cyning* [good king] and his deeds. Until this point, *Gar-dene* [Spear-Danes] is governed only by its relationship to what *we gefrunon* [we have heard]. At the poem's outset, then, the recollection of the existence of the Spear-Danes is dependent on the "we" who hear (or have heard) the story of their glories. Without this "we"—the second group hypothesized by the text—there might not be stories of the Spear-Danes at all. They require the transmission of narrative to be remembered.[4]

The "we" of *Beowulf's* opening lines stands in stark contrast to the "oure occian" that appears in the *Man of Law's Tale,* discussed in the preceding chapter. Rather than highlighting a community that endures across time, *Beowulf* emphasizes the fragility of this "we" and its composition. The poem characterizes the group designated by "we" through its knowledge: it has been the audience of the stories in question.[5] The stories are comprised of narratives about

---

3. For the grammatical complexity of these lines, see Blockley, *Aspects of Old English Poetic Syntax,* 195–213. Gates notes that these opening lines "[invite] reflection on community and deeds through memory" ("Discursive Murders," in Tracy, *Medieval and Early Modern Murder,* 55).

4. My interest in the possible resonances of these lines was first piqued by Carol Braun Pasternack, who made the argument that the intial "we" of the poem—for a brief moment—leads a reader or listener to expect that "we" ourselves are Spear-Danes. Pasternack, "Is Beowulf Postmodern Yet? A Roundtable."

5. See Liuzza, who argues that "the first-person plural [assumes] a common identity with his audience" ("Monuments, Memory, and History," in Johnson and Treharne, *Readings in Medieval Texts,* 92).

Spear-Danes, Scyld, and deeds of glory performed in the past. What is absent from its bounds is the story of *Beowulf* itself. The story of the hero commences after these introductory lines: therefore, "we" have not heard of Beowulf, or at least have not heard of him yet. Further complicating matters, the "we" who have heard these stories depends on a conflation of the time of the poem's narration and the time during which these stories are set. The poem implies that the "we" in question is temporally remote from not only the earlier events of Scyld Scefing's life but also the stories told about him.[6] Extended through the iterations of multiple performances, this "we" is always subject to the end of either the poem or its reading and the dispersal of its audience(s).[7]

Even the network of Spear-Dane stories that are part of this body of knowledge is fragile. *Beowulf* frames the text as a narrative with an audience that has heard or read other stories, related to but distinct from the heroic matter at hand. To a modern reader, of course, the frame that includes us as part of this "we" is fictive. We have not necessarily heard of the glories of the Spear-Danes, and though we know analogues for the story of Beowulf, there is no extant direct source.[8] Even at the time of its writing, however, the community designated by "we have heard" was narratively constructed by the references to Scyld Scefing and his childhood, career, and death.[9] The community that "has heard" the stories of Scyld is not the community Scyld himself created; rather, this narrative refers outward to a different set of peoples and times, and a community that inherits both the conditions of the past and the stories told about it.[10] Its placement at the beginning of *Beowulf* belies this disconnection. Moreover, although it is written in Old English, *Beowulf* is not about England or its inhabitants.[11] It relates a narrative about what Nicholas Howe has termed the English "ancestral homeland,"[12] but in doing so, it also creates

---

6. Most famously, Tolkien argues that *Beowulf* was "when new [. . .] already antiquarian" ("Monsters and the Critics," in *Beowulf*, trans. Heaney, ed. Donoghue, 138).

7. See Gates, who notes that this raises questions about "what *wē* as a community are supposed to recall about the stories *wē* know about the Danes," ("Discursive Murders," 56).

8. See Harris, "Nativist Approach," in Aertson and Bremmer, *Companion to Old English Poetry*; North, *Origins of Beowulf*; Frank, "Germanic Legend," in Godden and Lapidge, *Cambridge Companion to Old English Literature*. See also Niles, *Beowulf*; Dumville, "*Beowulf* and the Celtic World."

9. This is not, of course, to say that stories about Scyld did not circulate. Rather, I argue that what matters most deeply about such stories is how they function *in the present story*—their narratological effect on the poem.

10. See Frank, "Sense of History," in *Beowulf*, trans. Heaney, ed. Donoghue.

11. See Orchard, *Critical Companion*, 203–37.

12. See Howe, *Migration and Mythmaking*, 143–80. Howe argues that *Beowulf* refers to an "ancestral homeland" best described as preconversion Germania. The poet "has a culturally imposed concern with the continuing history of the pagan north because it offers some vision of what the Anglo-Saxons might have become had they not made their exodus" (146).

a new community of listeners through narrative. As a result, it demonstrates the pervasive power of shared narratives in such communities.

Why include a text like *Beowulf* in this study? *Beowulf* is not a translation.[13] Yet *Beowulf* deploys a myriad of translation *effects* to imagine possible communities. A hybrid product of orality and textuality, tradition and innovation, *Beowulf* is a textual space in which the process of community formation and dissolution is worked out through the telling and retelling of stories.[14] This process becomes legible because of the translation effects that indicate its operation. By following their signal, we see how the poem creates a vision of—and a warning about—communities that rely on such narratives to survive even as they fundamentally misunderstand them. That these misunderstandings are rooted in the inherent possibility of alterations—intentional or not—each time knowledge is passed from one person or medium to another simply underscores how thematically essential translation and its effects are to the poem.

Because of the unique status of *Beowulf* in this study—a text that is not a translation but that partakes of the same cultural logic as traditional translations—the translation effects used in the poem take a different form than many of those described in previous chapters. *Beowulf*'s translation effects highlight moments in which inherited narratives are actively passed down within the poem. This admittedly more metaphorical dimension of translation effects draws attention to narrative transmission even when linguistic difference is elided. The translation effects in *Beowulf* emphasize not the ability of narratives to shore up communities but rather the often-unintended consequences of relying on such stories to build group identities. These inherited narratives are most prominent in the poem's famed "digressions," segments of the poem that do not actively involve the exploits of Beowulf in the narrative present.[15] Despite their divergence from the poem's plot, the digressions are intimately related to *Beowulf*'s purpose, amplifying and refining the major foci of the poem.[16]

In this chapter, I examine several of these episodes in detail. I argue that because these digressions are often framed as inherited narratives that empha-

---

13. See, among others, Howe, 174: "Its language bears no mark of translation."

14. See Foley, *Traditional Oral Epic*; Niles, *Beowulf*.

15. See Bonjour, *Digressions in Beowulf*. More recently, Cronan has suggested using the term "para-narrative" rather than digression ("Narrative Disjunctions," 460). I retain the traditional term because it highlights the critical side-lining of received narratives. For a reading of how digressions intersect with history and memory in the narrative, see Liuzza, "Monuments, Memory, and History," in Johnson and Treharne, *Readings in Medieval Texts*.

16. For example, see Karkov and Farrell, "Gnomic Passages of *Beowulf*"; Parks, "Ring Structure and Narrative Embedding"; Crépin, "L'Espace du texte."

size the stories of communities that for one reason or another are threatened and do not endure, they demonstrate how the poem thematizes narrative transmission and its vicissitudes. The sheer number of these stories demonstrates the poem's pervasive obsession with such fragility. Moreover, they reveal a latent conflict in the text between human communities and the seemingly outside forces that threaten to disperse them. By systematically tracing the connections between humans, monsters (the Grendelkin and the dragon), objects (swords, treasure, the earth), and animals (particularly the Beasts of Battle), I highlight this thematic fragility of communities in the poem. The narrative digressions become the territory in which *Beowulf* explores the construction of human group identities and the affiliations on which such identities rely, whether such affiliations are explicit or covert.

The translation effects in *Beowulf*, I argue, foreground collectivity—a grouping that includes both human and nonhuman actors—rather than community.[17] Such groupings include associations that occur over a longer temporal span than the human communities in the poem are either aware of or account for in their activities. Collectivity therefore underlies, and in several cases undermines, the stability of communities in the poem. Ultimately, these human group identities are as contingent as the "we" without whom their stories would have no listener.

SYMPATHY FOR THE DEVIL

My consideration of the translation effects in *Beowulf* moves from narratives that focus on the more human participants in collectivity to those that focus on the less human ones. These narratives depend on different kinds of temporality, while also relying on figures of both narrative inheritance and the failure of community. I begin with Grendel, who through his catastrophic entrance into the hall repeatedly upsets King Hrothgar's hopes of establishing a more stable community. Grendel's attack introduces the mythic time of the biblical narrative of origins into the poem, muddling distinctions between Christian and non-Christian times and peoples.[18]

---

17. I borrow the terms "collective" and "collectivity" from Actor-Network Theory. See, for example, Latour, *Reassembling the Social* and *Pandora's Hope*. I am not the first to apply a new materialist lens to the poem. For thing theory, see Paz, "Unreadable Things in *Beowulf*." For an approach that draws on the idea of "vibrant" objects, see Hostetter, "Disruptive Things." For a useful introduction to new materialism and the premodern text, see Robertson, "Medieval Things."

18. See Osborn, "Scriptural History." Osborn argues, moreover, that a lack of understanding of Christian, revealed knowledge dooms the characters of the poem (979).

The first translation effect in this part of the poem takes the form of the Creation Song of the scop, recited in the hall just before Grendel's attack. The scop's story retells the Genesis version of the creation of the world. In addition to being an inherited narrative, the Creation Song functions as a translation effect because it draws attention to a moment in which linguistic and cultural differences are elided (similar to the absence of translation among the merchants in the *Man of Law's Tale,* examined in Chapter Four). The biblical version of Genesis—familiar not just to modern critics but also to the poem's audience—would necessitate some form of translation, which the poem performs without remarking on it.[19] Moreover, the poem's version of the creation story continues beyond the one that appears in Genesis 1.1, including the narrative of Cain and Abel that occurs later in Genesis. In this context, monsters, through their proximity to and conflict with human communities, come to signify the longer temporal spans of collectivity that the translation effects in *Beowulf* reveal.[20]

The Creation Song emphasizes Grendel's proximity to Heorot. Through a series of narrative juxtapositions, the poem simultaneously relates a foundational myth and encourages its audience to reinterpret it. It does so by framing its subject as a meditation on how human communities cohere by expelling alterity.[21] Here, the translation effect is indicated in its most trenchant form: a single phrase, "sægde se þe cuðe" (90b) [he said, he who knew] that indicates narrative transmission. Forming a boundary between the scop's song and the narrative of the rest of *Beowulf,* this line establishes both the point of view that governs the Creation Song and the boundaries that limit the story's circulation. The point of view this phrase emphasizes—that of humans—is already identified as only one possible point of view for the narrative. Because Grendel—"se þe in þystrum bad" (87b) [he who in darkness dwelled]—hears the narrative of creation, its meaning changes from a story of Christian origins to a story of unending enmity between human beings and monsters. Grendel's presence at its recitation makes the destruction of community a direct result of the narrative that attempts to exclude him.

---

19. The note in *Klaeber's Beowulf* gives the consensus on this allusion, declaring it "obviously based on Gen.1." (121n90–98).

20. See Niles, *Beowulf,* 183: "The Grendel episode [. . .] is presented in terms that identify it as a latter-day resurfacing of a feud that began with Cain's killing of Abel and resumed with the giants' war against God." See also Adam Miyashiro, "Homeland Insecurity." Miyashiro relates the Grendelkin not only to biblical history but to biopolitics and theories of sovereignty.

21. My argument here follows O'Brien O'Keeffe, who argues that "Grendel is at his most terrifying not in the marches but in the place of men. [. . .] It is the grotesque parody of the human in Grendel which repels us and draws us forward" ("Transformations and the Limits of the Human," 492).

While the Creation Song relates a very specific shared narrative, it also generates narrative ambiguities. These ambiguities result from a relationship between men and monsters that exists on a temporal scale that exceeds the experience of a single human life. The song explains the proper position of humans in the world as part of God's creation, proclaiming that

> se ælmihtiga eorðan worh(te),
> wlitebeorhtne wang, swa wæter bebugeð,
> gesette sigehreþig sunnan ond monan
> leoman to leohte landbuendum
> (92–95)

> the Almighty made the earth, the brightly-beautiful plain which the waters surround; he set victory-triumphant the sun and the moon, lights to make light for the land-dwellers.

The presence of a predominantly Christian narrative in Hrothgar's court complicates the understanding of whether the Danes, Hrothgar, or simply the poet himself is Christian.[22] Regardless of the religion practiced in Heorot, the scriptural reference serves as a moment of temporal heterogeneity, a mixing of times that is indicated by a story that might not even be possible to tell.

The Creation Song's seeming insistence on a Christian God and worldview finds an intensification in its juxtaposition with the allusion to the narrative of Cain and Abel in lines 107b–10. Most critical interpretations of the text suggest that the conjunction of this story and the attack on Heorot makes the distinction between humans and the Grendelkin more firm by situating their mutual enmity in biblical history.[23] The event can also be read typologically: the hall at Heorot becomes a kind of church and Grendel's attack is similar to the attack of Cain on Abel (which could also represent attacks on the church by unholy forces).[24] These readings assert a distinction between

---

22. Cavill argues that the poem expresses the view of the writer in this section, who allows "the Danish *scop* [to] sing of the creation as the writer believed it really happened" (Cavill, "Christianity and Theology," in Cavill, *Christian Tradition*, 25). Osborn argues that the truths the Creation Song conveys are not truths that must apply to the poem's characters; rather, the recitation of the song creates a kind of temporal heterogeneity (Osborn, "Scriptural History," 974–75). See also Benson, "Pagan Coloring of *Beowulf*," in Baker, *Beowulf: Basic Readings*; Irving, "Nature of Christianity"; Major, "Syncretism in *Beowulf*;" Irving, "Christian and Pagan Elements," in Bjork and Niles, *Beowulf Handbook*.

23. Cohen argues, "The giant builds the home [. . .] but the giant destroys the home too" (*Of Giants*, 10). See also Niles, *Beowulf*; Friedman, *Monstrous Races*, 84.

24. See Helder, "Song of Creation," 252–53.

Cain's kin, which includes the Grendelkin, and the humans against whom they fight. However, the narrative juxtaposition of the song of creation and Grendel's attack reaches beyond a reflexive mirroring of the Genesis story by highlighting the problematic proximity of Grendel to the poem's human protagonists. The disjunctive association of the two is amplified by the story of Cain and his kin.

These two creation narratives—that of humans and that of monsters—demonstrate the temporal depth that intrudes into the narrative present of *Beowulf*.[25] Whereas the scop's Creation Song introduces the typical catalogue of creation, the story of Cain and his exile from humanity is one of counter-creation. Because Cain kills his favored brother, he is subsequently "marked" for not only murder but fratricide: "Þone cwealm gewræc / ece drihten, þæs þe he Abel slog" (107b-108) [the eternal Lord avenged that death, because he slew Abel].[26] Medieval authors considered this "mark of Cain" to be the origin of monsters, and thus to solidify the difference between monsters and human beings.[27] The poem confirms this view, noting that after the crime and Cain's subsequent exile a variety of monsters arise:

> Þanon untydras   ealle onwocon,
> eotenas ond ylfe   ond orcneas,
> swylce gi(ga)ntas,   þa wið Gode wunnon
> lange þrage.
> (111–14a)

> From that one all kinds of monsters were born, giants and elves and evil spirits, and also giants, who long struggled against God.

Grendel is one of these creatures, and he dwells at the margins of human society in the moorlands that lie outside of Heorot.[28] In one sense, there is outright opposition between the world within the hall and the world that Grendel inhabits; as Jennifer Neville argues, the world outside the hall is the place of monsters, darkness, and chaos.[29] Yet the question of perspective must be

---

25. "The mythic past is thus important for its potential 'presentness' as well" (Niles, *Beowulf*, 183). See also Frank, "Sense of History," in *Beowulf*, trans. Heaney, ed. Donoghue.

26. See Friedman, *Monstrous Races*, 95; Orchard, *Pride and Prodigies*.

27. See Friedman, *Monstrous Races*; Cohen, *Of Giants*; Mittman, *Maps and Monsters*.

28. The poem describes him as "se þe moras heold, / fen ond fæsten; fifelcynnes eard / wonsæli wer weardode hwile" (103b–105) [he who held the moors, the fens and the swamps; the unhappy man occupied for a time the home of monsters].

29. Neville, *Representations of the Natural World*. See also Bintley, "Where the Wild Things Are," in Bintley and Williams, *Representing Beasts*.

examined: the world outside the hall signifies such negative things from a human perspective, the only perspective the poem can adequately address. On a purely textual level, the poem posits two groups that stand in outright opposition to one another, humans and monsters, with the clear suggestion that the reader or listener ought to be on the side of humans. Yet even as it juxtaposes these groups, the poem also models the link between them and the temporal point of view necessary to ascertain it. From the human point of view of community, Grendel represents the chaos which comes from outside the hall to disrupt life within it. Put into a larger temporal context, however, it becomes clear that Grendel's connection to the human community he attacks predates the specific situation of Heorot. He is connected to humans as a result of his lineage: his proximity, theologically, is inscribed in the story of Cain and the monsters that proceed from him.[30]

The placement of the Creation Song alongside the story of how monsters were created emphasizes a longer view of history that is not confined to the time of humans and their halls. Grendel's proximity to the hall proceeds from a view that exceeds the knowledge of the characters in the poem. It encourages the reader to acknowledge not only the close relationship of monsters and humans but also the possible iniquities that can come from it. The poem creates this possibility through an ambiguity in the point of view from which the audience metaphorically hears the creation sequence: from within the hall or outside of it. Is the reader or listener meant to be inside with the warriors or outside with Grendel? The paired phrases mentioned previously suggest how complex this question really is. The scop's narrative begins at line 90b, with "sægde, *se þe cuðe*" [he said, *he who* knew] (*emphasis mine*). The conjunction of this phrasing with one that appears three lines earlier, "*se þe* in þystrum bad," (87b) [*he who* in darkness dwelled] (*emphasis mine*), reveals the possibility that the reader or listener can "hear" the Creation Song as Grendel does—that is, from the point of view of "he who in darkness dwelled" and "dogora gehwam dream gehyrde / hludne in healle" (88–89a) [each of days heard joy, noise in the hall].[31] The earlier line conditions the reception of the Creation Song, in part because the song in question is repeatable. Grendel hears the noise more than once—possibly quite often.[32] The designation

---

30. Saltzman argues that the relationship between Grendel and Cain is related to the "criminality of concealment" that both participate in ("Secrecy and the Hermeneutic Potential," 41).

31. As O'Brien O'Keeffe argues, Grendel takes on increasing reality and threat as he approaches the hall ("Tranformations and the Limits of the Human," 492). Cronan links Grendel's first attack to his anger at the hall ("Essential Incongruities," 634).

32. Lerer argues that Grendel "has taken back the landscape, made himself now the ruler of this stead" ("On fagne flor," in Kabir and Williams, *Postcolonial Approaches*, 87).

"each of days" can thus comprise a dual set of references. It refers to the lapse between the first time the noise of the hall was overheard by Grendel and the present in which it provokes his attack. Moreover, it refers to the iterative nature of the noise in the hall.[33] Rather than representing an isolated incident, this part of the poem describes a recurring event that builds to the attack on Heorot. The sweet singing and harp-noise (lines 89–90)—the song of *he who knew*—are framed by the agony that the music causes for Grendel—*he who* dwells in darkness but also *he who* must know the song after all those recountings. The two become difficult to separate.

By putting the attack on Heorot within the context of Grendel hearing and being provoked by the hall joys of the human beings therein, and by drawing attention to its iterative nature, the poem pushes its reader to consider the monster's relationship to his human prey. Moreover, it asks the reader to question how long that relationship has lasted and therefore how much noise Grendel has endured and for how long.[34] Grendel's prolonged presence outside the hall changes the reception of the Creation Song in part because the narrative has a longer history that includes monsters like him alongside the humans who are the poem's protagonists. Grendel hears and responds violently to the human song that excludes him.[35] This episode thus highlights a gap in the knowledge of human communities, a gap through which the monster can make a riotous and disastrous reassertion of his connection to them.[36] The question that remains concerns the consequences of that longer temporality in the poem's present. When Grendel hears and reacts to the hall joys and song, the past enmity between monsters and humans becomes a present concern of the community he attacks, regardless of whether it has the temporal perspective necessary to acknowledge it.

These connections are the same ones that doom all human attempts to construct meaning in a frame of reference larger than the purely human.[37]

---

33. Hill describes the iterative nature of these hall-songs as "the kind of song here apparently sung daily" ("Social and Dramatic Functions," 310).

34. Grendel's pain from the hall noise is depicted quite forcefully in the 2008 Zemeckis film *Beowulf*. See also Lerer, who suggests that the noise hurts Grendel ("On fagne flor," in Kabir and Williams, *Postcolonial Approaches*, 85–86), and Cronan, "Essential Incongruities."

35. See Scribner, who argues that "it is possible that his rage is actually roused at the content of the song" ("Signs, Interpretations, and Exclusion," in Wehlau, *Darkness, Depression, and Descent*, 119). For a reading of the opposition between the hall and Grendel (as well as between human and monstrous history), see Saltzman, "Community, Joy, and the Intimacy of Narrative," in Remein and Weaver, *Dating Beowulf*.

36. For more on the monster's repeated irruption into the present of society and literature, see Cohen, "Monster Culture (Seven Theses)" in Cohen, *Monster Theory*, 3–25.

37. Hill argues that "we are always in complex, emotionally fraught [. . .] circumstances—no more so than in the very first mention of hall-songs, of repeated joy that aurally and mentally pains a creature of darkness" ("Social and Dramatic Functions," 310).

Through the narrative juxtaposition of creation and creation counternarrative, the poem shifts the emphasis from a single story of creation and destruction to the larger pattern within which the singular act occurs. The community-forming function of the Creation Song as a translation effect is clear. By retelling a received narrative, the scop reiterates what all members of the community share and therefore what binds them together. Yet the revelation of the rest of the story—of Cain and Abel, of monsters—demonstrates that the same longer history evoked to solidify a community can also destroy it, precisely because of what that inherited narrative leaves out.

This preoccupation with the ways in which the past intrudes in the narrative present of *Beowulf* repeatedly demonstrates how longer temporal spans— and the narratives that inhabit them—undermine human attempts to create stable identities for their communities. Take, for example, the oft-considered depiction of the building of Heorot (81b–85). By representing the creation and destruction of the hall in close proximity to one another and immediately before relating the story of all creation, the poem undermines the human attempt to create a lasting community by exposing the longer expanse of time that renders such attempts meaningless. Heorot is "heah ond horngeap," (82a) [high and horn-gabled] and "healærna mæst" (78a) [the best of halls].[38] Because Hrothgar "beagas dælde" (80b) [gave out rings] there, generating and strengthening the bonds that solidify community, it seems as though Heorot has an auspicious beginning. Yet the poem barely completes its description of the hall's construction before it describes its destruction: "heaðo-wylma bad / laðan liges" (82b–83a) [war-tides awaited, loathsome flames]. Even at the moment it is built, Heorot awaits its fiery end. The destruction of the hall is revealed to be the product of an intra-familial feud: "se ecghete aþumsweoran" (84) [the sword-hate of sworn oaths]. This echoes Grendel's intrusion into the hall from which he and his kin have been exiled. Oath-swearing (*aþ-swaring*) and sword-hate (*ecg-hete*) emphasize that it is a failure of community that will eventually destroy the possibility of a lasting fortress.[39] Such a failure raises the question of whether words and sworn oaths can *ever* be severed from sword-hate and destruction.[40] Although Beowulf is sent to save Heorot and its denizens from destruction by Grendel, the hall will still be destroyed—by humans,

---

38. For a reading of the architectural resonances of Heorot, see Garner, *Structuring Spaces*, 21–23. For the role of memory in the destruction of Heorot, see Liuzza, "Monuments, Memory, and History," in Johnson and Treharne, *Readings in Medieval Texts*, 97.

39. See Neville, *Representations of the Natural World*, 57.

40. The conjunction of oaths and sword-hate implies feud, which in the poem often results from a failed kinship alliance. Orchard compares this section to Beowulf's predictions about Freawaru (Orchard, *Critical Companion*, 241–42).

not monsters. Even if Grendel is "born to lose" in his encounter with Beowulf, the correlative is not that the Danes at Heorot are born to win.[41]

Heorot's fiery fate serves to amplify the effects of the Creation Song and the creation counternarrative. It also highlights the way collectivity underlies, and in this case undermines, human communities. The certainty that Heorot will not survive in the long term calls into question the efficacy of Beowulf's fight against Grendel in the short term. Beowulf arrives in Heorot to save the hall from an outside intruder, but the hall's destruction will ultimately come from within it—in the intrafamilial feud that consigns it to flames. This kind of cyclical violence that permeates the world of *Beowulf* is found as easily inside the hall as outside of it, but by juxtaposing the introduction of Grendel and the destruction of Heorot the poem calls into question the human belief that such cycles can be interrupted.[42] Set opposite the ambiguities of the two Creation Songs, the certainty of destruction calls the utility of fighting the Grendelkin into question because the effect of both monsters outside the hall and humans inside it is similar. The hall will not survive. Destruction—Grendel, fire, or feud—was already part of creation long before human voices sang of it. Yet Grendel's presence alludes to a longer history that accounts for his connection to Hrothgar and his men. This connection promises the failure of community before it can ever form and marks the futility of human attempts to interpret their world in any lasting way. Such relationships are foregrounded in the retold stories that surround and condition human communities in the poem. They are made legible through translation effects that remind the audience of narratives the characters cannot know, or do not remember.

THE LAY OF THE LAST SURVIVOR

The translation effect that connects the story of men to the story of monsters demonstrates one way in which human beings interact with an alterity that threatens their survival. Just as Grendel's arrival in the hall indicates a longer history that retains some power over human beings despite their ignorance of it, the Lay of the Last Survivor articulates and transmits multiple histories that exceed human understanding and knowledge. This translation effect—an inherited narrative from a long-dead people—highlights the effects of temporality on material culture. It also draws human communities into close contact with a nonhuman world.

---

41. Niles, *Beowulf*, 183.

42. For a reading of feud culture and its ties to social exchange and cyclical violence, see Baker, *Honor, Exchange, and Violence*.

The Lay of the Last Survivor begins the movement into the final battle scene of the poem and into the eventual death of both Beowulf and his people. The Lay relates the lament of a lone survivor who mourns the loss of his people in the aftermath of a catastrophic event, while he inters their treasure in a hoard. Although the Last Survivor is not part of any of the poem's other communities, the context of the Lay and the content of its lament indicate a key moment in the poem's articulation of the relationship between community and collectivity. Analyzed in its poetic context as the beginning of the end for Beowulf and the human community he leads, the Lay outlines the connections forged between humans and objects and thus exposes the relevance of the past for the future of human communities.[43] It demonstrates the disastrous consequences of human ignorance and the inability to understand that objects attach humans not only to one another but also to forces beyond themselves.

The disasters that befall human communities in the Lay invite speculation about their causes. From a critical standpoint, these calamities are most often considered in relation to the theme of mourning that dominates the end of *Beowulf*.[44] Critical treatments of the Lay have, among other topics, focused on the identity of the speaker, the structure of his words, his relationship with the dragon, and the consequences of the digression (2221–2323) for Beowulf and the Geats.[45] For some, the Lay describes a funeral; for others, it outlines a curse on the contents of the hoard that features centrally in it. Nearly all critics agree, however, that the Lay's dominant theme is irrevocable loss.[46]

In the Lay, the poem presents both the burial of a treasure hoard and the poetry occasioned by its deposit. A story within the larger story of *Beowulf*, the Lay stages the dissolution of human communities by focusing on material objects and animals that were once part of that community.[47] Although the

---

43. Hostetter argues that the lay is a "poetic study of objects and their relationship to the human actors who create and value them"—a relationship complicated by the "vibrancy" of such objects ("Disruptive Things," 55).

44. Bjork and Niles, *Beowulf Handbook*, 209. See also Bonjour, *Digressions in Beowulf*.

45. See also Parks, "Ring Structure and Narrative Embedding"; Hieatt, "Modþryðo and Heremod."

46. See Glosecki, *Shamanism and Old English Poetry*; Owen-Crocker, *Four Funerals in Beowulf*, 61–84; Orchard, *Critical Companion*; Thormann, "Poetics of Absence," in Foley, *De Gustibus*.

47. Borges calls this type of narrative embedding "a fiction within a fiction" ("When Fiction Lives," in *Selected Nonfictions*, 160). Although this term is not necessarily accurate for the Lay, it does serve to highlight the storytelling aspect of the digression. This technique is one Borges often used himself, and he describes two ways that such a fiction within a fiction might occur. The first firmly delineates the boundaries of the two, and is "as banal as the occurrence, in reality, of someone reading aloud or singing" (160). However, in a more complicated version, such as that found in *The Thousand and One Nights*, the interpolated fictions bleed into the larger fiction of the story and vice versa when "the king hears his own story

Lay may or may not describe an actual funeral, the materials found in it constitute buried treasure or grave goods. Because of the association with loss and death, the objects within the hoard can be read in much the same way that one might read a burial hoard. It helps observers—or in this case, listeners or readers—at a remove from its initial interment to understand what mattered to the culture that buried it. In archaeology, these burial hoards function, metonymically, in a manner similar to poetry: "A burial is itself not reality and is not meant to be; like poetry, it is a palimpsest of allusions, constructed in a certain time and place."[48] Although here Martin Carver focuses his analysis of treasure in burials on the excavation of early medieval English grave goods,[49] his assertion also suggests a method for pursuing the analysis of poetry composed about these hoards. Within what Carver describes as the "palimpsest" of interwoven allusions, the allusions themselves merit careful analysis. A larger set of connections emerges in the Lay, connections that function in direct opposition to the human desire for enduring community. They do so through a translation effect: a retold story that should seem familiar, passed down to articulate a loss.

The narrative concerning the hoard and the words used to describe it emphasize the human and monstrous connections formed with treasure as well as the legitimacy of both the treasure's burial and the dragon's subsequent hoarding. *Beowulf* describes the hoard as *ærgestreona* (2232b) [very old treasure], emphasizing its ancient provenance. This treasure is not unique; rather, the poem notes "Þær wæs swylcra fela / in þam eorðse(le)" (2231b–32a) [There were many such (hoards) in the halls of the earth]. The final lines of the poem describing Beowulf's burial and Wiglaf's decision to rebury the hoard with the fallen king similarly make clear the familiar nature of hoards.[50] As the "eormenlafe æþelan cynnes" (2234) [great leavings of a race of princes], the objects are considered *hordwyrðe* (2245b), literally hoard-worthy.[51] These descriptions

---

from the queen's lips. He hears the beginning of the story, which includes all the others, and also—monstrously—itself" (161).

48. Carver, "Burial as Poetry," in Tyler, *Treasure in the Medieval West*, 37.

49. Carver, 25–48.

50. See especially lines 3166–68: "Forleton eorla gestreon eorðan healdan, / golde on greote, þær his nu gen lifað / eldum swa unnyt, swa hit (æro)r wæs" [They let the earth hold the treasure of earls, gold in the ground, where it now still lives, as useless to men as it was before].

51. *Hordwyrðe* is one of four related words used in *Beowulf* that denote treasure, along with *hord-wela* (hoarded wealth), *hord-weorþung* (honored with treasure), and *hord-maððum* (treasure hoard).

each serve to strengthen the sense that hoards are a relatively common occurrence in the world of the poem.⁵²

The first line of the Lay further strengthens this sense of worthiness: "Heald þu nu, hruse, nu hæleð ne m(o)ston / eorle æhte" (2247–48a) [Hold now, you earth, now that warriors are no longer able to, the treasure of earls]. The Last Survivor apostrophizes the earth as the inheritor of his deposited treasures. Yet the earth is also their progenitor: "hyt ær on ðe / gode begeaton" (2248b–49a) [good men took it from you long ago]. The Survivor's actions thus complete a cycle: he gives the treasure back to the earth, which is also where it came from in the beginning.⁵³

In its articulation of this cycle, the lament outlines the connections between objects and the humans who use them as well as between objects and nonhuman entities.⁵⁴ Crucially, it does so using a translation effect: in this case, the assertion of the reported speech of the survivor from a remove of three hundred years or more, a remove that makes direct citation impossible. The digression is an inherited narrative, one that by necessity brings a story from the distant past into contact with the poetic present. It exists as a kind of reported speech, but we have no access to the chain of transmission that brings this narrative into the poem. We may suspect linguistic difference, but the poem does not dramatize it or its consequences. Yet the rhetoric of a translation effect—the identification of the Lay as a story we have heard before that comes to us across a long temporal span—is still present. It foregrounds the temporally heterogeneous connections between humans and nonhumans that are at the core of such narrative moments in *Beowulf.*

The cycle the Lay articulates encompasses both continuity and change, and has a direct effect on our understanding of the relationship between humans and nonhumans in the poem. Objects used in human communities—ring mail, swords, and helmets—are destined to return to the earth from which they were initially taken:

---

52. Niles argues that "the poet dwells with evident delight on the splendor of the hoard" ("Ring Composition," 928). Dean emphasizes that the treasure hoard is not *merely* a treasure hoard but rather represents "the communal experience, memory and history of the people whose last representative put the treasure there" ("Beowulf and the Passing of Time," 294).

53. Creed argues that the Lay begins "with what can be best characterized as an apostrophe, perhaps even an incantation—an address to *hruse,* the earth. [. . .] [The opening lines] suggest a circle: hold now what long ago you held [. . .] The entire final third of *Beowulf* can be characterized as a circling back to the ritual performed near its beginning by the Last Survivor" ("Beowulf and the Language of Hoarding," in Redman, *Medieval Archaeology,* 164).

54. Hostetter argues, however, that "the economic predominates over the world of *Beowulf,* where treasured items circulate in exchange for loyalty and great deeds" ("Disruptive Things," 44).

> Sceal se hearda helm   (hyr)stedgolde
> fætum befeallen;   feormynd swefað,
> þa ðe beadogriman   bywan sceoldon;
> ge swylce seo herepad,   sio æt hilde gebad
> ofer borda gebræc   bite irena,
> brosnað æfter beorne.   Ne mæg byrnan hring
> æfter wigfruman   wide feran,
> hæleðum be healfe.
> (2255–62a)

> The hard helm shall lose its decoratively wrought gold; the polishers sleep, who should polish the battle-helm. The same shall befall the battle-coat, which abided in battle over the breaking of shields, the bite of iron-swords, [it] decays after the warrior. Nor may the ring mail fare far, along with its battle-warrior: [it stays by] the side of the warriors.

The poem's poignant exposition of the hoard's contents emphasizes uses that have expired. The coat of mail will rust, unable to protect anyone from the *bite irena* [bite of iron-swords] that may have felled its former owner. The decorated helmet will lose its precious plating without the men who are meant to take care of it. Each object the Lay catalogues has a use that human beings have given to it. A human worker must polish the helmet, a human hand must wield the sword, and a human body must wear the ring-mail.[55] Without the *feorhcynn* (2266a) [living men], dispatched by death in war that saw these things employed, the Survivor envisions objects as worthless, bereft—literally without use.

More striking still are the items that the poem deems lost and that apparently cease to exist without a human context:

>   Næs hearpan wyn,
> gomen gleobeames,   ne god hafoc
> geond sæl swingeð,   ne se swifta mearh
> burhstede beateð.   Bealocwealm hafað
> fela feorhcynna   forð onsended.
> (2262b–66)

---

55. Hostetter notes that the speaker "does not lament the owners" of the artifacts; "rather it is the missing servants whose absence imperils the warrior caste" ("Disruptive Things," 57).

There is no harp's joy, play of the gleewood, nor does any good hawk swing through the hall, nor does the swift horse stamp in the city-stead. A baleful death has sent forth many living men!

Humans use harps to sing songs; with their death, such music must also cease. The formulation of these statements, however, makes the existence of not just harp music but also the hawk and horse themselves inextricable from human perceptions of them. The poem predicates the presence of the hawk on the existence of a hall it can fly through, and thus on the continued existence of humans. The same is true of the horse. There are no horses that stamp in the city-stead, and we can infer that the reason is because, like the hall, the continued existence of the city-stead depends on the survival of humans. However, although the human perception of these creatures dominates the lament voiced in the Lay, the poem's insistence on a vision of these creatures within human community does not necessarily preclude their existence outside of it. The hawk might fly and the horse stamp, elsewhere.

In this retelling of the expected fate of objects and animals, the emphasis on places integral to human community (such as the hall and the city-stead) highlights the limits of a perspective based solely on humans. The loss of human lives deprives both objects and animals of their former functions, yet the hawk and the horse do not fall as easily into the past as the disintegrating helmet and mail. The persistence of these animals in the poem suggests that from the perspective of a collectivity nothing is truly lost: being hoarded is as meaningful a state of being for a sword as participating in battle.[56] But the cyclical nature of the relationship between the past of the sword, the mail within the earth, and their futures (to be returned to the earth and to become dust) is not entirely consonant with the description of the hawk and the horse. A more dynamic interpretation of these animals and objects is merited, one that looks critically at why objects outlive the communities they serve.

Gillian Overing suggests that certain kennings in *Beowulf*—called incomplete kennings—function metonymically, letting a representative part of the whole come to the fore (such as the *hring-stefn*, the ringed prow, standing in for the boat as a whole).[57] The *feormynd* (2256b) [polisher], without whom the helmet will vanish, stands in for the community in which the warrior who wore it once lived. The *byrnan hring* (2260b) [mail coat] can stand in for the lost warrior, as can helmets and swords. Even in its present state of disuse, the ring mail bears a clear relationship to the men who once wore it.

---

56. See Ferhatović, who argues in *Borrowed Objects* that the dragon's relationship to the hoard is similar to modern instances of hoarding (143–63).

57. Overing, *Language, Sign, and Gender*, 20.

The ring mail cannot move from its resting place—"ne mæg byrnan hring / æfter wigfruman wide feran" (2260b–61) [nor may the ring mail fare far, after its battle-warrior]—precisely because it stays "hæleðum be healfe" (2262a) [by the side of the warrior] it was meant to protect, who is now dead and cannot "fare far" either. This association between the dead warrior and the ring mail allows one to stand in for the other, the man's stillness reflected in the stillness of his protective armor. Even the silence of the *hearpan wyn* (2262b) [harp's joy] and the cessation of *gomen gleobeames* (2263a) [the play of the gleewood] can stand in for the men who used the harp to make music. The harp and the gleewood, like the people who used them, return to dust—or more precisely, to the earth from which they came.[58]

But what can be made of the hawk and the horse? Jeffrey Cohen has argued persuasively that animals in medieval literature must be read as more than mere figures, "reference and reflection, insubstantial allegories in which we discover ourselves."[59] A purely allegorical approach to the horse and the hawk reflects its human framework—the horse and hawk, like the helmet and mail before them, only represent human loss. Although the human perception of these creatures dominates the lament voiced in the Lay, the poem's insistence on a vision of these creatures within human community does not necessarily preclude their existence outside of it.

Rather, like the cycle articulated through the initial address to the earth, the hawk and the horse reveal the enmeshment of human concerns in larger structures that circumscribe them. The Last Survivor's attitude toward treasure is complicated by the lines that occur directly before the Lay. Describing the state of mind of the Last Survivor before he voices his lament, the poem asserts that he already knew "þæt he lytel fæc longgestreona / brucan moste" (2240–41b) [that he would enjoy the long-accumulated treasures for a short interval of time].[60] Given that his entire community has been eradicated, it seems likely that the Last Survivor already knows this because (as in other Old English poems) life and its materials are ultimately *læne* or lent.[61] The earth apostrophized by the Last Survivor once held the treasure and will do so again. Unlike the treasure, however, the good hawk and swift horse do not

---

58. See Foley, *Immanent Art*.

59. Cohen, *Medieval Identity Machines*, 42. For further studies of the role of the animal in creating human identities, see Steel, *How to Make A Human*; Crane, *Animal Encounters*.

60. Both the translation and the interpretation of this line are difficult. I follow the translation of the passage used by the editors of the fourth edition of *Klaeber's Beowulf*: "He expected [that] the same [fate as had overtaken his relatives would overtake him] viz. that he would be permitted to enjoy the ancient treasures only a short time" (239n2239–41).

61. See, for example, "The Wanderer" in Krapp and Dobbie, *Exeter Book*. See also BT, s.v. *læne*.

decay. Although they will eventually die, their ending is not narrated in the Lay alongside the disintegration of the material objects in the hoard. After the deaths of the humans who used them, the hawk and the horse can continue to exist outside the human structures in the poem. This status—that of creatures associated with human use but not reducible to it—becomes a helpful model for interpreting the dragon's role in the poem.[62]

The dragon takes up occupancy of the hoard not long after the Last Survivor disappears. The survivor presumably meets the same fate as the rest of his people: sooner or later, he dies. In any case, the dragon "finds" the hoard, an action the poem describes with the Old English word *findan*. The semantic range of *findan* (used at 2270b in the third-person preterite *fond*) includes overtones not only of our modern English usage "to find" but also "to invent, imagine, devise, contrive, order, dispose, arrange, or determine." This range of meanings suggests that there is some kind of volition present on the part of the dragon, an active searching which leads the dragon to find the hoard.[63] That volition matters, in part because of the poem's attitude toward dragons and their hoarding behavior. The verse that narrates the dragon's relationship to the hoard does so with a peculiar familiarity:

> He gesecean sceall
> (hea)r(h on) hrusan, þær he hæðen gold
> warað wintrum frod; ne byð him wihte ðy sel.
> (2275b–77)

He shall seek out the heathen-temple in the ground, where he, wise in winters, guards the heathen gold. He is not a whit the better for it.

These lines have the tone of gnomic utterance: this is knowledge passed down, inherited. A similarly structured instance of gnomic verse in *Maxims II* makes an analogous claim: "Draca sceal on hlæwe, / frod, frætwum wlanc" (26b–27a) [The dragon ought to be in the barrow, old and proud of its treasures].[64] That this verse represents received wisdom becomes clearer by reference to its context in *Maxims*:

---

62. Neville argues that the "monstrous" is not necessarily distinct from or used in opposition to the "natural" as such, and so provides an important first step in redefining the category of "what is natural" as opposed to what is not (Neville, *Representations of the Natural World*).

63. See DOE, s.v. *findan*.

64. Text of *Maxims II* is drawn from Dobbie, *Anglo-Saxon Minor Poems*. I am obviously not the first to make this connection: see Ferhatović, *Borrowed Objects*, 149; Cronan, "Narrative Disjunctions," 472, among others.

> Sweord sceal on bearme,
> drihtlic isern. Draca sceal on hlæwe,
> frod, frætwum wlanc. Fisc sceal on wætere
> cynren cennan. Cyning sceal on healle
> beagas dælan.
> (25b-29a)

> The sword ought to be in the lap, the lordly iron. The dragon ought to be in the barrow, old and proud of its treasures. A fish ought to bring forth his progeny in the water. The king ought to give out rings in the hall.

The dragon's place and function seem completely natural—even, in certain senses, obligatory.[65] The dragon belongs in a treasure hoard. It holds this position as rightfully as a king gives out rings in the hall, a benchmark of early medieval English society.[66] Regardless of what other attributes the dragon might have, the narrator assumes that its proper place is in the hoard.[67]

The overlap in gnomic wisdom between *Beowulf* and *Maxims* is particularly revealing because such knowledge is clearly meant to be something that the poem's fictive "we" has heard before. We encounter received wisdom in the form of an inherited narrative, a story about dragons and their activities. By reference to the *Maxims* tradition, we begin to recognize another kind of translation effect, one meant to help shore up the human communities of *Beowulf* in the face of the difficulties and dangers they encounter. The list of ways in which one might expect the world to work creates an inherited set of expectations that give order to an otherwise chaotic world—a kind of narrative that makes community possible.[68] One of those expectations—the natural behavior of dragons—holds within itself the potential for human dissolution in a world that is not made solely for human beings.

The poem's final observation regarding the dragon suggests that despite the obligatory sense of the dragon's occupation of the hoard, the dragon itself does not benefit from its possession of the gold: "ne byð him wihte ðy sel" (2277b) [he is not a whit the better for it]. This assertion seems at odds with

---

65. *Sculan* has a variety of meanings, including senses of debt, obligation, or adherence to law or custom—it often conveys the same force as "shall" or "ought" in modern English usage. BT, s.v. *sculan*[8]. Cronan also argues that the dragon is drawn to the hoard because of its *hæðen* properties (Cronan, "Narrative Disjunctions," 472).

66. Hill, *Cultural World in Beowulf*, 135–37.

67. See Bonjour, *Digressions in Beowulf*; Niles, "Ring Composition."

68. See Neville, *Representations of the Natural World*.

the gnomic wisdom discussed above.[69] Yet, by juxtaposing such maxims about the dragon's position in the hoard with the idea that the dragon does not benefit from its acquisition, the poem points to the insufficiency of a viewpoint that bemoans the treasure's lack of use. This valuation judges the dragon's behavior and finds its use of the treasure wanting. The standard by which the dragon does not profit, however, is a human one. It is also limited: a comparison with another creature who does not profit from its use of human objects demonstrates the insufficiency of this view.

The "bookworm riddle" of the Exeter book begins to clarify the insufficiency of a human-centered explanation of the dragon by enforcing the connection between the wisdom such gnomic statements articulate and the expected nature of the relationships they describe.[70] Number 47 in the Krapp and Dobbie edition of the Exeter Book, this first-person riddle describes the work of a bookworm or book moth devouring a parchment page in a codex, which is described succinctly in the line: "moððe word fræt" (1a) [a moth ate words].[71] This creature notably does not benefit from the words it consumes by eating the book's material pages, a point described in words that echo *Beowulf*'s lines about the dragon's lack of profit: "Stælgiest ne wæs / wihte þy gleawra þe he þam wordum swealg" (5b-6) [The thievish guest was not a whit the wiser because he swallowed those words]. The Old English riddle suggests that, like the dragon, the moth takes something that belongs to humans—words—but is not made better by them. The moth, that is, does not learn from the knowledge it consumes. However, the earlier lines of the riddle, which introduce the strange occurrence of a moth eating words, suggest that this phenomenon and its effects are not necessarily something to lament: "Me þæt þuhte / wrætlicu wyrd (1b-2a) [To me that seemed a wondrous fate]. *Wrætlic*, as defined in Bosworth Toller, can mean "wondrous" or "curious"—but also carries connotations of a state of being, including one of "wondrous excellence" or being "beautiful, noble, excellent, [or] elegant."[72] Most importantly, the fact that the moth does not gain from its action does not imply that this action is unequivocally negative or evil. Rather, the moth's meal is part of *wyrd*, or fate—it is simply "what happens."[73]

---

69. See Chickering, *Beowulf*, 359. See also Irving, *Rereading Beowulf*; Clark, "Relaunching the Hero"; Taylor, "Dragon's Treasure in *Beowulf*."

70. For new approaches to thinking about the bookworm/moth riddle, see Zweck, "Silence in the Exeter Book Riddles"; Foys, "Undoing of Exeter Book Riddle 47" in Caie and Drout, *Transitional States*.

71. Old English text of the bookworm riddle is from Krapp and Dobbie, *Exeter Book*.

72. BT, s.v. *wræt-lic*.

73. BT, s.v. *wyrd*.

The similarity of a moth who is not made wiser by the words it eats to a dragon who is not made better by the treasure it guards further suggests that we can understand the dragon's role as the hoard's guardian as a natural—perhaps even neutral—occurrence.[74] The dragon is not made better by his possession of the treasure, but the poem does not suggest that this is improper. Indeed, as Denis Ferhatović points out, the dragon's "attachment" to the hoard "indicates otherwise. He appreciates it in some mysterious, reptilian way."[75] The voice that comments upon the dragon's lack of activity comes from a speaker who expects treasures to be distributed and rings to be dealt out. In short, it is a product of the human expectation of what treasure is and how it should be circulated within a human community. Such a reading is not without its precursors. Patricia Dailey notes that the dragon raises crucial questions about the role of the human in *Beowulf*: "Treasure is guarded both by men and by monsters, raising the question, for whom is it proper to guard, to live in peace, to defend and protect kin and belongings? Is it truly a mark of what is proper to man?"[76] These questions are central to understanding the relationship between the dragon and the hoard, as well as its impact on Beowulf's time as King of the Geats in the narrative present of the poem.

Yet the dragon's connection to the hoard also draws attention to how objects make meaning differently based on who (or what) is associated with them. A hoard can mean different things when used, referred to, or affected by different actors—humans, monsters, animals, or even other objects. As a result, the hoard's meaning transforms several times in this section of the poem. In the Last Survivor's lament, the hoard is all that remains of a people who have been destroyed. When the dragon occupies it, the hoard becomes a forbidden stockpile of treasure watched over by a jealous guardian. Finally, when a thief seeking treasure invades the hoard, it becomes the source of the dragon's fury and a symbol of human destruction. While the Lay of the Last Survivor exemplifies a human-centered interpretation of events by foregrounding the devastation that surrounds its speaker, the thief's role in this story emphasizes collectivity and the multiplicity of meanings that accrue to objects that humans seek to control and use.

The dragon's connection to the hoard arises in a time that is beyond human understanding, a *preohund wintra* (2278b) [three-hundred-year] span.

---

74. See McGalliard, "Poet's Comment in *Beowulf*."
75. Ferhatović, *Borrowed Objects*, 149.
76. Dailey, "Questions of Dwelling," 205. Dailey's argument regarding the "insubjective" bears some similarity to a theory of collectivity in *Beowulf*. Nowhere is this more apparent than in a reading of the dragon as an entity that dwells in its own barrow-like hall with its hoard, protects its treasure, and seeks retribution for loss.

Daniel Calder argues that this expanse is crucial to the dragon's seeming universality, suggesting that the dragon "does not seem to exist within the limits of human time."[77] The thief's intrusion into the hoard, and the dragon's subsequent rage, belies this assertion: the dragon might have a longer temporal purview than the humans of the poem, but their temporalities do intersect, disastrously. Put another way, human community as mourned in the Lay is bound up in the larger frame of collectivity regardless of human ability to detect or understand its presence. The actions of the thief are emblematic of this myopic approach. The poem describes this character as *an* (2280b) [alone]. Widely considered to be part of the ring structure of the poem,[78] the phrase that introduces the thief's action when he steals the cup—"oð ðæt hyne an abealch" (2280b) [until a lone (man) angered (the dragon)]—is similar to those used in introducing both Grendel ("oð ðæt an ongan / fyrene frem(m)an, feond on helle" [100b-101] [until a certain one began to perform evil, a fiend from hell]) and the dragon ("oð ðæt (a)n ongan, / deorcum nihtum draca rics[i]an" [2210b-11] [until a certain one, a dragon, began to rule in the dark of the night]).[79] Because the thief is also described as alone, the temptation is to see this man as we see Grendel and the dragon.[80] He seems to be singular and unassociated with any group.

Yet the framing of the line changes this view. While both Grendel and the dragon begin to attack human beings, the thief is already caught up in a web of associations present even at the lexical level. The dragon waits "oð ðæt hyne an abealch" [until a lone (man) angered (the dragon)]. The thief's action when he takes the cup from the dragon's hoard underscores a crucial distinction that must be made in order to understand the narrative function of these episodes within the poem: the distinction between community and collectivity. The thief creates a connection between humans and the dragon through its treasure, and this connection highlights the conflict between community—defined as connections only between humans—and collectivity, which encompasses the connections not only between humans but also between humans, objects, and monsters.

The action the thief takes in bringing the cup to Beowulf is motivated by a desire for reentry into human community of the kind that Raymond Williams

---

77. Calder, "Setting and Ethos," 29.

78. See Niles, "Ring Composition."

79. The uses of the word *an* often designate actors within the poem who are profoundly "alone." Included among these are Beowulf (at 425 and 431), Sigemund (at 888), the Last Survivor (at 2237 and 2268), Hreðel (at 2461), and Wiglaf (2599) after his compatriots abandon Beowulf in the dragon fight.

80. Orchard argues that the dragon and Grendel are also presented in "precisely parallel terms" (*Critical Companion*, 64).

defines: a positive term that describes the connections between human beings in society.[81] It relies on largely invisible social forces to hold the association in question together.[82] It is, moreover, a *uniformly* positive term, a status that Williams argues distinguishes it from other words describing human groups.[83] Williams's definition of community is one way to understand the thief's action. The thief steals the cup from the dragon in order to *mandryhtne bær* (2281b) [bring it to his lord]. The thief's action is clearly purposeful: the cup is used to *bene getiðad* (2284b) [garner a favor]. The favor is likely a form of pardon from exile, based on the following clarification that Beowulf granted a favor *feasceatum men* (2285a) [for the destitute (or wretched) man]. The cup is used as a price for entrance into the human community of Beowulf and the Geats; however, the cup bears other associations with it, including with the hoard and the dragon that guards it.[84]

The narrative juxtaposition of the thief's action with the dragon's rage, framing the affective valuation of human material culture in the Lay, highlights the insufficiency of a purely human vision of community. The disparate events and times by which the hoard, the dragon, the thief, and the Geats are linked bring to light the larger network of associations that includes humans and human communities but is not limited to them.[85] By suggesting that a broad range of entities—including human, nonhuman, technical, and textual ones—comprise the social world, the concept of collectivity complicates the narrative of society in *Beowulf*. The poem highlights the human struggle to create community through political alliances, the telling of stories, and the giving of treasure, yet closer examination of these actions reveals that such things are part of a larger network that is not primarily or even predominantly based on human associations.

Taking this view broadens our notion of agency by demonstrating how dragons and treasure can affect humans as much—or more—than other humans can. The relative diversity of actors in this network highlights another key distinction between the two configurations: collectivity, unlike community, can help solidify or perpetuate human groups but does not have to func-

---

81. Williams, *Keywords*, 76.

82. See Latour, *We Have Never Been Modern*; for the resistance of objects to these forces, see Hostetter, "Disruptive Things."

83. For Williams, the word community "seems never to be used unfavorably," a feature that distinguishes it from "all other terms of social organization" (*Keywords*, 76).

84. Such associations might also include a curse laid on the gold. See Hostetter, "Disruptive Things," 59.

85. For a comprehensive study of collectivity and its relationship to human ideas of community, see the following: Latour, *Reassembling the Social*; Callon, "Elements of a Sociology of Translation" in Law, *Power, Action, and Belief*; Law, "Ordering, Strategy and Heterogeneity."

tion in consonance with human desire. In *Beowulf*, the same object can link communities in one context and later form the basis for another context in which the same communities fall apart. The result is the foreboding sense of the future that lingers in the poem. The future invoked through the grouping of a collectivity is always already threatening the dispersal of human groups, precisely because it does not create a stable ground for human identity. Like the "we" that frames the opening of the poem, these identities are contingent on the situation in which they are found and the actors with whom they become associated. The instability of these identities in *Beowulf* becomes a concern when humans are connected to a larger history to which they have no access, as in the Lay.

In the Lay, treasure constitutes a crucial point of connection between humans and the entities around them: nature, the earth, and natural creatures. Moreover, both the treasure and the connection it facilitates persist across time. The collectivity—which includes the thief, the stolen treasure, and the dragon that guards it—endures beyond the community that the thief desires and the dragon destroys. *Beowulf* juxtaposes the multiple contexts associated with the treasure and thereby emphasizes the limits of the community into which the thief wishes to return. Elsewhere in the poem, the giving and receiving of treasures forms connections between different humans. For example, Wealtheow gives Beowulf the neck ring in return for his slaying of Grendel, and Beowulf gives gifts in the hall and is thus considered a good king.[86] The thief's use of the cup, on the other hand, brings the wrath of the dragon into the hall. When he takes the cup for his own reasons, he acts in ignorance of the larger history of the hoard and the network that includes the dragon: the very inherited narrative that surrounds the Lay of the Last Survivor. The thief bears the cup to his lord in hope of rejoining a human community; however, through the cup, he (unintentionally) creates a link between his people, the hoard, and the dragon. The dragon, bereft of a single part of its treasure, turns its anger outward toward the humans connected to the thief who caused the loss. In short, while the dragon appears as a threat from outside of the human world, it is intimately connected to the constitution of this world. It is already implicated in the human world through the various uses to which treasure is put.

Even in the midst of the dragon's attack, the temporality of collectivity is essentially veiled from the perspective of the poem's characters. Beowulf's

---

86. See *Beowulf* lines 1192–1231. Dailey posits objects like the necklace Wealtheow gives to Beowulf as a "living inheritance"—the work of the neck ring is established in the poem's present, but is also affected by both past and future uses to which it has been or will be put ("Questions of Dwelling," 208).

understanding of his encounter with the dragon, voiced after the theft of the cup, highlights how the limited human perception of time leads to an emphasis on community rather than collectivity:

> Gewat þa twelfa sum   torne gebolgen
> dryhten Geata   dracan sceawian;
> hæfde þa gefrunen   hwanan sio fæhð aras,
> bealonið biorna;   him to bearme cwom
> ma(ð)þumfæt mære   þurh ðæs meldan hond.
> (2401–5)

> Then, one of twelve, grievously angry, the lord of the Geats sought out the dragon. He had then learned by asking how the feud began, the evil fires of men; to him in his lap came the great treasure cup, through the hand of an informer.

In these lines, Beowulf learns "by asking" (*gefrignan*) that the dragon's actions are a direct consequence of those taken by the thief. He does so through a story that the thief passes on. The great treasure, originally meant as a gift to secure reentry into community, is offered by an informer who may even be the very person who took the cup from the hoard in the first place.[87] The informer does not give the cup to Beowulf as a symbol of remorse or a request for a favor, but as an answer to Beowulf's implied question, "How did the dragon's rampage begin?" The treasure has a history, and when the thief tries to use it to reenter a human community, he bears with the cup its long association with the dragon and the hoard. The very meaning of the cup changes through this dual association with both humans and monsters. At first, the cup signals inclusion and possible reentry into community. The association with the dragon, however, changes the gesture of intended peace-making into a provocation to revenge, one that will result in Beowulf's eventual demise.

The Lay of the Last Survivor and the segment of *Beowulf* that surrounds it emphasize the interconnections between humans, dragons, and treasure. In so doing, the poem highlights the insufficiency of a purely human vision

---

87. Although the identity of the "informer" is somewhat disputed, two main possibilities dominate the criticism. First, that the person in question is the lord of the thief. The second is that *meldan* refers to the thief himself, who gives the cup to Beowulf and thus implicates himself in the chain of events that both precede and follow its presentation. For the first interpretation, see Anderson, "Treasure Trove in *Beowulf*." For the second, see Biggs, "Some Fictions of Geatish Succession." See also Cherniss, *Ingeld and Christ*.

of treasure's significance. Crucially, it does so through a translation effect: a received narrative from a destroyed culture that sets the stage for the connections between humans and nonhumans that precipitate the crisis in the final portion of the poem. As Roberta Frank argues, "There is nothing natural about a sense of history" in this poem.[88] The collectivity that connects the dragon, human communities, and treasure is part of a much longer sense of history made present in *Beowulf* through inherited narrative, a history that exceeds or precedes human understanding of its depth.[89]

By pushing the reader or listener to acknowledge this longer sense of history as well as the beings—such as the dragon—that inhabit it, the poem concomitantly encourages the reader to enact the narrative distance that such historical longevity implies. This kind of longevity alludes to the existence of deep time within the poem, a periodization "too long to be readily comprehensible to minds used to thinking in terms of days, weeks, and years—decades at most."[90] This deep time is on a scale not immediately perceptible to humans, modern or medieval, and its existence in *Beowulf* is presented by the entities that by their nature experience its breadth: dragons, gold in the ground, and the earth itself. Such a longer view necessitates the readerly understanding that humans are not the central figure in the *longue durée*.[91] The digressions—in their function as translation effects—can therefore be accounted for as narrative objects that "translate" between different modes of narrative time. They bring together groups and entities that seem unassociated in the poem's present but that are actually closely connected when they are considered in terms of longer temporal spans. In the Lay of the Last Survivor, the deep time of *Beowulf* makes legible a history of the hoard that is not limited to human use; rather, humans are simply part of the collectivity that includes the dragon and his keeping of the hoard, as well as the earth and its role in keeping the objects in their elemental state.

---

88. Frank, "Sense of History," in *Beowulf*, trans. Heaney, ed. Donoghue, 168.

89. Frank, 167. Niles argues that *Beowulf*'s lack of geographical specificity is "balanced by an intricate, interlocking set of temporal relationships that lose nothing in depth for being left somewhat imprecise" (Niles, *Beowulf*, 180). See also Hanning, "*Beowulf* as Heroic History."

90. Gee, *In Search of Deep Time*, 3. Gee here paraphrases John McPhee's description of deep time in *Basin and Range*. In a literary context, see Dimock, *American Literature Across Deep Time*. For further reflection on the larger temporalities of *Beowulf*, see Hostetter, "Disruptive Things."

91. For the concept of the *longue durée* as it applies to historical inquiry, see Braudel, *On History*.

CONCLUSION

The juxtaposition of narratives of identity-formation in the opening segment of *Beowulf*, the Creation Song of the scop in Heorot as well as the monstrous genesis that accompanies it, and the Lay of the Last Survivor all highlight the destruction or dispersal of human communities and bring the poem's audience in line with another level of time that is implicitly present in the poem. This longer view demonstrates connections between humans and nonhumans across time rather than distinctions made by the characters or the narrator. By understanding group formation in *Beowulf* in terms of temporality, the final scenes of the poem reveal how collectivity emphasizes the interconnections that render the past both effective and destructive in its narrative present. Just as the Lay of the Last Survivor suggests a deeper past that intersects with the poem's temporal present, the Messenger's Speech explores the past which can and does assure the death of Beowulf as well as his people. In addition, the speech carefully outlines the broader context of human communities through its exposition of the connections between humans, corpses, and animals.

Divided into four main foci, the Messenger's Speech performs a complex analysis of the multiple forces at play in the downfall of Beowulf's people and the future that will see these elements come together cataclysmically in the association of the Geats with Beowulf's lifeless corpse. In the first part of the speech, the speaker surveys the scene after Beowulf's death, describing Wiglaf in his post-battle role as one who sits to preside over both the dead man and the dead dragon. Wiglaf "healdeð higemæðum heafodwearde, / leofes ond laðes" (2909–10a) [holds weary-minded the (role of the) head-guard of the loved one and the hated one]. The messenger then makes a prediction of what awaits the powerless Geats, noting that "nu ys leodum wen / orleghwile, syððan under[ne] / Froncum ond Frysum fyll cyninges / wide weorðeð" (2910b–2913a) [it is now for the people an expectation of a time of war, since the death of the king becomes widely known, to the Franks and the Frisians]. The messenger further describes the events that mark the beginning of the feud between the Swedes and the Geats, as well as the ultimate results of that feud (which include the annihilation of Beowulf's people). Finally, the speech segues to a lament, speaking of what some critics have termed the "beasts of battle" theme, in which ravens and wolves are given the final word over the warriors who have fallen.[92]

---

92. The "beasts of battle" is a common Germanic type scene. For more detailed consideration of the form and function of this trope, see Bonjour, "Beowulf and the Beasts of Battle"; Griffith, "Convention and Originality"; Honegger, "Form and Function"; Magoun, "Beasts of Battle in Anglo-Saxon Poetry."

Treasure connects Beowulf and his men with the dragon. In the Messenger's Speech and the aftermath of the final battle, however, the treasure undergoes one final shift in meaning. Beowulf intends for the gold to ensure the survival of his people. Wiglaf assigns the hoard a different destiny, and we learn that "ne scel anes hwæt / meltan mid þam modigan, ac þær is maðma hord, / gold unrime, grimme gecea(po)d" (3010b–12) [nor shall one part melt with that proud one, but that treasure hoard, uncounted gold, purchased grimly]. *Brond fretan* (3014b) [the fire shall eat] the remains of the hope of the Geats and leave the remaining warriors of the Geatish people to mourn their loss—and their impending fate—*golde bereafod* (3018b) [bereft of gold]. Meant to forge new bonds of loyalty, but placed on the pyre with Beowulf's body, the treasure becomes connected only to a corpse. As a result, any futurity it might have guaranteed for the community is cut off.

Although the poem underscores the connection of the gold with the corpse of Beowulf, certain scavengers also play a significant role in the speech and in the ultimate destruction of the Geats. By confronting the actions of the raven and the wolf in the beasts of battle scene, the poem's audience must also confront the endurance of these creatures beyond their human prey:

> ac se wonna hrefn
> fus ofer fægum   fela reordian,
> earne secgan   hu him æt æte speow,
> þenden he wið wulf   wæl reafode.
> (3024b–27)

> But the dark raven, eager over the fated men, will tell, will say to the eagle, how he succeeded at the meal, when he with the wolf plundered the slaughtered ones.

While the hawk and horse may return to their natural origin after the dispersal of human community in the Lay of the Last Survivor, the raven and the wolf remain at the scene of human loss in the Messenger's Speech. This moment in the poem—in addition to being reported speech in a very literal sense—is also a translation effect, although in this case the translation in question is imaginative rather than literal. The messenger relates what the raven will tell the eagle, and as Mo Pareles notes, "the speech appears before it is spoken, presumably at a physical distance from where it is spoken, and in the voice of a human being who does not attempt to approximate it closely."[93]

---

93. Pareles, "Animal Language," in Remein and Weaver, *Dating Beowulf*, 175.

To these removes I add that this is a narrative that requires translation (and thus interpretation), because even if the raven could speak, its speech would be fundamentally inhuman. Yet here we are made privy to these creatures' assessment of human prey, an inversion of the power structure that should assure human dominance.[94] Moreover, the narrative that the raven (figuratively) relates—that of "how he succeeded at the meal"—demonstrates the intrusion of the nonhuman into a configuration that initially appeared to be purely human.

The translation effect in this part of the Messenger's Speech—the relation of a narrative told by the raven to the eagle—also forces the poem's audience to reflect on the kinds of action that are proper to men or animals and to put human concerns into a longer temporality that does not necessarily need human action to sustain it. That the raven and the wolf reave or plunder (*reafian*) the corpses also disjunctively resonates with other moments in the poem in which humans undertake this action. At line 1212, the first use of *reafian* describes the actions undertaken by the Frisian warriors after a failed attack by Hygelac: "wyrsan wigfrecan wæl reafeden" (1212) [worse battle-warriors plundered the slaughtered]. *Reafian*, here, is a human action, undertaken in a human context, and performed upon humans. Frisian warriors plunder Geatish ones. At line 2985, a similar usage occurs in Wulf and Eofor's defeat of Ongenþeow: "Þenden reafode rinc oðerne, / nam on Ongenðio irenbyrnan / heard swyrd hilted ond his helm somod (2985–87) [Then the warriors plundered the other, took from Ongenþeow his iron byrnie, his hard sword hilt and also his helmet]. Human warriors take the things that matter in a human world by plundering bodies for war-gear. The wolf and the raven, by contrast, plunder human bodies for what such creatures value: meat.

The depiction of the wolf and the raven suggests that human plunder can be equated—at least lexically—with the actions of carrion eaters. This vision of desolation becomes an instantiation of collectivity because it sets human death in an animal context. Of particular importance, however, is that the messenger describes these beasts and their plunder *after* the details of the origins of the Swedish-Geatish feud.[95] The Messenger's Speech makes it clear:

---

94. Steel's work has long set the standard in understanding how human dominance over the animal establishes itself via violence against animal lives in the Middle Ages. See Steel, *How to Make A Human*. See further Pareles, "Animal Language," in Remein and Weaver, *Dating Beowulf*.

95. The poem tells us because of their pride (*for onmedlan*, 2926) the Geats originally sought out the Swedes in battle, thus beginning the disastrous series of events that leads to the poem's present. Hygelac is a key player in this action.

> Þæt ys sio fæhðo   ond se feondscipe,
> wælnið wera,   ðæs ða ic [wen] hafo,
> þe us seceað to   Sweona leoda,
> syððan hie gefricgeað   frean userne
> ealdorleasne.
> (2999–3003a)

> That is the feud, and the enmity, the slaughter-evil of men, that I believe will cause the Swedes to seek us out, as soon as they hear that our lord is lifeless.

These lines of the messenger's prophecy further strengthen the sense that warriors and animals are almost interchangeable because it places the beasts of battle scene within the same set of associations that links the Geats and the Swedes. Beowulf's body signifies differently as a corpse than it did while alive, when Beowulf was a warrior and a good king. Foreshadowing the fate of his soon-to-be-utterly-defeated men, Beowulf's corpse links the Geats of the poem's narrative present to a time of feud begun by Hygelac.[96] To the Swedes, the corpse means victory; to the Geats, death. But in the narrative of the beasts, the corpse signifies another level on which such events might be understood. The only real victors in the *longue durée* are the raven and wolf, who "succeeded at the meal." In the context of collectivity, humans become one group among many. The possibility of a future for human community is bound to the animals, monsters, and even corpses to which humans are connected—a collectivity made legible in the translation effects that transmit its narrative.

The opening lines of *Beowulf* stage a scene of narrative transmission in which the audience of the poem—in early medieval England as much as today is implicated in a process of retelling stories that "we have heard" before. By understanding the digressions in *Beowulf* as translation effects—textual evocations of retold stories that have important ramifications for community formation or destruction—we gain a critical vantage point from which to address both the endurance of the past and the lingering sense of loss within the poem. The stories retold in the digressions amplify the poetic themes of heroism, greatness, feud, and loss. They also outline the connections that lead from heroic achievement to the disasters of feud between human beings and between human beings and monsters. These connections place the poem in a longer historical framework that is not always accessible to the characters within it, an emphasis on the *longue durée* that provides a way of thinking

---

96. See lines 2923–3015.

about *Beowulf* that is responsive to the poem's concerns beyond its human subject matter. By understanding the digressions within *Beowulf* as translation effects, we gain access to the collectivities that engulf the human communities of the poem. This vantage point, in turn, creates the possibility of a poem that meditates on problems larger than heroic deeds and human loss. In such a reading, *Beowulf* becomes a poem about interconnection.

CODA

[...] the Saxon barrow-makers,
living among the wrecks of Roman buildings
they could not copy
or restore, saw themselves as late arrivers, as an *after-folk*
living on the graves of a greater folk
who'd gone before. *Where is the horse, where the rider,*
some now-nameless Saxon wrote,
grieving for a people who his own forebears
had annihilated, assimilated,
or driven into the sea.

—James Arthur, "A Local History"[1]

IN THE PRECEDING PAGES, I have sought to demonstrate that the traces of intervention medieval translators leave in their work are not only meaningful as cultural artefacts but themselves create meaning. By signaling the process of narrative transmission as it occurs, translation effects allow modern scholars to better perceive the work that translation performs both within the period and beyond it. Translations thus reveal their imagined textual communities as fundamentally expansive, extending in time and geographical space, in ways that we have only begun to explore.

My work has moved from the literal to the metaphorical, in order to demonstrate the ubiquity of translation effects in medieval literature. In the Old English *Orosius*, the use of a single discourse marker, *cwæð Orosius*, creates a temporally heterogeneous textual community that spans the temporal and spatial distance from Late Antique Rome to early medieval England. In Ælfric of Eynsham's *Lives of the Saints*, the circulation of stories from Bede's *Historia Ecclesiastica* becomes a force within the narratives of the saints, linking holy men and women from England to a longer and larger tradition, one whose narrative import spreads even to the soil of the land itself. The figure of translation lies alongside its reality in the Ælfrician homiletic corpus of manuscripts: discourse markers such as "þ[æt] is [. . .] on englisc" indicate

---

1. Arthur, "Local History," 40, in *Suicide's Son*.

literal translations in the *De Octo Vitiis* tradition. In the same manuscripts, emendations and marginalia refer to the circulation of stories in a narrative ecosystem that exceeds the immediate environs and time of the Old English homilies, engaging traditions that span both later English language narratives as well as French ones. Chaucer's *Man of Law's Tale,* taken alongside its analogues in Trevet's *Chronicle* and Gower's *Confessio Amantis,* demonstrates how the rhetoric of linguistic difference and the translation effects that do—or do not—signify its presence change the nature of the communities that each text imagines as it looks back to English historical figures and moments.

Beowulf, then, seems a fitting place to conclude this monograph about the circulation of stories despite its temporal dislocation at the end of a book for which it might have, chronologically, marked a beginning. As I observed in my introduction, *Beowulf* stands at the start of the "English canon," inaugurating the thousand or more years of the standard "*Beowulf*-to-Virginia Woolf" survey course. Yet, as I observe in my final chapter, *Beowulf* makes an uneasy alliance with those who wish to use it as a foundation for community formation. It invokes a narrative tradition, to be sure; however, in doing so it also shows how these narratives exceed the human capacity to control their circulation. Tales like the Lay of the Last Survivor connect humans to longer temporalities and the collectivities that inhabit them. In searching for a stable ground on which to build a community, the humans of the poem circulate stories they believe they understand. It is only the view of the poet that allows the poem's audience to see what its characters cannot: that the ground that looks stable is always already shifting.

As a final example, take Grendel's arrival from the *mearc* in which he makes his home. The monster enters Heorot again, this time to face Beowulf himself:

>   Raþe æfter þon
> on fagne flor   feond treddode,
> eode yrremod;   him of eagum stod
> ligge gelicost   leoht unfæger.
> (724–27)[2]

Quickly after that, on the decorated floor, the fiend trod, went with an angry mind; from his eyes, most like a flame, came a hideous light.

---

2. Old English text of *Beowulf* is from Fulk et al., *Klaeber's Beowulf.*

Seth Lerer eloquently argues for one notion of the past signaled by *on fagne flor*, suggesting that the decorations are in fact the remnants of a tiled mosaic floor of Roman origin.[3] Although the poem is not clear as to the floor's provenance, Lerer sees this moment as deeply evocative, with the floor serving a role as "a memory of magnificence, an allusion to something old, rich, artistic, and alien."[4] Lerer's analysis draws on postcolonial theory in order to understand the significance of the ruins that permeate the poem *Beowulf*—the stone-paved streets, the decorated floors, even the arched stone of the dragon's barrow.[5] Each of these material objects are the remains of the past, carried over, narrated, and *translated* from one time into another. That the characters do not understand their import is no matter: as translation effects, they remind the reader or listener of the poem that objects have histories and that in telling their stories, or even alluding to them, those histories are brought into contact with the present. Those stories, that is, can have a power that transcends time.

Indeed, the possibility of material translation effects haunts *Beowulf*, in the swords whose stories create the grounds for further feuds and the neck rings that spell disaster for their wearers.[6] These remnants of the past are part of what Lerer identifies as "a poetry of *pulvis*, a poetry of things left in the dust."[7] And *Beowulf* itself, he argues, becomes this kind of poetry: it "remains a ruin, charred and fractured, barely legible at times."[8] Its very illegibility becomes the impulse for poetic invention. Lerer's exploration of the postcolonial *Beowulf*—and the legacy that Seamus Heaney wrought when he translated it as such—is one that fundamentally asks what to do with the ruins of English literary history, itself built on the "ruined edifice" of *Beowulf*.[9]

Yet how do we build that literary tradition out of "a poetry of things left in the dust"? I argue that translation makes this question as complex as the Roman ruins that permeate the Beowulfian world. When Grendel treads the floor at Heorot, he becomes part of a longer story: a story of how ruins get handed down, with or without the narratives that would contextualize them

---

3. Lerer, "On fagne flor," in Kabir and Williams, *Postcolonial Approaches*. For mosaic floors in early medieval England, see Cramp, "*Beowulf* and Archaeology."

4. Lerer, "On fagne flor," in Kabir and Williams, *Postcolonial Approaches*, 84.

5. Lerer, 86–87.

6. See lines 2041–69, in which Beowulf imagines a scenario where the words of an old warrior to a young warrior regarding the former ownership of a battle sword reignite a feud between warring parties. See also lines 1197–1201, in which the poet invokes the *Brosinga mene* as an analogue for the neck ring given to Beowulf by Wealhtheow. Hygelac will later be wearing this neck ring when he dies.

7. Lerer, "On fagne flor," in Kabir and Williams, *Postcolonial Approaches*, 98.

8. Lerer, 98.

9. Lerer, 99.

as part of a specific kind of history.[10] As a result (and as Lerer's work shows), Grendel's own history becomes connected to the history of Rome's activities in England, despite the poem's setting in Scandinavia. Grendel is also connected, therefore, to the background of loss—"the wrecks of Roman buildings / they could not copy / or restore," as James Arthur's "A Local History" has it—that seems endemic to both the world within *Beowulf* and the world that created it.[11] The groupings imagined by the poem are not unidirectional: they stretch from its present to its past, and from that past into a future "we" who will inherit the narrative.

THIS BOOK ENTERS the modern world at a moment when, beyond the academic sphere, the narratives and histories of *Beowulf* and the other works in this monograph have been co-opted by white supremacists who seek to perpetuate the idea of monolithic medieval European identities—identities that are as historically bankrupt as they are morally vile.[12] Whatever their motivations, academics help to create these visions of the world whenever they give in to the temptation to look at these works as monoliths that yield but a single meaning, that are reducible to a historical setting or place, or that have a relationship to a source of culture or narrative that is unchanging in its signification and its work. These dual movements—first, to arrest and reduce the past and its works to a single time or meaning, and second, to mobilize that vision to create fictive histories for modern identities—betray a fundamental lack of understanding of the world from which they claim to draw. But misunder-

---

10. For the artistic and narrative effect of *spolia*, see Ferhatović, *Borrowed Objects*. My thoughts on the mosaic floor are deeply indebted to him, as well as to conversations with Irina Dumitrescu.

11. My understanding of time and ruins in Old English literature follows Liuzza's study of these tropes in *The Wanderer*. Like Lerer's poetry of *pulvis*, Liuzza emphasizes the interpretive impulse that arises from ruins: "Unlike their analogues in the tradition of Biblical exegesis, however, the ruins in *The Wanderer* are monuments not to the legibility but to the inscrutability of history, not to God's providential intervention but to the decline and decay of the earthly kingdom and the impermanence of human fame [. . .] they reveal the past not as a stable place from which the present takes it legitimate origin but as a place of loss, decay, silence, rupture, and brokenness, ultimately a warning to the present that our story will be told by the fragments we leave behind" ("Tower of Babel," 13).

12. The last several years have seen both a proliferation of such incidences—in which white supremacists explicitly align themselves with a monolithic and "pure" white European Middle Ages—as well as academics and others exposing and opposing their activities. A *very* partial bibliography of such pieces includes: Fellowship of Medievalists of Color, "On Race and Medieval Studies"; Livingstone, "Racism, Medievalism, and the White Supremacists of Charlottesville"; Bambury, "Medieval History Scholars"; Kim, "Teaching Medieval Studies in a Time of White Supremacy"; Lomuto, "White Nationalism and the Ethics of Medieval Studies."

standing is not the only issue. Rather, hermeneutic violence can bolster other kinds of violence, and so it is our responsibility as scholars not just to point out interpretive inaccuracy but to condemn the violence that it justifies. In the words of the Medievalists of Color Fellowship:

> We must continuously work to separate [medieval studies] from its links to nationalist and white supremacist impulses. At a time when such impulses have increased the rates of violence—rhetorical, psychological, and physical—in the US, UK, Europe, and elsewhere, we must ensure that the conditions for violence are not fostered within medieval studies. Indeed medieval studies must form a bulwark against such conditions.[13]

While this book does not take up the way modern communities deploy the medieval past for racist and violent ends, it nevertheless provides one starting point from which to counter simplistic interpretations of the past and their consequences. It shows that even for medieval people, such monoliths were already crumbling at the moment they were raised.

Gillian Overing reminds us of why *Beowulf* resounds so strongly in modernity and why we must continue to wrestle with its complexity even as it eludes our ability to pin it down:

> What [*Beowulf*] offers to a modern audience is not only an entry into [its] world, but a recognition of the radical, ethical dimensions of accepting emergence and multivalence. Again, this is not to argue that *Beowulf* gives any clear or moral directives about tolerance of the other. It is a poem largely about violence and fear, punctuated by moments of celebration where violence is controlled and fear is overcome. It regularly interrupts the various processes of becoming with resolution as violence, as death. But it is a poem about violence that continually wrestles with its subject, where celebration is always imbricated with fear, sorrow, foreboding; no moment is discrete. Creative tension and lack of resolution are endemic to the mode of its language, design and vision. One moment, place or thing is invested in another, and carries multiple meanings. In such a world it becomes both dishonest and simply *inappropriate* to solely praise, condemn or conclude. So to the student who asks why one thing in the poem seems to mean two, or three, or more things, or why one question opens up only further questions, the answer might be: get used to it—if you are able—and continue to wrestle

---

13. Fellowship of Medievalists of Color, "On Race and Medieval Studies."

with ambiguity. This is the mode of the poem, this is what it *does*. This is what it can do to and for our "now."[14]

Overing's point here is that *Beowulf*—like the mosaic floors its characters build upon but (perhaps) do not understand—is itself an accretion of times and traditions. It does not offer us a univocal understanding of the world it explores because such an understanding could not, did not, and does not exist: not in the time of the poem, not in the time of its composition, and not in any of the times of its reception. The best we, as critics, can do is to keep finding within the poem versions that respond to—and even contradict—the present uses to which the poem might be put.

And this, in the end, is what this book hopes to suggest about medieval literature more generally through its exploration of translation effects and the temporalities and communities they bring together, create, and even destroy. If translation was ubiquitous in the Middle Ages—and decades of scholarship have proven that it was—then the corollary is that the communities that these texts build draw on multilingual and multitemporal traditions. Translation effects demonstrate how narrative transmission can create and sustain communities based on such traditions; ignorance of the depth of these narratives can undermine attempts to build upon them. But in many cases, the inherited narratives of the Middle Ages can offer a glimpse not of monolithic identities that are unchanging across the centuries but of a profoundly interconnected world: a network of people, times, and stories.

---

14. Overing, "Beowulf: A Poem in Our Time" in Lees, *Cambridge History of Early Medieval English Literature*, 330–31.

BIBLIOGRAPHY

Alcuin. *The Bishops, Kings, and Saints of York*. Ed. Peter Godman. Oxford: Clarendon Press, 1982.

Allen, Elizabeth. "Chaucer Answers Gower: Constance and the Trouble with Reading." *English Language History* 64.3 (1997): 627–55.

Altman, Rochelle. "Hymnody, Graphotactics, and 'Cædmon's Hymn.'" *Philological Review* 34.2 (2008): 1–27.

Anderson, Benedict. *Imagined Communities: Reflections on the Origin and Spread of Nationalism*. London: Verso, 2006.

Anderson, Earl R. "Treasure Trove in *Beowulf*." *Mediaevalia* 3 (1977): 141–64.

Anlezark, Daniel. "Which Books Are 'Most Necessary' to Know? The Old English *Pastoral Care* Preface and King Alfred's Educational Reform." *English Studies* 98.8 (2017): 759–80.

Arthur, Ciaran. "Giving the Head's Up in Ælfric's *Passio Sancti Eadmundi*: Postural Representations of the Old English Saint." *Philological Quarterly* 92.3 (2013): 315–33.

Arthur, James. "A Local History." In *The Suicide's Son*, 39–40. Montréal: Véhicule Press, 2019.

Ashdowne, R. K., D. R. Howlett, and R. E. Latham, eds. *Dictionary of Medieval Latin from British Sources*. Oxford: British Academy, 2018.

Baker, Peter S. *Honor, Exchange, and Violence in* Beowulf. Cambridge: D. S. Brewer, 2013.

Bakhtin, Mikhail M. *The Dialogic Imagination: Four Essays*. Ed. Michael Holquist. Trans. Caryl Emerson and Michael Holquist. Austin: University of Texas Press, 1981.

Bambury, Brent. "Medieval History Scholars Are Suddenly on the Front Lines in the Fight against White Supremacists." *CBC Radio*, 29 September 2017. Available at https://www.cbc.ca/radio/day6/episode-357-little-rock-nine-historians-vs-neo-nazis-tabatha-southey-fired-robots-yuval-harari-and-more-1.4309188/medieval-history-scholars-are-suddenly-on-the-front-lines-in-the-fight-against-white-supremacists-1.4309219.

Barlow, Gania. "A Thrifty Tale: Narrative Authority and the Competing Values of the *Man of Law's Tale.*" *Chaucer Review* 44.4 (2010): 397–420.

Barney, Stephen, W. J. Lewis, J. A. Beach, and Oliver Berghof, trans. *The Etymologies of Isidore of Seville.* Cambridge: Cambridge University Press, 2011.

Bassnett, Susan. *Translation.* London: Routledge, 2014.

———. *Translation Studies.* London: Routledge, 2002.

Bately, Janet M. "King Alfred and the Old English Translation of *Orosius.*" *Anglia* 88 (1970): 435–60.

———. "The Literary Prose of King Alfred's Reign: Translation or Transformation?" In *Old English Prose: Basic Readings.* Ed. Paul Szarmach, 3–28. New York: Garland, 2000.

———, ed. *The Old English Orosius.* EETS, s.s. 6. Oxford: Oxford University Press, 1980.

———. "The Old English *Orosius.*" In *A Companion to Alfred the Great.* Eds. Nicole G. Discenza and Paul E. Szarmach, 313–43. Leiden: Brill, 2015.

———. "Those Books That Are Most Necessary for All Men to Know: The Classics and Late Ninth-Century England, a Reappraisal." In *The Classics in the Middle Ages: Papers of the Twentieth Annual Conference of the Center for Medieval and Early Renaissance Studies.* Eds. Aldo S. Bernardo and Saul Levin, 45–78. Binghamton, NY: Center for Medieval and Early Renaissance Studies, 1990.

———. "World History in the *Anglo-Saxon Chronicle*: Its Sources and Separateness from the Old English *Orosius.*" *ASE* 8 (1979): 177–94.

Bede. "The Story of Cædmon." In *The Norton Anthology of English Literature: Volume A, The Middle Ages.* Ed. Stephen Greenblatt, 29–32. New York: W. W. Norton, 2012.

Beer, Jeanette, ed. *Medieval Translators and Their Craft.* Kalamazoo, MI: Medieval Institute Publications, 1989.

———, ed. *Translation Theory and Practice in the Middle Ages.* Kalamazoo, MI: Medieval Institute Publications, 1997.

Benjamin, Walter. "The Task of the Translator." In *Selected Writings, Volume 1: 1913–1926.* Eds. Marcus Bullock and Michael W. Jennings, 253–63. Cambridge, MA: Belknap Press, 2002.

———. "Theses on the Philosophy of History." In *Illuminations.* Ed. Hannah Arendt. Trans. Harry Zohn, 253–64. New York: Schocken Books, 1968.

Benson, Larry. "The Pagan Coloring of *Beowulf.*" In *The Beowulf Reader.* Ed. Peter S. Baker, 35–50. New York: Routledge, 2000.

———, ed. *The Riverside Chaucer.* Boston: Houghton Mifflin, 1987.

Biggs, Frederick. "*Beowulf* and Some Fictions of Geatish Succession." *ASE* 32 (2003): 55–77.

Bintley, Michael D. J. "Where the Wild Things Are in Old English Poetry." In *Representing Beasts in Early Medieval England and Scandinavia.* Eds. Michael D. J. Bintley and Thomas J. T. Williams, 205–28. Woodbridge: Boydell, 2015.

Bittner, Rudiger. "Augustine's Philosophy of History." In *The Augustinian Tradition.* Ed. Gareth B. Matthews, 345–60. Berkeley: University of California Press, 1999.

Bjork, Robert E., and John D. Niles, eds. *A Beowulf Handbook.* Lincoln: University of Nebraska Press, 1997.

Block, Edward A. "Originality, Controlling Purpose, and Craftsmanship in Chaucer's *Man of Law's Tale.*" *PMLA* 68.3 (1953): 572–616.

Blockley, Mary. *Aspects of Old English Poetic Syntax: Where Clauses Begin.* Urbana: University of Illinois Press, 2001.

Blumenfeld-Kosinski, Renate, Luise von Flotow, and Daniel Russell, eds. *The Politics of Translation in the Middle Ages and the Renaissance.* Ottawa: University of Ottawa Press, 2001.

Bonjour, Adrien. "Beowulf and the Beasts of Battle." *PMLA* 72.4 (1957): 563–73.

———. *The Digressions in Beowulf.* Medium Aevum Monographs. Oxford: Blackwell, 1950.

Borges, Jorge Luis. "When Fiction Lives in Fiction." Trans. Esther Allen. In *Selected Non-Fictions*. Ed. Eliot Weinberger, 160–62. New York: Penguin, 2000.

Bosworth, Joseph, and T. Northcote Toller, eds. *An Anglo-Saxon Dictionary Based on the Manuscript Collections of the Late Joseph Bosworth.* Oxford: Oxford University Press, 1898.

Bowers, John M. "Colonialism, Latinity, and Resistance." In *Chaucer: Contemporary Approaches*. Eds. Susanna Fein and David Raybin, 116–34. University Park: Pennsylvania State University Press, 2010.

Braudel, Fernand. *On History.* Trans. Sarah Matthews. Chicago: University of Chicago Press, 1980.

Breeze, Andrew. "The Celtic Gospels in Chaucer's *Man of Law's Tale*." *Chaucer Review* 32.4 (1998): 335–38.

British Library. "Cotton MS Julius E.vii." Available at http://www.bl.uk/manuscripts/Viewer.aspx?ref=cotton_ms_julius_e_vii_fs001ar.

British Library. "Cotton MS Vespasian D XIV." Available at http://www.bl.uk/manuscripts/Viewer.aspx?ref=cotton_ms_vespasian_d_xiv_f004r.

Brooks, Nicholas P. *Anglo-Saxon Myths: State and Church, 400–1066.* London: Hambledon Press, 2000.

Brown, Michelle P. *Understanding Illuminated Manuscripts: A Guide to Technical Terms.* Los Angeles and London: The J. Paul Getty Museum in association with the British Library, 1994.

Brown, Peter. *The Cult of the Saints: Its Rise and Function in Latin Christianity.* Chicago: University of Chicago Press, 1981.

Bryan, Elizabeth J. *Collaborative Meaning in Medieval Scribal Culture: The Otho Laȝamon.* Ann Arbor: University of Michigan Press, 1999.

Burrow, J. A. "A Maner Latyn Corrupt." *Medium Ævum* 30.1 (1961): 33–37.

Bussières, Michelle. "Etude d'un Receuil Hagiographique en Vieil Anglais, MS British Library Cotton Julius E.vii." Ph.D. Diss., Université de Poitiers, 2004.

Butler, Emily. *Language and Community in Early England: Imagining Distance in Medieval Literature.* New York: Routledge, 2017.

Cain, Christopher M. "'þæt is on englisc': Performing Multilingualism in Anglo-Saxon England." In *Imagining Medieval English: Language Structures and Theories, 500–1500*. Ed. Tim William Machan, 81–99. Cambridge: Cambridge University Press, 2016.

Calder, Daniel G. "Setting and Ethos: The Pattern of Measure and Limit in *Beowulf*." *Studies in Philology* 69.1 (1972): 21–37.

Callon, Michel. "Some Elements of a Sociology of Translation: Domestication of the Scallops and the Fishermen of St. Brieuc Bay." In *Power, Action, and Belief: A New Sociology of Knowledge?* Ed. John Law, 196–233. Boston: Routledge, 1986.

Cameron, Angus, Ashley Crandell Amos, Antonette diPaolo Healey, et al., eds. *Dictionary of Old English: A to I Online.* Toronto: Dictionary of Old English Project, 2018.

Campbell, Emma. "The Scandals of Medieval Translation: Thinking Difference in Francophone Texts and Manuscripts." In *The French of England: Essays in Honour of Jocelyn Wogan-Browne*. Eds. Thelma Fenster and Carolyn P. Collette, 38–54. Cambridge: D. S. Brewer, 2017.

———. "The Time of Translation in Wauchier de Denain's *Histoire des moines D'Égypte*." *Florilegium* 31 (2014): 1–29.

Campbell, Emma, and Robert Mills. *Rethinking Medieval Translation: Ethics, Politics, Theory.* Cambridge: D. S. Brewer, 2012.

Carver, Martin. "Burial as Poetry: The Context of Treasure in Anglo-Saxon Graves." In *Treasure in the Medieval West*. Ed. Elizabeth M. Tyler, 25–48. York: York Medieval Press, 2000.

Cavill, Paul. "Christianity and Theology in *Beowulf*." In *The Christian Tradition in Anglo-Saxon England: Approaches to Current Scholarship and Teaching*. Ed. Cavill, 15–40. Cambridge: D. S. Brewer, 2004.

Cawsey, Kathy. "Disorienting Orientalism: Finding Saracens in Strange Places in Late Medieval Manuscripts." *Exemplaria* 21.4 (2009): 380–97.

Chase, Colin. "Saints' Lives, Royal Lives, and the Date of *Beowulf*." In *The Dating of Beowulf*. Ed. Chase, 161–71. Toronto: University of Toronto Press, 1981.

Chenard, Marianne Malo. "King Oswald's Holy Hands: Metonymy and the Making of a Saint in Bede's *Ecclesiastical History*." *Exemplaria* 17.1 (2005): 33–56.

Cherniss, Michael D. *Ingeld and Christ: Heroic Concepts and Values in Old English Christian Poetry*. The Hague: de Gruyter Mouton, 1972.

Chickering, Howell D. *Beowulf: A Dual Language Edition*. New York: Anchor Books, 2006.

Christie, Edward. "Self-Mastery and Submission: Holiness and Masculinity in the Lives of the Anglo-Saxon Martyr-Kings." In *Holiness and Masculinity in the Middle Ages*. Eds. P. H. Cullum and Katherine J. Lewis, 143–57. Toronto: University of Toronto Press, 2004.

Clark, David. "Relaunching the Hero: The Case of Scyld and Beowulf Re-opened." *Neophilologus* 90.4 (2006): 621–42.

Clayton, Mary, ed. and trans. *Two Ælfric Texts: "The Twelve Abuses" and "The Vices and Virtues."* Cambridge: D. S. Brewer, 2013.

Clemoes, Peter, ed. *Ælfric's Catholic Homilies: The First Series; Text*, EETS, s.s. 17. Oxford: Oxford University Press, 1997.

———. "The Cult of Saint Oswald on the Continent." In *Bede and His World: The Jarrow Lectures, 1958–1993*. Ed. Michael Lapidge, 587–610. London: Aldershot, 1994.

Cohen, Jeffrey Jerome. *Medieval Identity Machines*. Minneapolis: University of Minnesota Press, 2003.

———. "Monster Culture (Seven Theses)." In *Monster Theory: Reading Culture*. Ed. Cohen, 3–25. Minneapolis: University of Minnesota Press, 1996.

———. *Of Giants: Sex, Monsters, and the Middle Ages*. Minneapolis: University of Minnesota Press, 1999.

Colgrave, Bertram, and R. A. B. Mynors, eds. *Bede's Ecclesiastical History of the English People*. Oxford: Clarendon Press, 1969.

Collier, Wendy. "The Tremulous Worcester Hand and Gregory's *Pastoral Care*." In *Rewriting Old English in the Twelfth Century*. Eds. Mary Swan and Elaine M. Treharne, 195–208. Cambridge: Cambridge University Press, 2000.

Cooney, Helen. "Wonder and Immanent Justice in the *Man of Law's Tale*." *Chaucer Review* 33.3 (1999): 264–87.

Cooper, Christine F. "'But algates therby was she understonde': Translating Custance in Chaucer's *Man of Law's Tale*." *Yearbook of English Studies*, 36.1 (2005): 27–38.

Copeland, Rita. *Rhetoric, Hermeneutics, and Translation in the Middle Ages: Academic Traditions and Vernacular Texts*. Cambridge: Cambridge University Press, 1995.

Correale, Robert M., and Mary Hamel, eds. *Sources and Analogues of the Canterbury Tales*, Vol. 2. Cambridge: D. S. Brewer, 2009.

Cramp, Rosemary J. "*Beowulf* and Archaeology." *Medieval Archaeology* 1 (1957): 57–77.

———. "The Making of Oswald's Northumbria." In *Oswald: Northumbrian King to European Saint.* Eds. Eric Cambridge and Clare Stancliffe, 17–32. Stamford: Paul Watkins, 1995.

Crane, Susan. *Animal Encounters: Contacts and Concepts in Medieval Britain.* Philadelphia: University of Pennsylvania Press, 2013.

Creed, Robert P. "Beowulf and the Language of Hoarding." In *Medieval Archaeology: Papers of the Seventeenth Annual Conference of the Center for Medieval and Renaissance Studies.* Ed. Charles L. Redman, 155–67. Binghamton, NY: SUNY, Binghamton University Press, 1989.

Crépin, Andre. "L'Espace du texte et l'esprit liturgique dans la civilisation vieil-anglaise." In *Liturgie et espace liturgique,* 49–58. Paris: Didier-Erudition, 1987.

Crick, Julia. "English Vernacular Script." In *The History of the Book in Britain,* Vol. 1. Ed. Richard Gameson, 174–86. Cambridge: Cambridge University Press, 2012.

Cronan, Dennis. "Essential Incongruities in Grendel's Final Attack." *RES* 68.286 (2017): 633–49.

———. "Narrative Disjunctions in *Beowulf.*" *English Studies* 99.5 (2018): 459–78.

Cubitt, Catherine. "Ælfric's Lay Patrons." In *A Companion to Ælfric.* Eds. Hugh Magennis and Mary Swan, 165–92. Leiden: Brill, 2009.

———. "Sites and Sanctity: Revisiting the Cult of Murdered and Martyred Anglo-Saxon Royal Saints." *Early Medieval Europe* 9.1 (2000): 53–83.

———. "Universal and Local Saints." In *Local Saints and Local Churches in the Early Medieval West.* Eds. Alan Thacker and Richard Sharpe, 423–53. Oxford: Oxford University Press, 2002.

Curtius, Ernst Robert. *European Literature and the Latin Middle Ages.* Princeton: Princeton University Press, 1973.

Da Rold, Orietta. "Cambridge, University Library, Ii.1.33." In *The Production and Use of English Manuscripts 1060 to 1220.* Eds. Orietta Da Rold, Takako Kato, Mary Swan, and Elaine Treharne. University of Leicester, 2010. Available at https://www.le.ac.uk/english/em1060to1220/mss/EM.CUL.Ii.1.33.htm.

Da Rold, Orietta, Takako Kato, Mary Swan, and Elaine Treharne. "Principles of Description." In *The Production and Use of English Manuscripts 1060 to 1220.* Eds. Da Rold, Kato, Swan, and Treharne. University of Leicester, 2010. Available at https://www.le.ac.uk/english/em1060to1220/catalogue/principles.htm.

Da Rold, Orietta, and Mary Swan. "Linguistic Contiguities: English Manuscripts 1060–1220." In *Conceptualizing Multilingualism in England, c. 800–c. 1250.* Ed. Elizabeth M. Tyler, 255–70. Turnhout: Brepols, 2011.

Dagenais, John. *The Ethics of Reading in Manuscript Culture: Glossing the* Libro de Buen Amor. Princeton: Princeton University Press, 1994.

Dailey, Patricia. "Questions of Dwelling in Anglo-Saxon Poetry and Medieval Mysticism: Inhabiting Landscape, Body, and Mind." *New Medieval Literatures* 8 (2006): 175–214.

Damon, John E. "*Desecto Capito Perfido:* Bodily Fragmentation and Reciprocal Violence in Anglo-Saxon England." *Exemplaria* 13.2 (2001): 399–432.

———. *Soldier Saints and Holy Warriors: Warfare and Sanctity in the Literature of Early England.* Aldershot: Ashgate, 2003.

Davis, Kathleen. "National Writing in the Ninth Century: A Reminder for Postcolonial Thinking about the Nation." *JMEMS* 28.3 (1998): 611–37.

———. "The Performance of Translation Theory in King Alfred's National Literary Program." In *Manuscript, Narrative, Lexicon: Essays on Literary and Cultural Transmission in Honor of Whitney F. Bolton.* Eds. Robert Boenig and Kathleen Davis, 149–70. Lewisburg, PA: Bucknell University Press, 2000.

———. *Periodization and Sovereignty: How Ideas of Feudalism and Secularization Govern the Politics of Time*. Philadelphia: University of Pennsylvania Press, 2008.

———. "Time behind the Veil: The Media, the Middle Ages, and Orientalism Now." In *The Postcolonial Middle Ages*. Ed. Jeffrey Jerome Cohen, 105–22. New York: Palgrave, 2000.

Dean, Paul. "Beowulf and the Passing of Time: Part II." *English Studies* 75.4 (1994): 293–302.

Dearnley, Elizabeth. *Translators and Their Prologues in Medieval England*. Cambridge: D. S. Brewer, 2016.

de Hamel, Christopher. *The British Library Guide to Manuscript Illumination: History and Techniques*. Toronto: University of Toronto Press, 2001.

Delany, Sheila. "Womanliness in *The Man of Law's Tale*." *Chaucer Review* 9.1 (1974): 63–72.

Dimock, Wai Chi. *Through Other Continents: American Literature Across Deep Time*. Princeton: Princeton University Press, 2006.

Dinshaw, Carolyn. *How Soon Is Now? Medieval Texts, Amateur Readers, and the Queerness of Time*. Durham, NC: Duke University Press, 2012.

———. "New Approaches to Chaucer." In *The Cambridge Companion to Chaucer*. Eds. Piero Boitani and Jill Mann, 270–89. Cambridge: Cambridge University Press, 2003.

———. "Pale Faces: Race, Religion, and Affect in Chaucer's Texts and Their Readers." *Studies in the Age of Chaucer* 23 (2001): 19–41.

Discenza, Nicole Guenther. "Alfred's Verse Preface to the *Pastoral Care* and the Chain of Authority." *Neophilologus* 85.4 (2001): 625–33.

———. *Inhabited Spaces: Anglo-Saxon Constructions of Place*. Toronto: University of Toronto Press, 2017.

———. *The King's English: Strategies of Translation in the Old English Boethius*. Albany: State University of New York Press, 2005.

———. "The Old English *Bede* and the Construction of Anglo-Saxon Authority." *ASE* 31 (2002): 69–80.

Djordjević, Ivana. "Mapping Medieval Translation." In *Medieval Insular Romance: Translation and Innovation*. Eds. Judith Weiss, Jennifer Fellows, and Morgan Dickson, 7–23. Cambridge: D. S. Brewer, 2000.

Dobbie, Elliot Van Kirk, ed. *The Anglo-Saxon Minor Poems*. ASPR, Vol. 6. New York: Columbia University Press, 1942.

Donoghue, Daniel. *Old English Literature: A Short Introduction*. Oxford: Blackwell, 2004.

Dugas, Don-John. "The Legitimization of Royal Power in Chaucer's 'Man of Law's Tale.'" *Modern Philology* 95.1 (1997): 27–43.

Dumitrescu, Irina. "Bede's Liberation Philology: Releasing the English Tongue." *PMLA* 128.1 (2013): 40–56.

Dumville, David N. "*Beowulf* and the Celtic World: The Uses of Evidence." *Traditio* 37 (1981): 109–60.

———. "Kingship, Genealogies, and Regnal Lists." In *Early Medieval Kingship*. Eds. P. H. Sawyer and Ian N. Wood, 72–104. Leeds: University of Leeds, 1979.

Ellard, Donna Beth. *Anglo-Saxon(ist) Pasts, postSaxon Futures*. Earth: punctum books, 2019.

Fafinski, Mateusz. "Faraway, So Close: Liminal Thinking and the Use of Geography in the Old English *Orosius*." *Studia Warmińske* 56 (2019): 423–37.

Faulkner, Mark. "Ælfric, St. Edmund, and St. Edwold of Cerne." *Medium Ævum* 77.1 (2008): 1–9.

Fellowship of Medievalists of Color. "On Race and Medieval Studies." *Medievalists of Color*, 1 August 2017. Available at http://medievalistsofcolor.com/statements/on-race-and-medieval-studies/.

Ferhatović, Denis. *Borrowed Objects and the Art of Poetry: Spolia in Old English Verse*. Manchester: Manchester University Press, 2019.

Fineman, Joel. *Shakespeare's Perjured Eye: The Invention of Poetic Subjectivity in the Sonnets*. Berkeley: University of California Press, 1986.

———. *The Subjectivity Effect in Western Literary Tradition: Essays Toward the Release of Shakespeare's Will*. Cambridge, MA: MIT Press, 1991.

Fisher, Matthew. *Scribal Authorship and the Writing of History in Medieval England*. Columbus: The Ohio State University Press, 2012.

Fleming, Robin. *Kings and Lords in Conquest England*. Cambridge: Cambridge University Press, 1991.

Foley, John Miles. *Immanent Art: From Structure to Meaning in Traditional Oral Epic*. Bloomington: Indiana University Press, 1991.

———. *Traditional Oral Epic: The Odyssey, Beowulf, and the Serbo-Croatian Return Song*. Berkeley: University of California Press, 1990.

Foot, Sarah. "The Making of *Angelcynn*: English Identity before the Norman Conquest." *Transactions of the Royal Historical Society* 6 (1996): 25–49.

Foys, Martin K. "The Undoing of Exeter Book Riddle 47: 'Bookmoth.'" In *Transitional States: Cultural Change, Tradition, and Memory in Medieval England*. Eds. Graham Caie and Michael D. C. Drout. Tempe: ACMRS Publications, 2018.

———. *Virtually Anglo-Saxon: Old Media, New Media, and Early Medieval Studies in the Late Age of Print*. Gainesville: University Press of Florida, 2010.

Frank, Roberta. "The *Beowulf* Poet's Sense of History." In *Beowulf: A Verse Translation*, 2nd Ed. Trans. Seamus Heaney. Ed. Daniel Donoghue, 168–82. New York: W. W. Norton, 2019.

———. "Germanic Legend in Old English Literature." In *The Cambridge Companion to Old English Literature*. Eds. Malcolm Godden and Michael Lapidge, 88–106. Cambridge: Cambridge University Press, 1991.

Frankis, John. "King Ælle and the Conversion of the English: The Development of a Legend from Bede to Chaucer." In *Literary Appropriations of the Anglo-Saxons from the Thirteenth to the Twentieth Century*. Eds. Donald Scragg and Carole Weinberg, 74–92. Cambridge: Cambridge University Press, 2000.

———. "Languages and Cultures in Contact: Vernacular Lives of St. Giles and Anglo-Norman Annotations in an Anglo-Saxon Manuscript." *Leeds Studies in English*, n.s. 38 (2007): 101–33.

———. "Varieties of Language Contact in Anglo-Saxon Manuscripts." In *Crossing Boundaries: Interdisciplinary Approaches to the Art, Material Culture, Language and Literature of the Early Medieval World*. Eds. Eric Cambridge and Jane Hawkes, 258–62. Oxford: Oxbow Books, 2017.

Frantzen, Allen. *Before the Closet: Same-Sex Love from* Beowulf *to* Angels in America. Chicago: University of Chicago Press, 1998.

Franzen, Christine. *The Tremulous Hand of Worcester: A Study of Old English in the Thirteenth Century*. Oxford: Clarendon Press, 1991.

Friedman, John Block. *The Monstrous Races in Medieval Art and Thought*. Syracuse, NY: Syracuse University Press, 2000.

Fulk, R. D., Robert E. Bjork, and John D. Niles, eds. *Klaeber's Beowulf,* 4th ed. Toronto: University of Toronto Press, 2008.

Garner, Lori Ann. *Structuring Spaces: Oral Poetics and Architecture in Early Medieval England.* South Bend, IN: University of Notre Dame Press, 2011.

Gates, Jay Paul. "Discursive Murders: The St. Brice's Day Massacre, *Beowulf,* and *Morðor.*" In *Medieval and Early Modern Murder: Legal, Literary, and Historical Contexts.* Ed. Larissa Tracy, 47–76. Woodbridge: Boydell Press, 2018.

Geary, Patrick. *The Myth of Nations: The Medieval Origins of Europe.* Princeton: Princeton University Press, 2003.

Gee, Henry. *In Search of Deep Time: Beyond the Fossil Record to a New History of Life.* Ithaca, NY: Cornell University Press, 1999.

Glosecki, Stephen. *Shamanism and Old English Poetry.* New York: Garland, 1989.

Gneuss, Helmut, and Michael Lapidge. *Anglo-Saxon Manuscripts: A Bibliographical Handlist of Manuscripts and Manuscript Fragments Written or Owned in England up to 1100.* Toronto: University of Toronto Press, 2014.

Godden, Malcolm R., ed. *Ælfric's Catholic Homilies, The Second Series; Text.* EETS, s.s. 6. Oxford: Oxford University Press, 1979.

———. "The Anglo-Saxons and the Goths: Rewriting the Sack of Rome." *ASE* 31 (2002): 47–68.

———. "Did King Alfred Write Anything?" *Medium Ævum* 76.1 (2007): 1–23.

———, ed. and trans. *The Old English History of the World: An Anglo-Saxon Rewriting of Orosius.* Dumbarton Oaks Medieval Library 32. Cambridge, MA: Harvard University Press, 2016.

———. "The Old English *Orosius* and Its Sources." *Anglia* 129.3–4 (2011): 297–320.

Greenblatt, Stephen, ed. *The Norton Anthology of English Literature: Volume A, The Middle Ages.* New York: W. W. Norton, 2012.

Gretsch, Mechthild. *Ælfric and the Cult of the Saints in Late Anglo-Saxon England.* Cambridge: Cambridge University Press, 2005.

Griffin, Miranda. "The Time of the Translator in the *Ovide Moralisé.*" *Florilegium* 31 (2014): 31–53.

Griffith, Mark S. "Convention and Originality in the Old English 'Beasts of Battle' Typescene." *ASE* 22 (1993): 179–99.

Gunn, Victoria. "Bede and the Martyrdom of St. Oswald." In *Martyrs and Martyrologies: Papers Read at the 1992 Summer Meeting and 1993 Winter Meeting of the Ecclesiastical History Society.* Ed. Diana Wood, 57–66. Oxford: Blackwell Publishers, 1993.

Hahn, Thomas. "Early Middle English." In *The Cambridge History of Medieval English Literature.* Ed. David Wallace, 61–91. Cambridge: Cambridge University Press, 1999.

Hall, Thomas N. "Ælfric as Pedagogue." In *A Companion to Ælfric.* Eds. Hugh Magennis and Mary Swan, 193–216. Leiden: Brill, 2009.

Hamaguchi, Keiko. "The Cultural Otherness of Custance as a Foreign Woman in the *Man of Law's Tale.*" *Chaucer Review* 54.4 (2019): 411–40.

Hanna, Ralph. "Lambeth Palace Library, MS 487: Some Problems of Early Thirteenth-Century Textual Transmission." In *Texts and Traditions of Medieval Pastoral Care: Essays in Honour of Bella Millet.* Eds. Catherine Innes-Parker and Cate Gunn, 78–88. York: York Medieval Press, 2009.

Hanning, Robert W. "*Beowulf* as Heroic History." *Medievalia et Humanistica,* n.s. 5 (1974): 77–102.

Hare, Kent G. "Heroes, Saints and Martyrs: Holy Kingship from Bede to Ælfric." *The Heroic Age: A Journal of Early Medieval Northwestern Europe* 9 (2006): 23 paragraphs. Available at http://www.heroicage.org/issues/9/hare.html.

Harris, Joseph. "A Nativist Approach to *Beowulf*: The Case of Germanic Elegy." In *Companion to Old English Poetry*. Eds. Hank Aertson and Rolf H. Bremmer, 45–62. Amsterdam: VU University Press, 1994.

Harris, Stephen J. "The Alfredian World History and Anglo-Saxon Identity." *JEGP* 100.4 (2001): 482–510.

———. *Race and Ethnicity in Anglo-Saxon Literature*. New York: Routledge, 2003.

Hastings, Adrian. *The Construction of Nationhood: Ethnicity, Religion, and Nationalism*. Cambridge: Cambridge University Press, 1997.

Hayward, C. T. R., trans. *Saint Jerome's Hebrew Questions on Genesis*. Oxford: Clarendon Press, 1958.

Helder, William. "The Song of Creation in *Beowulf* and the Interpretation of Heorot." *English Studies in Canada* 13.3 (1987): 243–55.

Heng, Geraldine. *Empire of Magic: Medieval Romance and the Politics of Cultural Fantasy*. New York: Columbia University Press, 2003.

Hieatt, Constance B. "Modþryðo and Heremod: Intertwined Threads in the *Beowulf*-poet's Web of Words." *JEGP* 83.2 (1984): 173–82.

Hill, John M. *The Cultural World in Beowulf*. Toronto: Toronto University Press, 1995.

———. "The Sacrificial Synecdoche of Hands, Heads, and Arms in the Anglo-Saxon Heroic Story." In *Naked before God: Uncovering the Body in Anglo-Saxon England*. Eds. Jonathan Wilcox and Benjamin C. Withers, 116–37. Morgantown: West Virginia University Press, 2003.

———. "The Social and Dramatic Functions of Oral Recitation and Composition in *Beowulf*." *Oral Tradition* 17.2 (2002): 310–24.

Hill, Joyce. "Beyond the Obvious: Ælfric and the Authority of Bede." *Studies in Medieval History* 27 (2015): 39–54.

Hobson, Jacob. "Translation as Gloss in the Old English *Boethius*." *Medium Ævum* 86.2 (2017): 207–23.

Hodges, Kenneth. "Why Malory's Launcelot Is Not French: Region, Nation, and Political Identity." *PMLA* 125.3 (2010): 556–71.

Holdsworth, Carolyn. "Frames: Time Level and Variation in 'The Dream of the Rood.'" *Neophilologus* 66.4 (1982): 622–28.

Holsinger, Bruce. "The Parable of Cædmon's 'Hymn': Liturgical Invention and Literary Tradition." *JEGP* 106.2 (2007): 149–75.

Honegger, Thomas. "Form and Function: The Beasts of Battle Revisited." *English Studies* 79.4 (1998): 289–98.

Hostetter, Aaron. "Disruptive Things in *Beowulf*." *New Medieval Literatures* 17 (2017): 34–61.

Howe, John. "The Conversion of the Physical World: The Creation of a Christian Landscape." In *Varieties of Religious Conversion in the Middle Ages*. Ed. James Muldoon, 63–78. Gainesville: University Press of Florida, 1997.

Howe, Nicholas. *Migration and Mythmaking in Anglo-Saxon England*. New Haven, CT: Yale University Press, 1989.

———. "Rome: Capital of Anglo-Saxon England," *JMEMS* 34.1 (2004): 147–72.

Hsy, Jonathan. "'Oure Occian': Littoral Language and the Constance Narratives of Chaucer and Boccaccio." In *Europe and Its Others: Essays on Interperception and Identity*. Eds. Paul Gifford and Tessa Hauswedell, 215–24. Bern: Peter Lang, 2010.

———. *Trading Tongues: Merchants, Multilingualism, and Medieval Literature*. Columbus: The Ohio State University Press, 2013.

Hurley, Gina Marie. "Confession and the Creation of Community in Medieval Romance." PhD Diss., Yale University, 2020.

Hurt, James Riggins. "Ælfric and the English Saints." PhD Diss., Indiana University, 1965.

Irvine, Martin. *The Making of Textual Culture: 'Grammatica' and Literary Theory, 350–1100*. Cambridge: Cambridge University Press, 2006.

Irvine, Susan. "The Compilation and Use of Manuscripts Containing Old English in the Twelfth Century." In *Rewriting Old English in the Twelfth Century*. Eds. Mary Swan and Elaine Treharne, 41–61. Cambridge: Cambridge University Press, 2000.

Irving, Edward B., Jr. "Christian and Pagan Elements." In *A Beowulf Handbook*. Eds. Robert E. Bjork and John D. Niles, 175–92. Lincoln: University of Nebraska Press, 1997.

———. "The Nature of Christianity in *Beowulf*." *ASE* 13 (1984): 7–21.

———. *Rereading Beowulf*. Philadelphia: University of Pennsylvania Press, 1992.

Jakobson, Roman. "On Linguistic Aspects of Translation." In *The Translation Studies Reader*, 3rd Ed. Ed. Lawrence Venuti, 126–31. New York: Routledge, 2012.

Jerome. *Hebraicae quaestiones in libro Geneseos*. Eds. P. de Lagarde et al. Turnhout: Brepols, 1959.

———. "Letter to Pammachius." Trans. Kathleen Davis. In *The Translation Studies Reader*, 3rd Ed. Ed. Lawrence Venuti, 21–30. New York: Routledge, 2012.

Johnston, Michael, and Michael Van Dussen. *The Medieval Manuscript Book: Cultural Approaches*. Cambridge: Cambridge University Press, 2015.

Jordan, Timothy R. W. "Holiness and Hopefulness: The Monastic and Lay Audiences of Abbo of Fleury's *Passio Sancti Eadmundi* and Ælfric of Eynsham's *Life of Saint Edmund, King and Martyr*." *Enarratio* 19 (2015): 1–29.

Karkov, Catherine E., and Robert T. Farrell. "The Gnomic Passages of *Beowulf*." *Neuphilologische Mitteilungen* 91.3 (1990): 295–310.

Kaušikaitė, Greta, and Tatyana Solomonik-Pankrašova. "Vernacular Translation as *Enarratio Poetarum*: Cædmon's 'Hymn of Creation.'" *Respectus Philologicus* 26.31 (2014): 230–38.

Ker, N. R. *Catalogue of Manuscripts Containing Anglo-Saxon*. Oxford: Clarendon Press, 1957.

Kiernan, Kevin. "Reading Cædmon's 'Hymn' with Someone Else's Glosses." *Representations* 32 (1990): 157–74.

Kim, Dorothy. "Teaching Medieval Studies in a Time of White Supremacy." *In the Middle* (blog). 28 August 2017. Available at http://www.inthemedievalmiddle.com/2017/08/teaching-medieval-studies-in-time-of.html.

Kozuka, Yoshitaka. "Element Order in Old English Translation." In *Phases of the History of English*. Eds. Michio Hasaka, Michiko Ogura, Hironori Suzuki, and Akinobu Tani, 179–96. Bern: Peter Lang, 2013.

Krapp, George Phillip, ed. *The Junius Manuscript*. ASPR, Vol. 1. New York: Columbia University Press, 1931.

Krapp, George Phillip, and Elliot Van Kirk Dobbie, eds. *The Exeter Book*. ASPR, Vol. 3. New York: Columbia University Press, 1936.

Krappe, Alexander. "The Offa-Constance Legend." *Anglia* 61 (1937): 368–69.

Kratz, Dennis. "An Interview with Norman Shapiro." *Translation Review* 19 (1986): 27–28.

Kretzschmar, William A. "Adaptation and *anweald* in the Old English *Orosius*." *ASE* 16 (1987): 127–45.

Kruger, Steven F. "Conversion and Medieval Sexual, Religious, and Racial Categories." In *Constructing Medieval Sexuality*. Eds. Karma Lochrie, Peggy McCracken, and James A. Schultz, 158–79. Minneapolis: University of Minnesota Press, 1997.

Lapidge, Michael. *The Anglo-Saxon Library*. Oxford: Oxford University Press, 2006.

———. *The Cult of Saint Swithun*. Oxford: Oxford University Press, 2003.

———. "The Hermeneutic Style in Tenth-Century Anglo-Latin Literature." *ASE* 4 (1975): 67–111.

Latour, Bruno. *Pandora's Hope: Essays on the Reality of Science Studies*. Cambridge, MA: Harvard University Press, 1999.

———. *Reassembling the Social: An Introduction to Actor-Network Theory*. Oxford: Oxford University Press, 2005.

———. *We Have Never Been Modern*. Trans. Catherine Porter. Cambridge, MA: Harvard University Press, 1993.

Lavezzo, Kathy. *Angels on the Edge of the World: Geography, Literature, and English Community, 1000–1534*. Ithaca, NY: Cornell University Press, 2006.

———. "Beyond Rome: Mapping Gender and Justice in *The Man of Law's Tale*." *Studies in the Age of Chaucer* 24 (2002): 149–80.

Law, John. "Notes on the Theory of Actor-Network: Ordering, Strategy, and Heterogeneity." *Systems Practice* 5.4 (1992): 379–93.

Lazzari, Loredana. "Kingship and Sainthood in Ælfric: Oswald (634–642) and Edmund (840–869)." In *Hagiography in Anglo-Saxon England: Adopting and Adapting Saints' Lives into Old English Prose (c. 950–1150)*. Eds. Loredana Lazzari, Patrizia Lendinara, and Claudia Di Sciacca, 29–71. Turnhout: Brepols, 2014.

Lees, Clare. "In Ælfric's Words: Conversion, Vigilance and the Nation in Ælfric's *Life of Gregory the Great*." In *A Companion to Ælfric*. Eds. Hugh Magennis and Mary Swan, 271–96. Leiden: Brill, 2009.

Lees, Clare, and Gillian Overing. "Anglo-Saxon Horizons: Places of the Mind in the Northumbrian Landscape." In *A Place to Believe In: Locating Medieval Landscapes*. Eds. Lees and Overing, 1–26. University Park: Pennsylvania State University Press, 2006.

Legassie, Shayne Aaron. "Among Other Possible Things: The Cosmopolitanisms of Chaucer's 'Man of Law's Tale.'" In *Cosmopolitanism and the Middle Ages*. Eds. John Ganim and Shayne Aaron Legassie, 181–205. New York: Palgrave, 2013.

Le Goff, Jacques. *Medieval Civilization 400–1500*. Trans. Julia Barrow. Oxford: Blackwell Press, 1992.

Leneghan, Francis. "*Translatio Imperii*: The Old English *Orosius* and the Rise of Wessex." *Anglia* 133.4 (2015): 656–705.

Lerer, Seth. "Old English and Its Afterlife." In *The Cambridge History of Medieval English Literature*. Ed. David Wallace, 7–34. Cambridge: Cambridge University Press, 1999.

———. "'On fagne flor': The Postcolonial *Beowulf*, from Heorot to Heaney." In *Postcolonial Approaches to the European Middle Ages: Translating Cultures*. Eds. Ananya Jahanara Kabir and Deanne Williams, 77–102. Cambridge: Cambridge University Press, 2005.

Lindsay, W. M., ed. *Isidori Hispalensis Episcopi Etymologiarum sive Originum libri XX*. 2 vols. New York: Oxford University Press, 1911.

Liuzza, Roy M. "*Beowulf*: Monuments, Memory, and History." In *Readings in Medieval Texts: Interpreting Old and Middle English Literature*. Eds. David F. Johnson and Elaine Treharne, 91–108. Oxford: Oxford University Press, 2005.

———. "The Tower of Babel: *The Wanderer* and the Ruins of History." *Studies in the Literary Imagination* 36.1 (2003): 1–36.

Livingstone, Jo. "Racism, Medievalism, and the White Supremacists of Charlottesville." *New Republic*, 15 August 2017. Available at https://newrepublic.com/article/144320/racism-medievalism-white-supremacists-charlottesville.

Lomuto, Sierra. "White Nationalism and the Ethics of Medieval Studies." *In the Middle* (blog). 5 December 2016. Available at https://www.inthemedievalmiddle.com/2016/12/white-nationalism-and-ethics-of.html.

Lorden, Jennifer A. "Landscapes of Devotion: The Settings of St. Swithun's Early *Vitae*." *Anglo-Saxon England* 45 (2016): 285–309.

Machan, Tim William. "Chaucer as Translator." In *The Medieval Translator 4: The Theory and Practice of Translation in the Middle Ages*. Ed. Roger H. Ellis, 55–67. Cambridge: D. S. Brewer, 1989.

Maclean, Douglas. "King Oswald's Wooden Cross at Heavenfield in Context." In *The Insular Tradition*. Eds. Catherine E. Karkov, Michael Ryan, and Robert T. Farrell, 79–97. Albany: State University of New York Press, 1997.

Magennis, Hugh. "Ælfric's *Lives of the Saints* and Cotton Julius E.vii: Adaptation, Appropriation, and the Disappearing Book." In *Imagining the Book*. Eds. Stephen Kelly and John J. Thompson, 99–109. Turnhout: Brepols, 2005.

———. "Warrior Saints, Warfare, and the Hagiography of Ælfric of Eynsham." *Traditio* 56 (2001): 27–51.

Magoun, Francis P. "The Theme of the Beasts of Battle in Anglo-Saxon Poetry." *Neuphilologische Mitteilungen* 56.2 (1955): 81–90.

Major, C. Tidmarsh. "A Christian 'Wyrd': Syncretism in *Beowulf*." *English Language Notes* 32.3 (1995): 1–10.

Major, Tristan. "Ælfric of Eynsham and Self-Translation." In *Teaching and Learning Medieval Europe: Essays in Honor of Gernot R. Wieland*. Eds. Greti Dinkova-Bruun and Tristan Major, 83–110. Leiden: Brepols, 2017.

McGalliard, John C. "The Poet's Comment in *Beowulf*." *Studies in Philology* 75.3 (1978): 243–70.

McPhee, John. *Basin and Range*. New York: Farrar, Straus and Giroux, 1982.

McSparran, Frances et al., eds. *Middle English Dictionary: Online Edition in Middle English Compendium*. Ann Arbor: University of Michigan Library, 2000–2018. Available at http://quod.lib.umich.edu/m/middle-english-dictionary/.

Merrills, A. H. *History and Geography in Late Antiquity*. Cambridge: Cambridge University Press, 2005.

Michelet, Fabienne. *Creation, Migration, and Conquest: Imaginary Geography and Sense of Space in Old English Literature*. Oxford: Oxford University Press, 2006.

Miller, Thomas, ed. and trans. *The Old English Version of Bede's Ecclesiastical History of the English People*. Vols. 1–2. London: EETS, 1898.

Millett, Bella. "Chaucer, Lollius, and the Medieval Theory of Authorship." *Studies in the Age of Chaucer* 1 (1984): 93–103.

———. "The Pastoral Context of the Trinity and Lambeth Homilies." In *Essays in Manuscript Geography: Vernacular Manuscripts of the English West Midlands from the Conquest to the Sixteenth Century*. Ed. Wendy Scase, 43–64. Turnhout: Brepols, 2007.

Minkoff, Harvey. "An Example of Latin Influence on Ælfric's Translation Style." *Neophilologus* 61.1 (1977): 127–42.

———. "Some Stylistic Consequences of Ælfric's Theory of Translation." *Studies in Philology* 73.1 (1976): 29–41.

Minnis, Alastair. *The Medieval Theory of Authorship: Scholastic Literary Attitudes in the Later Middle Ages*. Philadelphia: University of Pennsylvania Press, 2010.

Mitchell, Bruce. "Cædmon's Hymn, Line 1: What Is the Subject of *Scylun* or Its Variants?" *Leeds Studies in English* 16 (1985): 190–97.

———. *Old English Syntax* Vols. 1–2. Oxford: Oxford University Press, 1985.

Mittman, Asa Simon. *Maps and Monsters in Medieval England*. New York: Routledge, 2006.

Miyashiro, Adam. "Decolonizing Anglo-Saxon Studies: A Response to ISAS in Honolulu." *In the Middle* (blog). 29 July 2017. Available at http:/www.inthemedievalmiddle.com/2017/07/decolonizing-anglo-saxon-studies.html.

———. "Homeland Insecurity: Biopolitics and Sovereign Violence in *Beowulf*." *Postmedieval* 11.4 (2020): 384–95.

———. "Our Deeper Past: Race, Settler Colonialism, and Medieval Heritage Politics." *Literature Compass* 16.9–10 (2019).

Nakley, Susan. *Living in the Future: Sovereignty and Internationalism in the* Canterbury Tales. Ann Arbor: University of Michigan Press, 2017.

———. "Sovereignty Matters: Anachronism, Chaucer's Britain, and England's Future's Past." *Chaucer Review* 44.4 (2010): 368–96.

Nelson, Ingrid. "Premodern Media and Networks of Transmission in the *Man of Law's Tale*." *Exemplaria* 25.3 (2013): 211–30.

Neville, Jennifer. *Representations of the Natural World in Old English Poetry*. Cambridge: Cambridge University Press, 1999.

Niles, John D. *Beowulf: The Poem and Its Tradition*. Cambridge, MA: Harvard University Press, 1983.

———. "Pagan Survivals and Popular Belief." In *The Cambridge Companion to Old English Literature*. Eds. Malcolm R. Godden and Michael Lapidge, 126–71. Cambridge: Cambridge University Press, 1991.

———. "Ring Composition and the Structure of *Beowulf*." *PMLA* 94.5 (1979): 924–35.

North, Richard. *The Origins of Beowulf: From Vergil to Wiglaf*. Oxford: Oxford University Press, 2006.

O'Brien, Bruce. *Reversing Babel: Translation Among the English during an Age of Conquests, c. 800 to 1200*. Newark: University of Delaware Press, 2011.

O'Brien O'Keeffe, Katherine. "*Beowulf* Lines 702b–836: Transformations and the Limits of the Human." *Texas Studies in Literature and Language* 23.4 (1981): 484–94.

———. "Graphic Cues for the Presentation of Verse in the Earliest Manuscripts of Bede's *Historia Ecclesiastica*." *Manuscripta* 31.3 (1987): 139–46.

———. "Orality and the Developing Text of Caedmon's *Hymn*." *Speculum* 62.1 (1987): 1–20.

———. *Visible Song: Transitional Literacy in Old English Verse*. Cambridge: Cambridge University Press, 1990.

O'Donnell, Daniel Paul. "Bede's Strategy in Paraphrasing Cædmon's 'Hymn.'" *JEGP* 103.4 (2004): 417–32.

Oosthuizen, Susan. *The Emergence of the English*. Leeds: ARC Humanities Press, 2019.

Orchard, Andy. *A Critical Companion to* Beowulf. Cambridge: D. S. Brewer, 2003.

———. "Poetic Inspiration and Prosaic Translation: The Making of *Cædmon's Hymn*." In *Studies in English Language and Literature: Doubt Wisely; Papers in Honour of E. G. Stanley*. Eds. M. J. Toswell and E. M. Tyler, 402–22. London: Routledge, 1996.

———. *Pride and Prodigies: Studies in the Monsters of the* Beowulf-*Manuscript*. Toronto: University of Toronto Press, 2003.

Orosius, Paulus. *Historiarum Adversum Paganos Libri Septem*. Ed. Karl Zangemeister. Leipzig: B. G. Teubner, 1889.

———. *The Seven Books of History against the Pagans*. Trans. Roy Deferrari. *The Fathers of the Church*, Vol. 50. Washington, DC: Catholic University of America Press, 1964.

———. *The Seven Books of History against the Pagans*. Trans. A. T. Fear. Liverpool: Liverpool University Press, 2010.

Osborn, Marijane. "The Great Feud: Scriptural History and Strife in *Beowulf*." *PMLA* 93.5 (1978): 973–81.

———. "Translation, Translocation, and the Native Context of 'Cædmon's Hymn.'" *New Comparison* 8.1 (1989): 13–23.

Overing, Gillian. "Beowulf: A Poem in Our Time." In *The Cambridge History of Early Medieval English Literature*. Ed. Clare A. Lees, 309–31. Cambridge: Cambridge University Press. 2013.

———. *Language, Sign, and Gender in Beowulf*. Carbondale: Southern Illinois University Press, 1990.

Owen-Crocker, Gale. *The Four Funerals in Beowulf and the Structure of the Poem*. Manchester: Manchester University Press, 2000.

Pareles, Mo. "What the Raven Told the Eagle: Animal Language and the Return of Loss in *Beowulf*." In *Dating Beowulf: Studies in Intimacy*. Eds. Daniel C. Remein and Erica Weaver, 164–86. Manchester: Manchester University Press, 2020.

Parkes, M. B. "The Influence of the Concepts of *Ordinatio* and *Compilatio* on the Development of the Book." In *Scribes, Scripts, and Readers: Studies in the Communication, Presentation, and Dissemination of Medieval Texts*, 35–70. London: Hambledon Press, 1991.

———. *Pause and Effect: An Introduction to the History of Punctuation in the West*. Berkeley: University of California Press, 1993.

Parks, Ward. "The Traditional Narrator and the 'I Heard' Formulas in Old English Poetry." *ASE* 16 (1987): 45–66.

———. "Ring Structure and Narrative Embedding in Homer and *Beowulf*." *Neuphilologische Mitteilungen* 89.3 (1988): 237–51.

Pasternack, Carole Braun. "Is Beowulf Postmodern Yet? A Roundtable." Paper Presented at the International Congress on Medieval Studies, Kalamazoo, MI, May 2006.

Paz, James. "Æschere's Head, Grendel's Mother, and the Sword that Isn't a Sword: Unreadable Things in Beowulf." *Exemplaria* 25.3 (2013): 231–51.

Pelle, Stephen. "Source Studies in the Lambeth Homilies." *JEGP* 113.1 (2014): 34–72.

Phillips, Susan E. "Chaucer's Language Lessons." *Chaucer Review* 46.1 (2011): 39–59.

Pinner, Rebecca. *The Cult of Saint Edmund in Medieval East Anglia*. Woodbridge: Boydell Press, 2015.

Pratt, Robert A. "Chaucer and *Les Cronicles* of Nicholas Trevet." In *Studies in Language, Literature, and Culture of the Middle Ages and Later*. Eds. E. B Atwood, A. A. Hill, and R. Willard, 303–11. Austin: University of Texas Press, 1969.

Putter, Ad. "Code-Switching in Langland, Chaucer, and the *Gawain* poet: Diglossia and Footing." In *Code-Switching in Early English*. Eds. Herbert Schendl and Laura Wright, 281–302. Berlin: DeGruyter, 2011.

Rajendran, Shyama. "Undoing 'the Vernacular': Dismantling Structures of Raciolinguistic Supremacy." *Literature Compass* 16.9–10 (2019).

Rambaran-Olm, Mary. "Anglo-Saxon Studies [Early English Studies], Academia, and White Supremacy." *Medium* (blog). 27 June 2018. Available at https://mrambaranolm.medium.com/anglo-saxon-studies-academia-and-white-supremacy-17c87b36obf3.

———. "Misnaming the Medieval: Rejecting 'Anglo-Saxon' Studies." *History Workshop*. 4 November 2019. Available at http://www.historyworkshop.org.uk/misnaming-the-medieval-rejecting-anglo-saxon-studies/.

Raybin, David. "Custance and History: Woman as Outsider in the *Man of Law's Tale*." *Studies in the Age of Chaucer* 12 (1990): 65–84.

Remein, Daniel C. "ISAS Should Probably Change its Name." Paper Presented at the International Congress on Medieval Studies, Kalamazoo, MI, May 2017. Available at https://www.academia.edu/34101681/_Isas_should_probably_change_its_name_ICMS_Kalamazoo_2017.

Reynolds, Susan. *Kingdoms and Communities in Western Europe, 900–1300*. Oxford: Oxford University Press, 1997.

———. "What Do We Mean by 'Anglo-Saxon' and 'Anglo-Saxons'?" *Journal of British Studies* 24.4 (1985): 395–414.

Ríkharðsdóttir, Sif. *Medieval Translations and Cultural Discourse: The Movement of Texts in England, France, and Scandinavia*. Cambridge: D. S. Brewer, 2012.

Robertson, Elizabeth. "The 'Elvyssh' Power of Constance: Christian Feminism in Geoffrey Chaucer's *The Man of Law's Tale*." *Studies in the Age of Chaucer* 23 (2001): 143–80.

Roberston, Kellie. "Medieval Things: Materiality, Historicism, and the Premodern Object." *Literature Compass* 5/6 (2008): 1060–80.

Rohrbacker, David. *The Historians of Late Antiquity*. London: Routledge, 2002.

Rossi-Reder, Andrea. "Embodying Christ, Embodying Nation: Ælfric's Accounts of Saints Agatha and Lucy." In *Sex and Sexuality in Anglo-Saxon England*. Eds. Daniel Calder, Carol Pasternack, and Lisa Weston, 183–202. Tempe: ACMRS, 2004.

Rowley, Sharon. "'Ic Beda' . . . 'Cwæð Beda': Reinscribing Bede in the Old English *Historia Ecclesiastica gentis anglorum*." In *Palimpsests and the Literary Imagination of Medieval England: Collected Essays*. Eds. Leo Carruthers, Raeleen Chai-Elsholz, and Tatjana Silec, 95–113. New York: Palgrave MacMillan, 2011.

Rutherford, Alexander. "The Anglo-Norman Chronicle of Nicolas Trivet: Text, with Historical, Philological and Literary Study." PhD Diss., University of London—Birkbeck, 1932.

Saltzman, Benjamin A. "Community, Joy, and the Intimacy of Narrative in *Beowulf*." In *Dating Beowulf: Studies in Intimacy*. Eds. Daniel C. Remein and Erica Weaver, 31–53. Manchester: Manchester University Press, 2020.

———. "Secrecy and the Hermeneutic Potential in *Beowulf*." *PMLA* 133.1 (2018): 36–55.

Sato, Kiriko "Ælfric's Lexical Alterations in His Adaptations from the Old English *Boethius*." *Neophilologus* 95.2 (2011): 305–11.

———. "Ælfric's Linguistic and Stylistic Alterations in His Adaptations from the Old English *Boethius*." *Neophilologus* 96.4 (2012): 631–40.

Schendl, Herbert, and Laura Wright, eds. *Code-Switching in Early English*. Berlin: DeGruyter, 2011.

Schibanoff, Susan. "Worlds Apart: Orientalism, Antifeminism, and Heresy in Chaucer's *Man of Law's Tale*." *Exemplaria* 8.1 (1996): 59–96.

Schiff, Randy P. *Revivalist Fantasy: Alliterative Verse and Nationalist Literary History*. Columbus: The Ohio State University Press, 2011.

Schipper, William. "A Worksheet of the Worcester 'Tremulous' Glossator." *Anglia* 105.1–2 (1987): 28–49.

Schliermacher, Friedrich. "On the Different Methods of Translating." In *The Translation Studies Reader*, 3rd Ed. Ed. Lawrence Venuti, 43–64. New York: Routledge, 2012.

Schott, Christine. "Intimate Reading: Marginalia in Medieval Manuscripts." Ph.D. Diss., University of Virginia, 2012.

Scribner, Matthew. "Signs, Interpretation, and Exclusion in *Beowulf*." In *Darkness, Depression, and Descent in Anglo-Saxon England*. Ed. Ruth Wehlau, 117–32. Kalamazoo, MI: Medieval Institute Publications, 2019.

Sisam, Celia. "The Scribal Tradition of the Lambeth Homilies." *RES* 2.6 (1951): 105–13.

Skeat, W.W. *Ælfric's Lives of the Saints*. Vols. 1–2. London: EETS, 1881.

Sklar, Elizabeth. "Ælfric's *Life of Saint Edmund*: Constructing a National Identity." *Medieval Perspectives* 17.2 (2002): 129–42.

Smith, Kathleen. "Writing, Rewriting, and Disrupting the Anglo-Saxon Past in Chaucer's *Man of Law's Tale*." In *Remembering the Medieval Present: Generative Uses of England's Pre-Conquest Past, 10th–15th Centuries*. Eds. Jay Paul Gates and Brian O'Camb, 195–214. Leiden: Brill, 2019.

Spearing, A. C. "Narrative Voice: The Case of Chaucer's *Man of Law's Tale*." *New Literary History* 32.3 (2001): 715–46.

Stahuljak, Zrinka. "Medieval Fixers: Politics of Interpreting in Western Historiography." In *Rethinking Medieval Translation: Ethics, Politics, Theory*. Eds. Emma Campbell and Robert Mills, 147–63. Cambridge: D. S. Brewer, 2012.

Stanbury, Sarah. "The *Man of Law's Tale* and Rome." *Exemplaria* 22.2 (Summer 2010): 119–37.

Stancliffe, Clare. "Oswald, 'Most Holy and Victorious King of the Northumbrians.'" In *Oswald: Northumbrian King to European Saint*. Eds. Eric Cambridge and Clare Stancliffe, 33–83. Stamford: Paul Watkins, 1995.

Stanley, Eric. "King Alfred's Prefaces." *RES* 39.155 (August 1988): 349–64.

Stanton, Robert. *The Culture of Translation in Anglo-Saxon England*. Cambridge: D. S. Brewer, 2002.

Stavsky, Jonathan. "Translating the Near East in the *Man of Law's Tale* and Its Analogues." *Chaucer Review* 55.1 (2020): 32–54.

Steel, Karl. *How to Make A Human: Animals and Violence in the Middle Ages*. Columbus: The Ohio State University Press, 2011.

Steiner, George. *After Babel: Aspects of Language and Translation*. Oxford: Oxford University Press, 1998.

———. "The Hermeneutic Motion." In *The Translation Studies Reader*, 3rd Ed. Ed. Lawrence Venuti, 156–161. New York: Routledge, 2012.

Stephenson, Rebecca. *The Politics of Language: Byrhtferth, Ælfric, and the Multilingual Identity of the Benedictine Reform*. Toronto: Toronto University Press, 2015.

Stock, Brian. *The Implications of Literacy: Written Language and Models of Interpretation in the Eleventh and Twelfth Centuries*. Princeton: Princeton University Press, 1983.

———. *Listening for the Text: On the Uses of the Past*. Baltimore: Johns Hopkins University Press, 1990.

Stodnick, Jacqueline. "Bodies of the Land: The Place of Gender in the *Old English Martyrology*." In *Writing Women Saints in Anglo-Saxon England*. Ed. Paul Szarmach, 30–52. Toronto: University of Toronto Press, 2013.

Strohm, Paul. *Theory and the Premodern Text*. Minneapolis: University of Minnesota Press, 2000.

Swan, Mary. "Ælfric's *Catholic Homilies* in the Twelfth Century." In *Rewriting Old English in the Twelfth Century*. Eds. Mary Swan and Elaine M. Treharne, 62–82. Cambridge: Cambridge University Press, 2000.

———. "London, Lambeth Palace, 487." In *The Production and Use of English Manuscripts 1060 to 1220*. Eds. Orietta Da Rold, Takako Kato, Mary Swan, and Elaine Treharne. University of Leicester, 2010. Available at https://www.le.ac.uk/english/em1060to1220/mss/EM.Lamb.487.htm.

———. "Preaching Past the Conquest: Lambeth Palace 487 and Cotton Vespasian A.xxii." In *The Old English Homily: Precedent, Practice, and Appropriation*. Ed. Aaron Kleist, 403–23. Turnhout: Brepols, 2007.

———. "Reading for the Ear: Lambeth Palace Library, MS 487, Item 10." *Leeds Studies in English* 41 (2010): 214–24.

Swan, Mary, and Elaine M. Treharne, eds. *Rewriting Old English in the Twelfth Century*. Cambridge: Cambridge University Press, 2000.

Sweet, Henry, ed. *King Alfred's West-Saxon Version of the Pastoral Care*. 2 vols. EETS, o.s. 45. London: Early English Texts Society, repr. 1958.

Taylor, Ann. "Contact Effects of Translation: Distinguishing Two Kinds of Influence in Old English." *Language Variation and Change* 20.2 (2008): 341–65.

Taylor, Jaime K. "Toward Premodern Globalism: Oceanic Exemplarity in Chaucer's *Man of Law's Tale*." *PMLA* 135.2 (2020): 254–71.

Taylor, Jane H. M. "Rewriting: Translation, Continuation, and Adaptation." In *Handbook of Arthurian Romance: King Arthur's Court in Medieval European Literature*. Eds. Leah Tether and Johnny McFayden, 167–81. Berlin: DeGruyter, 2017.

Taylor, Paul Beekman. *Chaucer Translator*. Lanham, MD: University Press of America, 1998.

———. "The Dragon's Treasure in *Beowulf*." *Neuphilologische Mitteilungen* 98.3 (1997): 229–40.

Thacker, Alan. "*Membra Disjecta*: The Division of the Body and the Diffusion of the Cult." In *Oswald: Northumbrian King to European Saint*. Eds. Eric Cambridge and Clare Stancliffe, 97–127. Stamford: Paul Watkins, 1995.

Thijs, Christine B. "Early Old English Translation: Practice Before Theory?" *Neophilologus* 91.1 (2007): 149–73.

Thormann, Janet. "The Poetics of Absence: The Lament of the Sole Survivor." In *De Gustibus: Essays for Alain Renoir*. Ed. John Miles Foley, 542–50. New York: Garland, 1992.

Timofeeva, Olga. "Translating the Texts Where 'et verborum ordo mysterium est': Late Old English Idiom vs. ablativus absolutus." *Journal of Medieval Latin* 18 (2009): 217–29.

Tolkien, J. R. R. "*Beowulf*: The Monsters and the Critics." In *Beowulf: A Verse Translation*, 2nd Ed. Trans. Seamus Heaney. Ed. Daniel Donoghue, 111–38. New York: W. W. Norton, 2019.

Traxel, Oliver M. *Language Change, Writing and Textual Interference in Post-Conquest Old English Manuscripts: The Evidence of Cambridge, University Library Ii.1.33*. Bern: Peter Lang, 2004.

Treharne, Elaine. "Ælfric's Account of St. Swithun: Literature of Reform and Reward." In *Narrative and History in the Early Medieval West*. Eds. Ross Balzaretti and Elizabeth M. Tyler, 167–88. Turnhout: Brepols, 2006.

———. "Cambridge, Corpus Christi College, 178." In *The Production and Use of English Manuscripts 1060 to 1220*. Eds. Orietta Da Rold, Takako Kato, Mary Swan, and Elaine Treharne. University of Leicester, 2010. Available at https://www.le.ac.uk/english/em1060to1220/mss/EM.CCCC.178.htm.

———. "Cambridge, Corpus Christi College, 303." In *The Production and Use of English Manuscripts 1060 to 1220*. Eds. Orietta Da Rold, Takako Kato, Mary Swan, and Elaine Treharne. University of Leicester, 2010. Available at https://www.le.ac.uk/english/em1060to1220/mss/EM.CCCC.303.htm.

———. *Living through Conquest: The Politics of Early English, 1020–1220.* Oxford: Oxford University Press, 2012.

———. "London, British Library, Cotton Vespasian D.xiv." In *The Production and Use of English Manuscripts 1060 to 1220.* Eds. Orietta Da Rold, Takako Kato, Mary Swan, and Elaine Treharne. University of Leicester, 2010. Available at https://www.le.ac.uk/english/em1060to1220/mss/EM.BL.Vesp.D.xiv.htm.

———. "Making Their Presence Felt: Readers of Ælfric, c. 1050–1350." In *A Companion to Ælfric.* Eds. Mary Swan and Hugh Magennis, 399–422. Leiden: Brill, 2009.

———. "Oxford, Bodleian Library, Hatton 116." In *The Production and Use of English Manuscripts 1060 to 1220.* Eds. Orietta Da Rold, Takako Kato, Mary Swan, and Elaine Treharne. University of Leicester, 2010. Available at https://www.le.ac.uk/english/em1060to1220/mss/EM.Ox.Hatt.116.htm.

Tyler, Elizabeth M. "Writing Universal History in Eleventh-Century England: Cotton Tiberius B.i, German Imperial History-writing and Vernacular Lay Literacy." In *Universal Chronicles in the High Middle Ages.* Eds. Michele Campopiano and Henry Bainton, 65–93. York: York Medieval Press, 2017.

Tyler, Elizabeth M., and Ross Balzaretti, eds. *Narrative and History in the Early Medieval West.* Turnhout: Brepols, 2006.

VanderBilt, Deborah. "Translation and Orality in the Old English *Orosius.*" *Oral Tradition* 13.2 (1998): 377–97.

Venuti, Lawrence. "Translation, Community, Utopia." In *The Translation Studies Reader.* Ed. Venuti, 468–88. New York: Routledge, 2004.

———. *The Translator's Invisibility: A History of Translation.* New York: Routledge, 2018.

Vleeskruyer, Rudolf, ed. *The Life of Saint Chad: An Old English Homily.* Amsterdam: North Holland Press, 1953.

Waite, Greg. "Translation Style, Lexical Systems, Dialect Vocabulary, and the Manuscript Transmission of the Old English Bede." *Medium Aevum* 83.1 (2014): 1–48.

Wakelin, Daniel. *Scribal Correction and Literary Craft: English Manuscripts 1375–1510.* Cambridge: Cambridge University Press, 2014.

Wallace, David. *Chaucerian Polity: Absolutist Lineages and Associational Forms in England and Italy.* Stanford, CA: Stanford University Press, 1997.

Warren, Michelle R. "Translation." In *Oxford Twenty-First Century Approaches to Literature: Middle English.* Ed. Paul Strohm, 51–67. Oxford: Oxford University Press, 2007.

Waterhouse, Ruth. "Discourse and Hypersignification in Two of Ælfric's Saints' Lives." In *Holy Men and Holy Women: Old English Prose Saints Lives and Their Contexts.* Ed. Paul Szarmach, 333–52. Albany: State University of New York Press, 1996.

Weaver, Erica M. "Formal Orders: Writing Poetry and Prose in Late Anglo-Saxon England." PhD Diss., Harvard University, 2018.

Weiss, Judith, Jennifer Fellows, and Morgan Dickinson, eds. *Medieval Insular Romance: Translation and Innovation.* Cambridge: D. S. Brewer, 2000.

Whitaker, Cord J. "Race and Racism in *The Man of Law's Tale.*" In *The Open Access Canterbury Tales.* Eds. Candace Barrington, Brantley Bryant, Richard H. Godden, Daniel T. Kline, and Myra Seaman. Available at https://opencanterburytales.dsl.lsu.edu/mlt1/.

Wilcox, Jonathan. "A Reluctant Translator in Late Anglo-Saxon England: Ælfric and Maccabees." *Proceedings of the Medieval Association of the Midwest* 2 (1994): 1–18.

Williams, Raymond. *Keywords: A Vocabulary of Culture and Society.* Oxford: Oxford University Press, 1985.

Wormald, Patrick. "Engla Londe: The Making of an Allegiance." *Journal of Historical Sociology* 7.1 (1994): 1–24.

Wynn, Phillip. "The Conversion Story in Nicholas Trevet's 'Tale of Constance.'" *Viator* 13 (1982): 259–74.

Zemeckis, Robert, dir. *Beowulf,* 2007; Hollywood, CA: Paramount Home Entertainment, 2008. DVD.

Zweck, Jordan. "Silence in the Exeter Book Riddles." *Exemplaria* 28.4 (2016): 319–36.

INDEX

Abbo of Fleury, 54–55, 63
Ælfric of Eynsham, 1, 15–16, 53–54; and protonationalism, 70n41. See also *Life of Oswald, King and Martyr* (Ælfric of Eynsham); *Lives of the Saints* (Ælfric of Eynsham)
Ælle, King, 145, 149
Æthelstan, King, 54, 63, 70n41
Alcuin, 68n35
Alfred of Wessex, King, 9; and the *Preface* to the *Pastoral Care*, 3–7, 5n2, 6n26, 14, 20n64, 58n13, 63; and the vocabulary of translation, 5n23, 55
Alfredian translations, 26–27, 29n15, 30; and sources, 39n37, 52. See also the Old English *Orosius*; *Preface* to the *Pastoral Care*
Angelcynn, 6, 56, 64
Anglo-Norman *Chronicle*, the (Trevet), 147–48; and Pope Gregory the Great, 148–49
"Anglo-Saxon," as a racist term, 12–13, 12n46, 12n48
Arthur, James, 183, 186
Augustine of Canterbury, 148
Augustine of Hippo, Saint, 28, 62; and Paulus Orosius, 28, 29n13, 34

Bakhtin, Mikhail, 51n53, 96n24, 103n58
Bately, Janet, 26, 28n11, 39n37
Bede: and apostate kings, 71–73; and Bishop Aidan, 73–74; and Edwin of Northumbria, 71; and Heavenfield, 83–86; and the *Historia Ecclesiastica*, 68; and *Life of Oswald*, 70–77; and Maserfeld, 85–87; and Mercian hostilities, 75–77; and Northumbrian identity, 70; and Oswald's death, 75, 79
Benedictine reform, 14, 63
Benedictine spirituality, 63
Beowulf, 12, 15, 17–18; building of Heorot, 161–62; and the Creation Song, 156–58; and the creation of monsters, 158; digressions, 155; Grendel, 156n20, 159–60; kennings, 167–68; opening lines of, 8–9, 151–54; and Roman ruins, 17; and translation, 154. See also dragons; the Lay of the Last Survivor; the Messenger's Prophecy
Borges, Jorge Luis, 163n47

Cadwalla, 69, 72, 75, 81
Cædmon's *Hymn*, 18, 24; in Bede's *Historia Ecclesiastica*, 20–23; in the *Norton*

· 209 ·

Anthology, 19–20; in the Old English *Bede*, 22; as reverse translation, 23

Chaucer, Geoffrey, 3n11, 11–12, 17, 126–27; and "anxiety of originality," 127n6; and Lollius, 2; *Troilus and Criseyde*, 2–3

christendom, 6, 29, 88

code-switching, 135n34, 138, 139

collectivity, 155, 155n17, 156, 162, 178; and animals, 180–81; and community, 163, 173–75, 176; and objects, 167, 172; and temporality, 175, 177

community of the page, 24, 91, 95, 113–14, 123–24

Confessio Amantis (Gower), 137–38; and code-switching, 139. See also Gower, John

Constance-legend, the, 127, 129, 129n17

conversion, 6, 76; in Chaucer's *Man of Law's Tale*, 17, 126–29, 132, 134, 135n34, 137–40, 143, 145, 146; of the Mercians, 76; of Northumbria, 71, 73–74; of Oswald, 72; of Rome, 26, 28, 51; in Trevet's Anglo-Norman *Chronicle*, 147–50

Copeland, Rita, 13, 30n22, 31n24

Davis, Kathleen, 4n18, 5, 5n21, 5n23, 6, 6n26, 55n7, 66n32, 73n51, 125–26, 130n19

Decollation of John the Baptist, 121–22

De Duodecim Abusivis Huius Seculi (Ælfric of Eynsham), 99n40, 105

deep time, 177

De Octo Vitiis (Ælfric of Eynsham), 91, 98–109, 114–15, 183–84

Discenza, Nicole Guenther, 30, 32n28, 39n38, 46

discourse markers, 16, 91, 99n45, 104–5, 107–9, 111, 183

domestication, in translation theory, 2, 57, 57n10, 59

dragons in *Beowulf*, 169–70; expected activities of, 170; and the thief, 173–74; and time, 172–73; and treasure, 178

Dream of the Rood, the, 49n50

Dunstan, 54, 64–65, 65n28

Edgar, King, 64–65

Frank, Roberta, 151, 177

glossing, 16, 91–98. See also Tremulous Hand of Worcester

Godden, M. R., 25n1, 29, 29n17, 46, 50n51; and the *cwæð* construction, 30

Gower, John, 17, 137–38, 139, 141n52, 142, 144, 145n61. See also *Confessio Amantis* (Gower)

Gregory the Great, Pope, 70n40, 146, 148–49, 149n70

Howe, Nicholas, 29, 29n15, 29n17, 136, 153, 153n12, 154n13

Hsy, Jonathan, 13, 14n52, 125n3, 132n27, 134n30, 138, 139, 139n46

Imagined Communities (Anderson), 8n34, 9, 9n37, 11, 14n52

intimacy of texts, 23n73, 91n1, 95. See also community of the page

Irvine, Martin, 3, 4, 5n21, 6n25, 21n66, 23n70, 31

Latin words: *transferre*, 21, 56

Latour, Bruno, 155n17, 174n82

Lay of the Last Survivor in *Beowulf*, 162–64; and animals, 166–69; apostrophe, 165; burial hoards, 164–65; objects, 165–67

Lerer, Seth, 94, 159n32, 160n34, 185

Life of Andrew (Ælfric of Eynsham), 117, 120, 122

Life of Oswald, King and Martyr (Ælfric of Eynsham): and apostate kings, 72–73; and Bede, 68; and Bishop Aidan, 73–74; and Edwin of Northumbria, 71; and Heavenfield, 69, 80–85; and the *heofonlic leoht*, 78; and the holy dust, 69; and Maserfeld, 75, 86–88; and Mercian hostilities, 76–77; and Oswald's conversion, 71–72; and Oswald's last words, 79

Lives of the Saints (Ælfric of Eynsham): *Æthelthryth*, 66; *Agnes*, 61; *Alban*, 66–67; *Basil*, 60; *Cecilia*, 60, 66; *De Memoria Sanctorum*, 99, 109, 113; *Edmund*, 53–56, 63–64; Latin *Preface* to, 57–58; Old English *Preface* to, 58–59; *Swithun*, 64–65; *Thomas*, 62

Man of Law's Tale, the (Chaucer), 15, 17, 125–26, 128–31, 149; and the *Britoun book*,

142–45; and language, 134; and merchants, 130–31, 134, 134n30–31, 135n34, 138

manuscripts: Cambridge, Corpus Christi College Library **178**, 99, 99n41, 104, 105; Cambridge, Corpus Christi College Library **303**, 99n40, 99n41, 104, 107n69, 108; Cambridge, University Library **Ii.1.33,** 92, 99, 99n43, 104, 105, 109–11, 113, 114, 115–16, 119–20, 124; Cambridge, University Library **Kk.6.16,** 23, 23n73; London, British Library Cotton Julius **E.vii,** 99, 99n43, 104, 105, 109–15; London, British Library Cotton Vespasian **D.xiv,** 99, 99n40, 99n44, 100–103, 104, 105, 106; London, Lambeth Palace Library **487,** 99, 99n41, 104–8, 114; Oxford, Bodleian Library Hatton **114,** 96–97, 99, 104; Oxford, Bodleian Library Hatton **115,** 96, 96n31; Oxford, Bodleian Library Hatton, **116,** 96; Saint Petersburg, Russian National Library **Q.v.I.18,** 23, 23n73

Maxims II, 169–70

Messenger's Speech in *Beowulf,* 178–79; and animal language, 179–80; and the Beasts of Battle topos, 179–81

Middle English words: *pes,* 145; *wenden,* 130; *voys,* 131

migration myth, early English, 136

multilingualism, 6, 14; in manuscripts, 91n1, 99n45, 118, 120, 123, 129n16; in Chaucer, 131

O'Brien O'Keeffe, Katherine, 21, 23n73, 93, 93n10, 100, 102n55, 156n21, 159n31

"Of the Noble Lady Constance" (Trevet), 131–32, 134–37; and the Briton Gospel book, 142, 144; and code-switching, 138–39

Old English words: *an,* 173; *areccan,* 45n45; *asecgan,* 45n45; *awendan,* 55; *cwide,* 40, 40n40; *fetian,* 83; *findan,* 170; *gefrignan,* 176; *gehwyrfan,* 22; *gemearcian,* 40; *læne,* 168; *niman,* 117; *nu,* 47n48; *reafian,* 180–81; *sculan,* 170; *spell,* 40, 40n40; *spellcwide,* 40, 40n40; *trahtnere,* 122; *wrætlic,* 171; *wyrd,* 171

orality, 34, 34n30, 154

Orosius, the Old English, 1, 10, 15–16, 25–27, 51–52, 183; and the absence of the Latin preface to, 30; address to the Romans, 46–49; Christianity, 36; the *cwæð Orosius* construction, 26–27, 29–30, 31; geographical preface to, 32–33; the "I heard" construction, 33–34, 35; *mid spellcwidum gemearcian,* 39–40, 40n40; the *nu,* 49–50; Roman historical inadequacy, 41–43; the temporality of history in, 43, 45; *translatio imperii, translatio studii,* 29n16; writing history, 37–40

Orosius, Paulus, 1, 20n13; and the evils of the past, 38, 44; and the *Historiarum Adversum Paganos Libri Septi,* 26, 28–29; the use of the passive voice, 34–35, 35n31

Overing, Gillian, 80, 167, 187–88

Penda, King of Mercia, 69, 75–77. See also *Life of Oswald, King and Martyr* (Ælfric of Eynsham)

punctus, to indicate translation, 91, 104, 106, 111, 114

Preface to the *Pastoral Care,* 3–6, 14, 20n64, 58n13, 63n21. See also Alfred of Wessex, King

proverbs, of Solomon, 121–22; of the *vilun,* 120–21

relics, 79–82

Riddle 47 ("bookworm"), 171–72

Rome, 6, 16, 28–30, 38–39, 43, 44n44, 48, 50, 51; and Chaucer's *Man of Law's Tale,* 127, 129–31, 133; and persecutions of Christians, 60–61; and Trevet's Anglo-Norman *Chronicle,* 148–49

ruins, 185, 186n11

"Saxons," in England, 128n14, 134, 139; outside of England, 135–36; and relationship to "Britons" 141, 144–45

Scyld Scefing, 152–53

source study, 10, 14

Stanton, Robert, 14, 92, 93n6, 94

stars, 45, 133

Stock, Brian, 8n35, 27, 91n1. See also textual community

temporality: 25, 33, 51n53; in *Beowulf,* 155, 160, 178; and Chaucer's *Man of Law's Tale,* 127; and collectivity, 175–76, 180; and the community of the page, 108n73; and material culture, 162; and narrative, 90, 155; and textual community, 91; of translation, 56, 59

textual community, 8, 8n35, 24, 27, 27n9, 46, 55, 61–62, 64, 90–91, 123–24, 183

translatio studii, translatio imperii, 5, 7, 7n28, 12, 13, 13n49; and glosses, 92, 93n6; and *The Man of Law's Tale,* 143n57; in marginalia, 122; and the Old English *Orosius,* 29n16, 30n22

translation effects, 1, 3, 7–12, 15–18, 183, 188; and Ælfric's *Lives of the Saints,* 55–56, 61, 65, 69, 75, 81; and *Beowulf,* 154–56, 162, 177, 181–82, 185; and Cædmon's *Hymn,* 18, 20–21; and Chaucer's *Man of Law's Tale,* 126–28, 130, 140, 150; and community, 28, 52, 61; and discourse markers, 104–5, 114–15; and glossing, 93, 96–97; and *litterae notabiliores,* 100–103; and manuscripts, 90–92, 98–100, 108–11; and marginalia, 115, 120, 123; and narrative, 162; and the Old English *Orosius,* 31–32; and ruins, 185; and temporality, 21, 51, 177, 181; and Trevet's Anglo-Norman *Chronicle,* 137

translation theory, 13–14, 55n7, 57

Translator's Invisibility (Venuti), 2, 2n3, 57n10

transparency, in translation theory, 2, 2n3, 2n6; and medieval authors, 2, 26

Tremulous Hand of Worcester, 92–98, 124

Trevet, Nicholas, 131; and Bede, 146

Venuti, Lawrence, 1n1, 2, 10, 57n10

Vie de Sainte Gilles, 121

Wanderer, the, 168n61, 186n11

Warren, Michelle R., 3n12, 7, 10–11, 92

white supremacists and the Middle Ages, 186, 186n12

Williams, Raymond, 173–74

INTERVENTIONS: NEW STUDIES IN MEDIEVAL CULTURE
Ethan Knapp, Series Editor

Interventions: New Studies in Medieval Culture publishes theoretically informed work in medieval literary and cultural studies. We are interested both in studies of medieval culture and in work on the continuing importance of medieval tropes and topics in contemporary intellectual life.

Translation Effects: Language, Time, and Community in Medieval England
MARY KATE HURLEY

Talk and Textual Production in Medieval England
MARISA LIBBON

Scripting the Nation: Court Poetry and the Authority of History in Late Medieval Scotland
KATHERINE H. TERRELL

Medieval Things: Agency, Materiality, and Narratives of Objects in Medieval German Literature and Beyond
BETTINA BILDHAUER

Death and the Pearl Maiden: Plague, Poetry, England
DAVID K. COLEY

Political Appetites: Food in Medieval English Romance
AARON HOSTETTER

Invention and Authorship in Medieval England
ROBERT R. EDWARDS

Challenging Communion: The Eucharist and Middle English Literature
JENNIFER GARRISON

Chaucer on Screen: Absence, Presence, and Adapting the Canterbury Tales
EDITED BY KATHLEEN COYNE KELLY AND TISON PUGH

Chaucer, Gower, and the Affect of Invention
STEELE NOWLIN

Fragments for a History of a Vanishing Humanism
EDITED BY MYRA SEAMAN AND EILEEN A. JOY

The Medieval Risk-Reward Society: Courts, Adventure, and Love in the European Middle Ages
WILL HASTY

The Politics of Ecology: Land, Life, and Law in Medieval Britain
EDITED BY RANDY P. SCHIFF AND JOSEPH TAYLOR

The Art of Vision: Ekphrasis in Medieval Literature and Culture
EDITED BY ANDREW JAMES JOHNSTON, ETHAN KNAPP, AND MARGITTA ROUSE

Desire in the Canterbury Tales
ELIZABETH SCALA

Imagining the Parish in Late Medieval England
　ELLEN K. RENTZ

Truth and Tales: Cultural Mobility and Medieval Media
　EDITED BY FIONA SOMERSET AND NICHOLAS WATSON

Eschatological Subjects: Divine and Literary Judgment in Fourteenth-Century French Poetry
　J. M. MOREAU

Chaucer's (Anti-)Eroticisms and the Queer Middle Ages
　TISON PUGH

Trading Tongues: Merchants, Multilingualism, and Medieval Literature
　JONATHAN HSY

Translating Troy: Provincial Politics in Alliterative Romance
　ALEX MUELLER

Fictions of Evidence: Witnessing, Literature, and Community in the Late Middle Ages
　JAMIE K. TAYLOR

Answerable Style: The Idea of the Literary in Medieval England
　EDITED BY FRANK GRADY AND ANDREW GALLOWAY

Scribal Authorship and the Writing of History in Medieval England
　MATTHEW FISHER

Fashioning Change: The Trope of Clothing in High- and Late-Medieval England
　ANDREA DENNY-BROWN

Form and Reform: Reading across the Fifteenth Century
　EDITED BY SHANNON GAYK AND KATHLEEN TONRY

How to Make a Human: Animals and Violence in the Middle Ages
　KARL STEEL

Revivalist Fantasy: Alliterative Verse and Nationalist Literary History
　RANDY P. SCHIFF

Inventing Womanhood: Gender and Language in Later Middle English Writing
　TARA WILLIAMS

Body Against Soul: Gender and Sowlehele *in Middle English Allegory*
　MASHA RASKOLNIKOV

www.ingramcontent.com/pod-product-compliance
Lightning Source LLC
Chambersburg PA
CBHW020653230426
43665CB00008B/427